Uncle John's
BATHROOM READER®
PLUNGES INTO
PENNSYLVANIA

Uncle John's BATHROOM READER Plunges into PENNSYLVANIA

Bathroom Readers' Institute

Ashland, Oregon

San Diego, California

Our "Regular" Readers Rave!

"*Uncle John's Bathroom Reader* has added a new dimension to my bathroom visits. Thank you."

—Mitchell

"I would just like to thank you for making me laugh. Since discovering your great series, I find myself visiting my bathroom more often. There is need of a new invention: Armrests in the toilet!"

—Caroline

"I think these books are the best in the world. I take them to school and show all my friends. Thank you for making my visits to the bathroom fun."

—Bobby

"Today my friend was asking me who my best teacher was. I said 'Uncle John.' He was confused and asked me if I was home-schooled. My response? No. I was bathroom-schooled. He went out and bought a copy. Thanks for the education!"

—Tyler

"Just thought I'd let you know what a great job you're doing. My whole family enjoys your books and our tradition has been to buy one, then two books at Christmastime for reading the next year. You've become so popular that we now have at least three new books in the bathroom, and it's only June!"

—Martha

"I absolutely love your books. But oddly, I've never read them in the bathroom. As soon as I get one, I have to read it cover to cover. Keep up the good work!"
—**Leanne**

"I just wanted to say how wonderful I have found the *Bathroom Readers*. I have bought several for friends and family, and they are truly addicted now. Everyone seems to spend an extra 10 minutes in the bathroom in order to read."
—**Lisa**

"You guys are the funniest I've ever read!"
—**Suzanne**

"Keep 'em coming! I am totally addicted to your books, currently owning 14. I was a teacher for 30 years, and am now a reference librarian. I suggested to my supervisor that we order your books for our local library collection, as they are the most consistently fascinating series on facts and trivia that I have ever come across. I have sung your praises to our librarian patrons on numerous occasions, so hopefully I have helped spawn a new generation of BR fanatics!"
—**Jack**

"I love your books and have read and reread and reread the *Bathroom Readers* I have. My wife tells me I am a warehouse of useless information, thanks in part to you guys."
—**Ben**

"I have many of your books and enjoy reading them at work. By the way, my job is making toilet paper."
—**Don**

Uncle John's Bathroom Reader
Plunges into Pennsylvania

"Bathroom Reader," "Portable Press," and
"Bathroom Readers' Institute" are registered trademarks of
Baker & Taylor, Inc. All rights reserved.

Some material was reprinted from the following titles: *Uncle John's
Ahh-Inspiring Bathroom Reader, Uncle John's All-Purpose Extra Strength
Bathroom Reader, Uncle John's Bathroom Reader Plunges into Great
Lives, Uncle John's Bathroom Reader Plunges into National Parks,*
and *Uncle John's Supremely Satisfying Bathroom Reader.*

For information, write The Bathroom Readers' Institute
P.O. Box 1117, Ashland, OR 97520
e-mail: mail@bathroomreader.com

ISBN-13: 978-1-59223-854-5/ISBN-10: 1-59223-854-8

Library of Congress Cataloging-in-Publication Data
Uncle John's bathroom reader plunges into Pennsylvania.
    p. cm.
  ISBN 978-1-59223-854-5 (pbk.)
1. Pennsylvania—Anecdotes. 2. Pennsylvania—Humor.
F149.6.U63 2009
974.8--dc22

                                                    2008042629

Printed in Canada
First printing: March 2009
09 10 11 12 13 14   10 9 8 7 6 5 4 3 2 1

Contents

Titans and Tycoons

Speaking Pennsylvanian

Name That Town

Stars of Sport

Quotable Notables

Puzzle These Out

Let Us Entertain You

Historical Heroics

Just for Fun

Highway Haunts

Mixed Bag

Quote Me

"Nowhere in this country, from sea to sea, does nature comfort us with such assurance of plenty, such rich and tranquil beauty as in those unsung, unpainted hills of Pennsylvania."

—Rebecca Harding Davis, author

Thank You!

The Bathroom Readers' Institute thanks the following
people whose hard work, advice, and assistance
made this book possible.

Gordon Javna

JoAnn Padgett

Melinda Allman

Amy Miller

Jeff Altemus

Brian Boone

Thom Little

Michael Brunsfeld

Julia Papps

Dan Mansfield

Susan Steiner

Lea Markson

Vickey Kalambakal

John Scalzi

Debbie K. Hardin

Gabriela Toth

Myles Callum

Jenness I. Crawford

Ryan Murphy

Scott Tharler

Julie, Elise, and
Transcontinental

J. Carroll

Debbie Pawlak

Kathryn Grogman

Kathryn Senior

Megan Kern

Jay Newman

John Dollison

Stuart Smoller

Toney Lee

Angela Kern

Bonnie Vandewater

Lisa Meyers

Amy Ly

Monica Maestas

Kait Fairchild

Sydney Stanley

Cynthia Francisco

Ginger Winters

Jennifer Frederick

Tom Mustard

Sophie, Bea, and Porter
the Wonder Dog

Preface

Welcome to Pennsylvania—the second state in the Union, the birthplace of commercial radio, and the leading U.S. producer of mushrooms. With credentials like these, it's no wonder we chose the Keystone State as the subject of our latest Bathroom Reader. We recruited a group of Pennsylvania aficionados to put together this collection of the most interesting stories the state has to offer. Read all about . . .

History: When we thought of Pennsylvania, the first thing that came to mind was history—few states have a closer link to the American Revolution. Philadelphia, of course, is home to the Liberty Bell, Independence Hall, and a whole lot more, but the rest of the state played an important role too: The winter that George Washington's army spent at Valley Forge was one of the colonists' greatest challenges, and the bitter dispute between Pennsylvania and Connecticut for the Wyoming Valley helped to define the states' current borders.

Sports: Whether you prefer hockey, baseball, or football, you'll find your team in these pages.

Business: Pennsylvania has been home to major businesses for more than a century. Whether they are building bridges, making ketchup, drilling for oil, or developing more efficient ways to make steel, Pennsylvanians are masters of innovation.

Hometowns: If you want to ride one of America's first roller coasters, visit the Pro Wrestling Hall of Fame, travel the country's first major toll road, or see where marshmallow Peeps are made, you can do it in Pennsylvania.

Say What?

We also asked around and found answers to some of the public's most burning Pennsylvania-related questions:

- Who invented Little League?
- Why do Swarthmore students run naked through their school at exam time?
- What's a Moravian Love Feast?
- Who was Pennsylvania's "Father of the Underground Railroad"?
- Where can you see a corpse made of lye soap and the thorax of John Wilkes Booth?
- Who named Philadelphia?
- How big is the King of Prussia mall?
- What town on the Monongahela River helped to inspire the Clean Air Act of 1970?
- How many pretzels do Pennsylvanians eat in a year?

From William Penn's Holy Experiment to heroes of the American Revolution to abolition and beyond, Pennsylvania's history is sweeter than all the chocolate at Hershey Park. So head over to South Philly for a cheesesteak, kick back with a bottle of Rolling Rock, and pull on that Penn State sweatshirt. It's going to be an awesome ride.

As always, go with the flow . . .

—Uncle John and the BRI staff

Museums of the Strange

*From preserved livers to ceramic elephants, Pennsylvania's got one
of the most bizarre collections of museums we've ever seen.*

Mister Ed's Elephant Museum (Orrtanna)

If you've ever wondered where you could be surrounded by
more than 6,000 elephants, this is the place. The owner, who
goes only by "Mister Ed," has been collecting elephant-related
things since 1967, when he got an elephant figurine as a wedding present. By 1975, his pachyderm menagerie had gotten so
big that it was taking up too much space in his house, so he
decided to put them in a museum. Highlights: an elephant
potty chair, a ceramic head with elephants coming out of it,
and a nine-foot-tall talking elephant named Miss Ellie.

Choo Choo Barn (Strasburg)

Strasburg native George Groff opened the Choo Choo Barn in
1961 as a way to raise money for his sons' college educations.
He'd been collecting model trains since 1945 and thought there
might be some money in displaying them. So he rented an old
building on Route 741, set up his trains, and hoped people
would come. They did: locals and tourists to Strasburg (in the
heart of Lancaster County) visited in droves. Originally just
600 square feet, the museum has since expanded to its current
1,700 square feet. The animated displays are its most impressive asset. Set up to resemble Lancaster County, there's an
Amish barn raising, a Ferris wheel, a ski lodge with ice-skaters,
and a three-minute-long fire scene in which a group of (miniature) firemen put out a real (miniature) house fire.

Mütter Museum (Philadelphia)

When it comes to weird museums, this one wins by . . . a bone. In 1858, local physician and professor Thomas Dent Mütter left $30,000 and a 1,700-piece collection of bones, plaster casts, and other medical-related items to the College of Physicians of Philadelphia to start a museum. The original museum opened in 1863 at the corner of Locust and 13th streets, but in 1908, when the displays outgrew their space, the college moved them to their current location on South 22nd Street. Today's exhibits showcase more than 20,000 objects, including a collection of brains, an Iron Lung, the "soap woman" (the body of a woman who died in the 19th century and was buried in soil containing chemicals that turned her remains into lye soap), and a plaster cast of history's most famous Siamese twins, Chang and Eng Bunker. But our vote for the weirdest? It's a tie: a cancerous growth removed from U.S. president Grover Cleveland's upper jaw, and the thorax of assassin John Wilkes Booth.

The Museum of Mourning Art (Drexel Hill)

In Drexel Hill's Arlington Cemetery—a century-old resting place for war veterans, local celebrities, and even a *Titanic* survivor—is a structure built to look like George Washington's Mount Vernon home. Inside is the Museum of Mourning Art is a collection of funerary items from history—everything from a 17th-century book with instructions of how to get to heaven, to an 18th-century cemetery gun that was rigged to fire when grave robbers tripped it. (It shot anyone who set it off, though, not just grave robbers, so the gun was quickly outlawed in England and the American colonies.)

Stoogeum (Spring House)

Off a small street that doesn't even show up on most maps is the Stoogeum, a museum dedicated to the Three Stooges. Gary Lassin opened the place in 2004 and likes to keep the business low-key. He doesn't have a staff or regular hours—anyone who wants to visit has to e-mail him for directions and to set up an appointment. But he does have one of the most impressive collections of Stooges memorabilia around today: nearly 100,000 artifacts. The three-story Stoogeum also houses a research library, a film storage vault, and a theater, and serves as the official headquarters of the Three Stooges Fan Club.

Insectarium (Philadelphia)

If you like creepy-crawlies, the Insectarium is for you. The museum opened in 1992 and today houses hundreds of thousands of insects (many live), including Madagascar hissing cockroaches, human face stinkbugs, velvet ants, and a foot-long walking stick. There's even a man-made spiderweb for kids to play on and a simulated kitchen infested with thousands of swarming cockroaches.

Did You Know?

On November 28, 1984, Ronald Reagan issued Presidential Proclamation 5284, which declared William Penn an honorary citizen of the United States. (Since Penn had been born in England, he never had "official" citizenship.)

Just the Facts

Here's a quick look at Pennsylvania.

Population (2008): 12,440,621

Capital: Harrisburg

State motto: "Virtue, liberty, and independence"

Nickname: The Keystone State

Land area: 44,816.61 square miles

Length: 283 miles

Width: 160 miles

Highest point: Mt. Davis—3,213 feet

Lowest point: Delaware River—sea level

Record low temperature: –42°F (1904)

Record high temperature: 111°F (1936)

Ratified the U.S. Constitution: December 12, 1787 (second after Delaware)

Number of U.S. representatives: 19

Number of counties: 67

Number of national forests: 1 (Allegheny National Forest)

Percentage of land covered by forest: Almost 60 percent (17 million acres)

Borders: New York, New Jersey, West Virginia, Maryland, Delaware, and Ohio

"Whiz Wit"

It doesn't matter how you order it—just don't call it a "steak and cheese."

Cheesesteak 101

The greasy, drippy sandwich that calls Philly home is more than just steak and cheese on a bun. To make a proper cheesesteak, you'll need to do the following: sauté thinly sliced beef (preferably ribeye) with melted cheese, and put the mixture on a crusty hoagie roll. You can put the cheese slices on top of the beef right before flipping it into the bun, or you can grill them together—the idea is to melt the cheese completely into the steak. Cheese choices include American, provolone, or Cheez Whiz, but Cheez Whiz is the favorite, by far. The most common additional ingredients: onions, green peppers, and mushrooms.

You can get grilled steak and cheese on a roll almost anywhere in the world, but Philly natives claim that you can't get a *real* cheesesteak outside of the city. One main reason is Amoroso's Baking Company, where most cheesesteak vendors get their rolls. Amoroso's rolls are distinctively flaky because its bakers use Philadelphia's alkaline drinking water, nicknamed "Schuylkill Punch."

Pat vs. Joe

Who made the first Philly cheesesteak? It depends on who you ask. In 1930, Pasquale "Pat" Olivieri was a hot dog vendor in South Philadelphia. One day, he put some beef on his grill next to the frankfurters, and a passing cabbie, lured by the aroma, asked for a steak sandwich. Soon, cabbies from around the city were stopping by Pat's cart for the sandwiches. Eventually, they got so popular that Pat opened a restaurant—Pat's King of Steaks—on Passyunk Avenue. It's still around, grilling 24 hours a day.

Story number two comes from Joe Vento, founder of Geno's Steaks, which opened across the street from Pat's in 1966. Pat may have been the first to put steak on a bun, but Vento claims that he was the first to put cheese in the sandwich, thereby inventing the cheesesteak.

Either way, the two restaurants have been competing for the title of best cheesesteak ever since. Both Joe Vento and Frank Olivieri (Pat's current owner and the founder's nephew) claim that theirs is the superior sandwich . . . even though neither has actually tried his competition. The rivalry is good-natured, though: Olivieri says that if Geno's ever went out of business, he'd "feel a void" and would have to buy his rival's store and reopen it so he could fight with himself.

Wit or Witout?

No matter what restaurant you choose, you'll want to keep some things in mind:

1. Order efficiently. Natives just name the cheese and whether they want their steaks "wit" onions or "witout." A standard order would be "Whiz wit."

2. There are variations on the traditional cheesesteak. Any of the following is acceptable:

- Pizza steak—served with mozzarella and pizza sauce.
- Western cheesesteak—served with barbecue sauce and jalapeños.
- Cheesesteak hoagie—served with lettuce and tomato.

- Cheesefake—for vegetarians.
- Cheesesteak spring rolls—the innards of a cheesesteak wrapped in a crispy, fried shell.
- South Street sushi—made by wrapping a slice of pizza from Lorenzo's around a cheesesteak from Jim's Steaks, both located on South Street.
- And if those are too mundane, the Barclay Prime Steakhouse on 18th Street offers a $100 cheesesteak made with Wagyu beef, foie gras, black truffles, and served "wit" champagne.

The Politics of Hunger

The cheesesteak is no longer just a humble sandwich—not only is it known around the world, it has also found itself at the center of several political scandals. While on the campaign trail in 2004, presidential hopeful John Kerry visited Philadelphia and ordered a cheesesteak . . . with Swiss cheese. The *Philadelphia Daily News* wrote, "In Philadelphia, ordering Swiss on a cheesesteak is like rooting for Dallas at an Eagles game." A few months later, George W. Bush said in a speech that he liked his cheesesteaks "Whiz wit." But a Philadelphia newspaper discovered that the president actually preferred American, prompting speculation about why he wanted to hide his cheese preferences.

Finally, in 2005, before Super Bowl XXXIX, Pennsylvania governor Ed Rendell bet Massachusetts governor Mitt Romney a Philly cheesesteak against a Boston lobster that the Pittsburgh Steelers would beat the New England Patriots. Romney turned down the wager, saying the cheesesteak "had no nutritional value." The Steelers took the title, but some Philadelphians are still smarting from the slight.

Fly That Flag

*Have you ever looked closely at the symbols on
Pennsylvania's state flag?*

The Design

- The seal in the center of the flag is Pennsylvania's coat of
  arms. Philadelphia iron merchant Caleb Lownes created it
  in 1778 for use on the colony's money. In 1799, the state
  legislature approved it for use on the Pennsylvania militia's
  flag.

- The coat of arms is different from the official state seal, but
  both incorporate some of the same images: the eagle, ship,
  plow, wheat bundles, and crossed olive branch and corn
  stalk.

The Images

- Because Pennsylvania was one of the colonies' early trade
  and agricultural hubs, the images on the state flag mostly
  symbolize the state's long history of commerce and farming.
  The harnessed workhorses, bundles of wheat, and plow
  represent agriculture; the ship represents trade.

- The eagle atop the crest shows Pennsylvania's commitment
  to being part of the United States, and the olive branch
  and corn stalk crossed at the bottom represent peace and
  prosperity.

- The state's motto—"Virtue, liberty, and independence"—
  appears on a red ribbon at the bottom.

The Color

- In 1907, the Pennsylvania's General Assembly officially adopted the state flag as we know it today. Until then, various groups (like Civil War soldiers) had made their own variations. But on June 13, 1907, the General Assembly laid down some rules: the flag would include the state's coat of arms embroidered on a blue background, which had to be the same color as the blue on the United States flag.

Did You Know?

The Philadelphia Phillies are the oldest continuous, one-name, one-city franchise in all of professional sports.

Make Way for the Black and Gold

The Pittsburgh Steelers got off to a slow start, but by the 1970s, they were an NFL powerhouse.

I n 1933, Pittsburgh resident Art Rooney paid $2,500 (the standard fee at the time) to begin a football franchise with the NFL. Legend has it—and Rooney has never denied it—that he won the money just days earlier betting on horses at the Saratoga Springs racetrack in New York.

The team's original name was the Pirates, the same moniker as the city's professional baseball team and in whose stadium the new football team played. Rooney changed the name to the Steelers before the 1940 season, in honor of the Pittsburgh steel industry.

From Down-and-Out to a Dynasty

The Steelers were ranked low in the standings for a long time. In their first 40 years, they made it to the playoffs just once, in 1947. During that time, they also had only five winning seasons.

But things changed in 1969 when Rooney hired Chuck Noll as head coach. Within a few years, the Steelers were a much better team. They made it to the playoffs in 1972 and 1973 and then, in 1974, won the AFC Championship game— and beat the Minnesota Vikings in the Super Bowl. Over the next six years, the Steelers made it to the Super Bowl four times . . . and won them all.

Since 1979, the Steelers have made it back to the Super Bowl twice: in 1995 (they lost to the Dallas Cowboys 27–17) and in 2006, when coach Bill Cowher, quarterback Ben Roethlisberger, running back Jerome Bettis, and wide receiver Hines Ward led the team to a 21–10 win over the Seattle Seahawks. The Steelers are one of only three teams in NFL history to win the Super Bowl five times. (The San Francisco 49ers and the Dallas Cowboys are the other two.)

Stellar Steeler Stats

- Pittsburgh has 17 members (including players, coaches, and owners) in the NFL Hall of Fame, the fourth-most of any team.
- In 1938, the Steelers signed running back Byron White, the only NFL player to later become a Supreme Court justice. (He served on the nation's highest court from 1962 until 1993.)
- The only German-born member of the NFL Hall of Fame: Ernie Stautner, a Steelers defensive tackle from 1950 until 1963. He played for 14 years and, though smaller than most NFL athletes, was among the league's most accomplished players. He's the only Steeler to ever have his number (70) officially retired by the team.
- John "Frenchy" Fuqua, a Steelers running back in the 1970s, was known as one of the flashiest dressers in the NFL. Off the field, he wore platform shoes—with live gold-fish in the water-filled, see-through heels.
- On November 16, 2008, the Steelers beat the San Diego Chargers by a score of 11–10. The Steelers got the unusual score of 11 by scoring three field goals for 9 points, and a safety, for 2. It was the first time in the NFL's history (12,837 games) that a match-up ended with an 11–10 score.

On the Road

Here are six Pennsylvania roadside attractions worth stopping for.

Shippensburg: Tiny World

Ernest Helm originally built Tiny World as a place for his cats to play in the backyard. The first structure: a Victorian house with a scratchable carpeted staircase. Since that first house, he's added many others: a church, a train station, a courthouse, a Texaco gas station (complete with little cars filling up), and more neighborhood houses. There are also two landscaped paths for visitors, and the whole thing is set on a hill, which Helm thinks adds to its appeal. According to him, "If it was on flat ground, it wouldn't look so good."

Bedford: The Coffee Pot

You can't miss the 17-foot-tall building shaped like a coffee pot on Route 30. Built in 1927, it used to be a quick stop for travelers on the Lincoln Highway—a place to get a cup of hot coffee or buy gas. But over the years, the enormous coffee pot fell into disrepair and nearly ended up being demolished in the 1990s. A local grassroots effort managed to save the structure, one of only five coffee pot–shaped buildings left in the United States. In 2004, it was completely renovated and relocated. Today, the Coffee Pot sits at the entrance to the Bedford Fairgrounds.

Erie: The Blockhouse

Mad Anthony Wayne was a Revolutionary War general, born in

Chester County, Pennsylvania, who served mostly in Canada but also had a brief stint at Valley Forge. In 1796, he died of a severe case of gout at a military post in Erie and was buried in a wooden coffin near the blockhouse—a tall, wooden defensive structure that often acted as a guard tower. That should have been the end of his story, but 12 years later, when his daughter was on her own deathbed, Wayne's family dug up his remains to transport the bones to Radnor for reburial in the family's Philadelphia plot about 400 miles away. But when they opened his coffin, they discovered that the body had hardly decomposed at all. Instead, it was almost perfectly preserved (save one foot). Moving the whole body so far would be difficult because the roads were rough and unpaved, the body was cumbersome, and the Waynes had only a small wagon. So the family's doctor came up with an unusual solution: he'd boil the body and then cut it up. The bones could go on to Radnor, and the flesh would be reburied near the blockhouse.

Over the years, the original blockhouse burned down, and the general's remains were accidentally dug up again. But finally in 1880, the State of Pennsylvania decided to erect a memorial at the spot of Wayne's death. Today, the blockhouse has been rebuilt and the structure dedicated to the general. Inside are a handful of exhibits, including a dummy in Wayne's likeness with an overturned bottle of whiskey (one of his favorite drinks) lying near his head.

Driftwood: Tom Mix's Outhouse

Tom Mix was a Pennsylvania-born Western movie star who made more than 300 movies—mostly in the silent era—before he died in a freak accident in 1940. (While driving in Arizona, he hit the brakes hard to avoid crashing into a ditch; a metal suitcase in the backseat flew forward, hit him in the head, and killed him.) Today, the Tom Mix Comes Home Museum in his birthplace of Driftwood includes all kinds of Tom Mix movie star memorabilia. Our favorite: the outhouse from his boyhood home.

Frackville: The Pioneer Pie Woman

Frackville's 15-foot-tall Pioneer Woman (holding a pie) has developed a roadside reputation as one of Pennsylvania's creepier attractions. Wearing a blank stare and a bright green dress, she stands outside Granny's Restaurant on West Coal Street. The child who clutches her skirt mostly looks like a young girl (in a dress and apron), but her face is that of an older man—and the toy she's holding is missing its head.

Hallam: World's Largest Shoe

In 1948, millionaire shoe manufacturer Mahlon N. Haines built this white house in the shape of a workshoe as an advertising gimmick for his company. It was a five-level working house—25 feet high, 48 feet long, with three bedrooms and two baths. Haines invited his employees to stay in it for their birthdays, anniversaries, and other special occasions; he also offered the house to any honeymooning couple from a town whose stores sold his shoes. (Nights in the shoe included full maid service, butler, cook, and chauffeur.)

Over the years, the Shoe House changed hands several times—it was an ice cream parlor for a while—but in 1987, Haines's granddaughter bought it and turned it into a museum dedicated to her grandfather.

More roadside attractions on page 271.

A Capital City

*Pennsylvania's state capital offers clean
living and a whole lot of history.*

Town: Harrisburg

Location: Dauphin County

Founding: 1791

Population (2008): 47,000

Size: 11.4 square miles

County Seat: Yes

What's in a Name?

The town was named for John Harris Sr. and Jr., a father and
son who were among the region's first white settlers. John Sr.
arrived around 1700 and set up a trading post (the first in the
area) and ran a successful ferry service across the Susquehanna
River. John Jr. laid out the town in 1785.

Claims to Fame:

- Stephen R. Reed has been mayor since 1981. In 2006, he
  was named the best mayor in the United States and the
  third-best in the world.

- Harrisburg is one of the "greenest" cities in the United
  States. In 2007, it received the state's Governor's Award for
  Environmental Excellence, having reduced energy costs and
  consumption by 60 percent.

- Harrisburg was a major troop dispatch point for the Union

army during the Civil War. The reason: it was a state capital and it was just 40 miles from the Mason-Dixon line, the border with the Confederacy.

- Camp Curtin (which today is uptown Harrisburg) processed and trained more soldiers during the Civil War than any other facility on either side.

- Harrisburg is the site of the largest indoor agricultural complex in the world. The Pennsylvania State Farm Show Complex covers more than 24 acres and hosts 200 farm, animal, and trade shows each year.

- There are two major American history museums in the city: the National Civil War Museum and the William Penn Museum.

- In his 1957 autobiographical novel *On the Road*, Jack Kerouac mentioned Pennsylvania's capital city: "That night in Harrisburg, I had to sleep in the railroad station on a bench; at dawn the station masters threw me out. I stumbled out of town with barely enough strength to reach the city limits. I knew I'd be arrested if I spent another night in Harrisburg. Cursed city!"

- The Pennsylvania state capitol building is regarded as one of the most beautiful in the nation. The 272-foot-wide dome atop the structure was modeled after the one on St. Peter's Basilica in Rome.

Did You Know?

Pennsylvania contains about 9 percent of all the wooded areas in the United States.

Pennsylvania-isms: The Basics

What is Pennsylvania-speak? Some of it is borrowed from Amish or eastern European influences, and some is just regional shorthand.

Term: It's all
Meaning: There isn't any more
Example: After you request chipped ham (thinly sliced ham), the guy at the deli counter tells you, "Sorry, but it's all."

Term: Leave
Meaning: Let
Example: "Hold on tight and don't leave go."

Term: Outen (or *close*) the light
Meaning: Shut off the light
Example: "Before you go to sleep, outen the light."

Term: Redd (also *red* or *read*)
Meaning: To straighten or tidy
Example: "After dinner, go on upstairs and redd up your room."

Term: What for
Meaning: Which
Example: "What for golf club are you gonna use on this shot?"

Term: 'N'at

Meaning: Etcetera, a shortened version of "and that."

Example: "For the barbecue, we bought hamburgers, kielbasa, buns, 'n'at."

Term: Let

Meaning: Leave

Example: "When you're done with the cereal, please let it on the table."

Term: Heyna (also *henna*, *ayna*, or *haynit*)

Meaning: Request for affirmation at the end of a sentence, meaning "Isn't that correct?"

Example: "Sure is hot today, heyna?"

Term: "Ho, butt!"

Meaning: "Yo, bud!" or "Hey, you!"

Example: Used when calling out to get someone's attention in a friendly way. "Ho, butt! How 'bout those Steelers?"

Term: Wash my hairs

Meaning: To shampoo one's hair

Example: "After wearin' my sweaty Pirates cap, I decided to wash my hairs, so they weren't all panked down [flattened]."

For more Pennsylvania-isms, turn to page 134.

Man of Steel

*Pennsylvania's self-made steel mogul Andrew Carnegie was
a philanthropist and business genius. But many people cite his
contempt for unions and the low salaries he paid his workers
as examples of capitalist greed. Hero or villain? Will
the real Andrew Carnegie please stand up?*

Child Laborer

Andrew Carnegie started out poor. His father, Will, was a
weaver and a pro-labor radical in his hometown of Dunfermline,
Scotland. But during the 1840s, when steam-powered looms
began to replace workers, Will Carnegie found himself without a
job and unable to support his family. So in 1848, 13-year-old
Andrew, his parents, and his younger brother set out for the
United States, hoping to improve their fortunes.

At first, life in their new home wasn't much better. The
Carnegies settled in Pittsburgh's smoky, soot-filled slums. Will
Carnegie went to work in a cotton factory, and Andrew got a
job at the same mill as a bobbin boy—he brought the weavers
empty spindles and took away the full ones. He hated the job;
the work was tedious and it kept him inside for more than 12
hours a day. But he took home $1.20 a week, money that his
struggling family needed.

At 14, Andrew got a new job as a messenger boy in a
local telegraph office. He now made $2.50 a week and spent
a lot of time running errands, giving him the chance to visit
Pittsburgh's libraries and theaters when he had messages for
them. He particularly liked the theater and always tried to take
its messages at night so he could stay and watch the shows.

These experiences helped instill in him an appreciation for culture and the arts that would last the rest of his life.

A Mogul on the Rise

Carnegie impressed his bosses at the telegraph office early on—he could decipher Morse code messages quickly without having to write them down. He also memorized the addresses and people to whom he delivered messages so that he could greet them on the street if he saw them. Before long, he'd moved up again: this time, Carnegie became the personal secretary and telegraph operator for Thomas A. Scott, an administrator at the Pennsylvania Railroad. Of the salary Scott paid him ($35 per month), Carnegie said later, "I couldn't imagine what I could ever do with so much money."

Over the next few years, Carnegie continued working his way up to higher positions—and better pay—at the railroad. Eventually, when Scott was promoted, Carnegie took over his job and became the head of the railroad's Pittsburgh division. Much of Carnegie's drive for success was out of necessity: by the time he was 20, his father had died and he was his family's only wage earner.

Carnegie also made some smart investments. His first success: $217.50 invested in Pullman sleeping railroad cars gave him a $5,000 return. Later, he made more successful investments in oil.

Say No to Strikers . . . Round One

His work at the Pennsylvania Railroad also brought him into contact with capitalism's ugly side. In 1856, Carnegie learned about an upcoming railroad strike when an informant told him about it and named the unions involved. Despite his own

history as a laborer (and his father's history as a labor sup-
porter), Carnegie told Thomas Scott about the union workers'
plans. The result: Scott fired all of the workers who were
planning to strike, and the walkout never happened. Andrew
Carnegie got a promotion.

Pumping Iron

When the Civil War broke out in 1861, Pittsburgh became
one of the Union's industrial centers, and its factories began
making cannons and gunboats. Thomas Scott got a job as a
military supervisor and brought Andrew Carnegie along. They
were in charge of overseeing the repair and maintenance of
telegraph and rail lines, which kept goods and communication
moving between officials in the North and the troops on the
battlefield.

When the war was over, Carnegie decided to leave the
Pennsylvania Railroad and open his own businesses. In 1865,
he founded the Keystone Bridge Company, which concentrated
on building iron railroad bridges to replace existing wooden
ones. This was nothing new, but Carnegie's business model
was—and it changed the way people sold iron. Previously, one
mill produced the original (or pig) iron, another converted it to
bars, and still others manufactured iron goods from those bars.
Carnegie took over all the processes, eliminating middlemen,
improving transportation costs, and bringing in high profits.

In 1867, he opened the Keystone Telegraph Company. Its
main project: stringing telegraph lines from railroad posts so
the entire state of Pennsylvania would have access to telegraph
communication. By 1868, Carnegie was making more than
$50,000 a year, almost 80 times as much as the average worker.

Creating Carnegie Steel

In 1868, Carnegie was doing so well that he toyed with the idea of retiring when he turned 35 in 1870. He wrote, "To continue much longer overwhelmed by business cares and with most of my thoughts wholly upon the way to make more money in the shortest time, must degrade me beyond hope of permanent recovery." Still, he started on a new business venture—this time, in steel.

In 1872, he built his first steel mill—what became the Carnegie Steel Company—near Pittsburgh. Using his experience in the iron industry, Carnegie transformed the American steel business. He used Britain's efficient new Bessemer steelmaking furnaces and cut costs by getting rid of middlemen, buying the iron-ore fields that provided raw materials, and buying railroads to transport ore to his steel plants.

These changes led to big profits for the company, but they also cut costs for consumers, and Carnegie's low-priced steel helped make the United States the world's industrial powerhouse. Carnegie steel was used to build skyscrapers, bridges, railroad tracks, and trains all over the country. And Carnegie himself became a celebrity, seen by the public as a self-made millionaire who also seemed to embrace his working-class roots. In 1886, Carnegie even wrote an essay for *Forum* magazine championing the right of workers to form a union. But that reputation was about to be stained by one of the most brutal conflicts in American labor history: the Homestead strike.

For the rest of the story, turn to page 78.

You Know You're a Pennsylvanian When . . .

- You drink pop, eat hoagies and chipped ham, and played at the crick as a kid.

- You stuff your Thanksgiving turkey with "filling," not stuffing or dressing.

- You tell people you're from PA, not Pennsylvania.

- You have only three spices in your house: pepper, salt, and Heinz ketchup.

- You're used to hearing horses' hooves on the street.

- You enjoy winter driving because the potholes are filled with snow.

- You pronounce Lancaster, Wilkes-Barre, and Lebanon correctly.

- You stock up on milk and bread at the first talk of snow.

- You know the Penn State cheer . . . even though you never went to school there. (Fight on, State!)

- You know that the summer street fairs signal the beginning of funnel cake season.

- You eat dinner for lunch.

- You can spell Bryn Mawr, Schuylkill, and Monongahela without looking them up.

An Insider's Guide to Reggie Jackson

Long before he became Mr. October, baseball's premier clutch hitter was just a kid from Wyncote, PA. Here's more about his early years and how he put his name into Major League Baseball's record books.

1. His father played in the Negro Leagues.

For the Jacksons, baseball was more than just a sport; it was also the family business. Reggie's father, Martinez "Marty" Jackson, was a talented second baseman who played for two seasons in the Negro Leagues in the 1930s with the Newark Eagles before becoming a tailor in Wyncote. Marty instilled in Reggie a love for the game and gave him a little extra incentive to become a star. "I told Reggie that if he didn't make the team, he'd have to work in my shop," he recalled. (Marty later carried business cards that read "Marty the Tailor, Father of the Famous Reggie Jackson.")

2. He was scouted when he was just 11 years old.

Reggie Jackson began playing softball in his backyard when he was 7 years old, and by the time he was 11, he had become so skilled that his reputation as a ballplayer spread beyond Wyncote. That year, while playing in a sandlot with his friends, a scout from the New York Giants approached him, gave the boy his card, and told him to look him up in a few years. Their relationship never advanced beyond that initial meeting, but the brief encounter helped inspire Jackson to pursue a career in professional baseball.

3. He went to high school with a future Israeli prime minister.

Jackson attended Cheltenham Township High School, the same school that graduated Israeli prime minister—and fellow southpaw—Benjamin Netanyahu. (Netanyahu's family lived in Pennsylvania for a few years in the early 1960s.) Jackson was a senior when Netanyahu was a freshman, so the two likely had very little interaction. But Mr. October was a classmate of Netanyahu's older brother, Yonatan. (Other Cheltenham Township High School alumni: poet Ezra Pound and comedian Bill Cosby.)

4. He attended Arizona State University on a football scholarship.

Jackson was a phenomenal halfback on Cheltenham's football team. His combination of speed and power attracted plenty of college scouts, and he eventually accepted a scholarship to play football at Arizona State University. But the team wasn't a good fit, and when coach Frank Kush tried to convert him into a defensive back after his freshman season, Jackson decided to quit and play baseball instead.

That proved to be a good decision. Jackson soon became the first college player to hit a ball out of Phoenix Municipal Stadium, the team's home field, and by 1966, he was named College Player of the Year by the *Sporting News*. Kansas City Athletics owner Charlie Finley was so impressed with Jackson's exploits that he selected him second overall in the 1966 Major League Baseball amateur draft and offered him a $95,000 signing bonus. Jackson accepted the offer and left college to go pro.

5. He gave rapper MC Hammer his nickname.

A youth named Stanley Burrell worked as a batboy for the Oakland Athletics from 1972 until 1980 and was around during Jackson's tenure with the team. On meeting Burrell, Jackson mentioned that the boy bore a striking resemblance to Hall of Fame outfielder "Hammerin'" Hank Aaron, and Jackson began addressing the youngster as "Hammer" for short. The nickname stuck, and Burrell combined it with MC (Master of Ceremonies) later when he began performing at local clubs and bars around San Francisco.

Career Stats

- Jackson played for 21 seasons with four major league teams: the Kansas City/Oakland Athletics (1967–75 and 1987), the Baltimore Orioles (1976), the New York Yankees (1977–81), and the California Angels (1982–86).

- He batted .262, hit 563 homeruns, and drove in 1,702 runs.

- He was a 14-time All-Star (1969, 1971–75, 1977–84).

- He was the American League Most Valuable Player in 1973, and he led the American League in home runs four times (1973, 1975, 1980, 1982).

- He was inducted into the Baseball Hall of Fame in 1993.

- He holds the record for most career strikeouts with 2,597 (a dubious achievement, but his only career record).

Rocky Road

Yo, Adrian! Here are some facts about the most famous movie ever to be set in Philadelphia.

- Sylvester Stallone wrote his first draft of *Rocky* in three days, though he rewrote it substantially before production. The original ending: during the climactic fight, Rocky decides he hates boxing, throws the fight, and quits the sport forever.

- Stallone's inspiration for the movie: a New Jersey boxer named Chuck Wepner who fought his way up through the lower rungs of boxing in the 1960s and 1970s to earn a title fight against Muhammad Ali in 1975. Wepner ultimately lost after 15 bloody rounds, but his gutsy performance brought him national attention.

- Producers Irwin Winkler and Robert Chartoff, working with the United Artists studio, offered Stallone $350,000 for the rights to produce *Rocky*. But Stallone wouldn't sign off unless he got to star in it, too. The compromise: Stallone would take the $350,000, provide rewrites through production, and accept "scale"—minimum wage—for acting: $350 a week.

- United Artists gave Winkler and Chartoff $2 million to make the film so they'd have enough money to hire a big star. When they learned that Stallone (who wasn't a big star at the time) would play the lead, they cut the budget in half.

- The role of Rocky's coach Mickey was played by Burgess Meredith (best known as the Penguin on TV's *Batman*). But Stallone wrote it for Lee J. Cobb, who turned it down because he felt the role was beneath him. Second choice:

Lee Strasberg, who wanted three times the $25,000 salary he was offered. Stallone's pick for Adrian: Carrie Snodgrass (*Diary of a Mad Housewife*). She also wanted more money than the film could afford, though, even turning down the part when Stallone offered her his entire salary. Susan Sarandon was also rejected (because she was "too beautiful"), so the part went to Talia Shire.

- Shooting lasted just 28 days. (Most movies take about 90.)

- The scene where Rocky and Adrian have their first date at an empty skating rink was written much differently at first. It was supposed to be packed with people celebrating Thanksgiving, but the production couldn't afford to pay 300 extras. So Stallone rewrote the scene to have Rocky and Adrian sneak into a closed rink. (It was shot in Santa Barbara, California, not Philadelphia.)

- The meatpacking plant where Rocky trains by punching sides of beef: Shamrock Meats in Vernon, California.

- Skating rink and meat lockers aside, most of the film was shot in and around Philadelphia. The restaurant scene where Rocky gets $500 in training money from his loan shark boss was filmed at Pat's King of Steaks on Passyunk Avenue. The scenes of Rocky running through the city were shot on the sly, without permits. And the reactions of bystanders (including the produce stand guy who throws Rocky an orange) are all real.

- For the prelude to the climactic fight scene between Rocky and Apollo Creed (Carl Weathers), producers tried to get several former boxing champions to sit in the audience. Only one showed up: Joe Frazier, who lived in Philadelphia.

- United Artists didn't like the first cut of the film, so the studio considered releasing it directly to television. But eventually United Artists gave in, released it to theaters—and *Rocky* earned more than $117 million at the box office. (That's the equivalent of $389 million today.)

- The movie was a massive hit by the time the Oscar nominations were announced in February 1977, so the fact that *Rocky* was nominated for some awards was not surprising. What was surprising: it got 10 nominations, a tie with *Network* for the most. Among the nominees were Stallone for screenwriting and acting, Shire for Best Supporting Actress, John G. Avildsen for directing . . . and the biggest prize of all, Best Picture. In all, it won three Oscars: Best Film Editing, Best Director, and Best Picture, beating out favorites *Network* and *All the President's Men*.

- Nine months after the film's release, its theme, "Gonna Fly Now," credited to the film's composer Bill Conti, hit #1 on the pop chart.

- Stallone wrote all five *Rocky* sequels (*Rocky II, Rocky III, Rocky IV, Rocky V,* and *Rocky Balboa*), and directed all except *Rocky V*.

- Rocky's "real" first name: Robert.

- The movie's most famous scene—Rocky running up the front stairs of a building—was shot at the Philadelphia Art Museum, where Rocky climbs 72 steps.

- Visiting the museum's steps to imitate the "Rocky run" is (unofficially) Philadelphia's most popular tourist attraction.

- In 1983, the city erected a nine-foot, 1,300-pound bronze statue of Rocky (with his arms raised) at the base of the museum's stairs. Stallone himself commissioned the statue.

The "Commonwealth" Thing . . .

If you look closely at the official documents and legal processes
of Pennsylvania, you'll see that it's not only a great state;
it's also something called a "commonwealth."

Origin of the Term "Commonwealth"

A "commonwealth" is a political entity with a government that
operates for the common weal (the common good), rather than
to benefit the rulers (kings, emperors, etc). This was a revolutionary idea in the 17th century, particularly for the British,
even though from 1649 to 1660, England itself was a commonwealth, rather than a monarchy. (The Brits beheaded Charles I
to do it.)

The term was commonly used during the American
Revolution because it signified that a state's residents saw
themselves as having a government legitimized by the people,
rather than by a monarchy.

State or Commonwealth?

Today, Pennsylvania is one of four U.S. states that still calls
itself a "commonwealth." (The others are Kentucky, Virginia,
and Massachusetts.) Pennsylvania's interchangeability of the
terms "commonwealth" and "state" goes back to 1776, when
the state's first constitution used both to refer to itself.
Additional state constitutions in 1790, 1838, 1874, and 1968
also used the terms interchangeably.

Rebel with a Cause

He's best known as the Quaker who founded Pennsylvania. But did you know that William Penn was once a highborn rebel who got tossed out of school and thrown into jail before his parents finally disowned him?

I f you want to go back to the beginning of Pennsylvania, there's only one man to start with: William Penn. He was born in London in 1644, and his father was an English admiral who was friendly with King Charles II. William served as his father's personal assistant and often delivered military messages to the monarch. That relationship seemed to assure young William's future as a favorite at court.

Seek and Ye Shall Find

But William Penn also had a spiritual side. At the time, the Anglican Church was Great Britain's state church; every citizen belonged to it. But at the age of about 20, Penn strayed from Anglicanism after he heard a talk by Thomas Loe, a Quaker missionary. Unlike Anglicanism, which emphasized loyalty to the church and the monarchy, the Quakers encouraged a direct and personal relationship with God, and believed that a person's conscience should be his moral authority, not directives from the church or king. Quakers also lived and dressed simply and, instead of formal services, held meetings during which both male and female parishioners meditated in silence until someone was "moved" to speak.

But there was no freedom of religion in 17th-century England. When he was a student, Penn spoke out at Oxford—attendance at the Anglican chapel was mandatory, and Penn was expelled for protesting the policy. His irritated father packed him off to school in France in the hopes that he would shape up into a proper young aristocrat. Eventually, William Penn returned to England, studied law, and appeared to be conforming to the mainstream. But at age 22, he shocked his family—and society—by officially becoming a Quaker.

A Plain People

Despite the Quakers' peaceful ways, most Anglican authorities considered them to be dangerous, mainly because the Quakers preached that all human beings were equal in the eyes of God. That meant a commoner was as important as a king or queen. Quakers also promoted peace and refused to fight in wars, a stance that brought them persecution in England. The treatment was taken so seriously that the Quaker Act of 1662 made it illegal for anyone to participate in Quaker meetings or refuse to attend Anglican church services.

In September 1667, William Penn was arrested at a Quaker meeting. Because he was an aristocrat, the police let him go. But when his parents heard the news, they disowned him.

The Champ

Penn ended up in prison several times for his Quaker activities—he even spent time in a cell in the Tower of London. But he refused to recant his beliefs. Instead, he used his time in prison to write pamphlets about the Quaker faith and religious liberty. His ideas eventually gained a wide audience throughout Europe, and when he lectured, huge crowds gathered to hear him.

William Penn received a windfall in 1681 when King

Charles II granted him a vast tract of land southwest of New Jersey, encompassing the area that is now Pennsylvania and Delaware. The story goes that the king was settling a debt he owed Penn's now-deceased father, but it's also possible that Charles wanted to rid England of Quakers in general and William Penn in particular. In any case, the religious rebel was given one of the world's largest land grants—and he knew exactly what he wanted to do with it.

The Great Law

Penn started planning his colony while crossing the Atlantic onboard the ship *Welcome*. In a document called "The Great Law"—which became Pennsylvania's constitution in 1701—he wrote a line that became a cornerstone of American culture. He stated that no person in the province

> shall be in any case molested or prejudiced in his or theire person or Estate because of his or theire Conscientious perswasion or practice nor be compelled to frequent or mentaine any Religious Worship place or Ministry contrary to . . . theire Religious perswasion.

The idea was revolutionary, and the pamphlet immediately made Pennsylvania a haven for people of persecuted faiths. It also offered men and women a level of religious liberty that was unusual in the Western world at the time.

A Holy Experiment

Penn arrived in his new colony on October 27, 1682. King Charles named the area Pennsylvania (or, "Penn's woods"). Penn called it his "Holy Experiment" because he wanted to create a New World utopia. At a time when many major cities were crowded and dirty, Penn created a blueprint for

Philadelphia that included parkland encircling its borders and space for each house to have a garden. He also did his best to maintain a peaceful relationship with the colony's neighbors— Penn met with leaders from the local Indian tribes and bought (rather than simply took) their land.

But perhaps most important, Penn tried to prevent tyranny by installing a representative government that consisted of two elected groups: one to pass laws, and another to ratify them. That government also guaranteed its citizens the right to secure private property, trial by jury, and a free press.

The Golden Age

Word of this new governmental experiment soon reached the other colonies and Europe. French writer Voltaire wrote, "William Penn might, with reason, boast of having brought down upon earth the Golden Age!" English commoners showed their support for Penn's "holy experiment" by moving to Pennsylvania. Quakers, of course, flocked there. But so did Jews, Catholics, and many marginalized Protestant sects, including Amish, Mennonites, Methodists, Dunkers, Moravians, and Presbyterians.

Although Pennsylvania was one of the last American colonies to be founded, it quickly became one of the most populated—by 1700, more than 20,000 people lived there— and Philadelphia grew into an urban center. Perhaps most importantly, Penn's radical experiment not only worked, but laid the foundation for another government that would be founded 100 years later: the United States.

Meet the Continental Congress

In the 18th century, Philadelphia was a hotbed of political activity.

These days, the United States Congress meets in Washington, D.C., but it's not the first congress the United States had. Before the U.S. Congress, there were three other congresses: the continental congresses, a group of delegates from the 13 British colonies that governed the young nation even before it was officially a nation. And all three congresses convened in Philadelphia.

The First Continental Congress

When it met: September 5–October 26, 1774

Why did it meet? In 1774, the colonists were chafing under British rule because of the Intolerable Acts, a series of punitive laws that came as a reaction to the Boston Tea Party the year before. The various acts included closing Boston Harbor until someone paid for all the dumped tea, replacing home rule of the Massachusetts Colony with direct control by the British government (until then, the British had mostly left the colonists alone), and forcing colonists to quarter British soldiers. The First Continental Congress met to decide what to do about the laws. Because they were still officially part of a British colony, the colonists had to meet in secret, and they decided that in response to the Intolerable Acts, they would boycott British goods beginning December 1, 1774, and suspend exports to Britain the following September unless the acts were repealed. They also decided to convene again in May.

What happened? The boycott went into effect. However, before the export suspension could begin, the Revolutionary War started and rendered the ban unnecessary.

Attendees: Fifty-six delegates from 12 colonies. (The colony of Georgia sat this one out because it was having trouble with the Creek tribe and needed the British army's help.) The delegates included John and Samuel Adams, Patrick Henry, and George Washington. Samuel Adams had proposed the idea of a congress in 1773 "to draw up a Bill of Rights and publish it to the world."

The Second Continental Congress

When it met: May 10, 1775–December 12, 1776, and then at various times and in various places in Pennsylvania and Maryland until 1781

Why did it meet? By this time, the Revolutionary War had broken out, and the Continental Congress acted as a provisional government for the colonies. It established a post office, printed money, built a navy, and appointed George Washington as commander in chief of the U.S. military. Initially, the colonies had just been fighting for representation within the British empire, but by July 1776, both the delegates to the congress and the individual colonial governments had decided they wanted the colonies to become an entirely independent nation.

What happened? This congress approved the Declaration of Independence and then began work on the Articles of Confederation, the United States' first constitution.

Attendees: Most of the same delegates who attended the First Continental Congress, though Ben Franklin and Thomas

Jefferson also participated this time. Georgia's representatives arrived on July 20, 1775.

The Third Continental Congress (a.k.a. the Congress of the Confederation)

When it met: March 1, 1781–March 4, 1789 (though it was in Philadelphia only until June 21, 1783)

Why did it meet? After the Second Continental Congress finalized the Articles of Confederation in 1781, the Congress of the Confederation took over the day-to-day business of running the new country. Its first major accomplishment: sending Benjamin Franklin, John Adams, John Jay, and others to negotiate peace with Britain. This culminated with the 1783 Treaty of Paris, which ended the war between Britain and its former colonies. After that, though, running the new country got harder because the Articles of Confederation didn't give the Congress of the Confederation much power. This led to the Constitutional Convention in Philadelphia in 1787, whose goal was to draft a document that would lay a foundation for a workable and powerful national government.

What happened? The Constitutional Convention gave rise to the current U.S. Constitution, which the states ratified in 1788. It went into effect on March 4, 1789, when the Congress of the Confederation disbanded and the U.S. Congress as we know it today came into being.

Attendees: Hundreds of elected representatives from the 13 states of the United States of America. The first presiding officer of the congress—called the "president"—was Samuel Huntington of Connecticut.

Revolutionary Documents: Common Sense

Philadelphia was the birthplace of three of the most important documents in American history: the Declaration of Independence, the U.S. Constitution, and Common Sense, a philosophical pamphlet by Thomas Paine, who turned complaining into an art form.

Friends in High Places

Thomas Paine's early years were unimpressive. Born in England in 1737, he dropped out of school by the time he was 12. He later worked as a corseter's apprentice, a seaman, and a tax officer, but he couldn't seem to find his niche. He did, though, excel as a writer. When Benjamin Franklin met Paine in London in 1774, Paine impressed Franklin with his ability to write passionately and clearly on political issues. Paine's most recent critique: an argument against his employer (England's tax office, for whom Paine tracked alcohol and tobacco smugglers and then collected taxes on their goods). Paine argued that the low wages the office paid led directly to corruption. Displeased with the criticism, Paine's employers had fired him.

Paine seemed a perfect protégé for Franklin, who was in England because tensions between the colonies and the mother country were high. Revolutionary ideas that were swirling in colonial cities seemed like a good fit for Paine, so the statesman urged him to start life over in America.

Paine arrived in Philadelphia in November 1774, with no job and no money, but he did have an impressive letter of introduction from Franklin. That opened doors for him, and within a year, Paine was working as an editor for the pro-Revolution *Pennsylvania Magazine*. He soon declared his loyalty to the Revolution and began writing a pamphlet to support its independence.

Just Common Sense

When the Revolutionary War began in April 1775, not all of the colonists wanted to separate from Britain. In fact, many considered themselves British citizens and urged their neighbors to remain loyal to the British monarchy. There was also disagreement at the time as to whether to merely fight for representation in the existing British government, or for complete independence. Thomas Paine believed in the latter, and in January 1776, he published a 47-page pamphlet called *Common Sense* that argued in favor of an all-out war with Britain.

Paine's experiences in England clearly influenced his opinions. He'd been poor and (he claimed) mistreated at the hands of the ruling monarchy. In *Common Sense*, he lashed out at the idea of obeying a king and called Britain's George III "the royal brute of England." He also told his readers that if the colonies remained a part of England, they would be dragged into European conflicts that had nothing to do with them. Instead, he argued, they needed to be an entirely separate country and should establish a republican government with a constitution that would spell out each citizen's liberties.

In Support of the Cause

Paine was convincing. By the summer of 1776, his pamphlet had sold half a million copies, and America's leaders were formally declaring their independence from England. Even though the profits from *Common Sense* could have made Paine rich, he used the money to buy supplies for the rebel troops.

Common Sense turned out to have a lasting impact on the Revolution. Not only did it inspire the public, it also inspired lawmakers. Paine's pamphlet directly influenced Thomas Jefferson, the primary author of the Declaration of Independence. (*More about that document on page 182.*)

Life After *Common Sense*

Thomas Paine stayed in Philadelphia and continued to write pamphlets throughout the war. He drafted several famous works, including 16 "Crisis" papers, which included now-famous lines like "These are the times that try men's souls" and encouraged the colonists to keep fighting. (George Washington gave his troops the first "Crisis" paper to read as a means of inspiration.)

When the war ended, Thomas Paine was on the side of victory, but he was penniless. Because he'd refused all money for his writing, he had little to show for his patriotic endeavors. In the 1780s, the State of Pennsylvania gave him 500 pounds, the State of New York gave him a plot of land, and he moved to a farm in New Rochelle, New York. He continued writing and working for freedom—in 1791, he wrote a pamphlet called *The Rights of Man*, in support of the French Revolution. Thomas Paine died in 1809 at the age of 72.

Did You Know?

According to the states's Department of Agriculture, Pennsylvania is the United States' second-largest producer of ice cream. (California is first.)

Behind the Hits

Philadelphian Will Smith first made a name for himself as the rapper "the Fresh Prince," and Boyz II Men rose to fame after scoring a hit with "Motown Philly." But Pennsylvania had been in the pop-music limelight before—thanks to nonPennsylvanians Billy Joel and Elton John.

"Allentown"

Until Billy Joel released this song in 1982, it seemed unlikely that the depressed, Rust Belt Allentown region in eastern Pennsylvania's Lehigh Valley could be the subject of a catchy pop tune. But Joel used the area as a metaphor for the effects of the industrial economic recession of the 1980s and charted a hit song in the process.

Why Allentown? The song's lyrics evoke the despair and disillusionment of an unemployed blue-collar worker, but Allentown wasn't the place Joel had in mind when he was writing the song. He'd read a magazine article about the decline of the steel industry in the Lehigh Valley, particularly in neighboring Bethlehem, which is mentioned in the first verse. But Joel thought "Allentown" sounded like a more generic name for an all-American town. In 2007, he said, "If I look at a map and I want to find where the heartland begins, I'd probably start right there in the Lehigh Valley . . . So the name Allentown worked for me as a heartland name."

It also worked with the chords and melody Joel had come up with in the early 1970s, while trying to write a song about his own hometown of Levittown, New York. As he tried to write that song, though, Joel discovered that Levittown seemed too boring to merit a pop song. The original lyrics went, "We're living here in Levittown/And there's really not much going down/And I don't see much when I look around/The trees are green/The dirt is brown." Joel put the song away until he played a series of concerts in Allentown, met the residents, and saw what was happening to the community. He said, "There was a kind of wearing on the area from what had happened in the steel industry." So he decided to write about that.

Did you know? "Allentown" isn't the only song about Allentown. Frank Zappa's 1975 song "200 Years Old" and a 1950s folk song by Irving Gordon, "Allentown Jail," both mention the town.

"Philadelphia Freedom"

Elton John had been a longtime fan of tennis player Billie Jean King, and they became friends after running into each other at various celebrity tennis tournaments. When King gave John a personalized tracksuit, he told her he would write a song for her. "Philadelphia Freedom" was a reference to King's team in the World Tennis League—the Philadelphia Freedoms.

What it's about: The song was, according to John, "one of the only times I tried to deliberately write a hit single," but it presented some problems for radio DJs: "Philadelphia Freedom" was 5 minutes and 41 seconds long. Many DJs had already vowed not to play any songs longer than four minutes because it complicated their playlists. (Accounting for commercials, the popular "14 hits in a row" hour-long format didn't work if songs were longer than four minutes.) John's song was so successful, though, that listeners demanded DJs play it anyway.

Did you know? In the end, the song's lyrics (by John's long-time lyricist Bernie Taupin) ended up not having any direct references to Billie Jean King, tennis, or sports at all. Instead, and in spite of being written by two English songwriters, "Philadelphia Freedom" had a patriotic quality with lines like "'Cause I live and breathe this Philadelphia freedom/From the day that I was born I've waved the flag." The lyrics resonated strongly with Americans—so much so that the song was used as an anthem for the U.S. bicentennial celebration a year later.

Did You Know?

In 1919, the Pennsylvania Railroad built the Hotel Pennsylvania in New York City. The luxurious 22-floor, columned structure was one of the most elaborate of its day. It originally contained more than 2,000 bathrooms and had tunnels underground that connected it to Penn Station across the street. Everyone from Duke Ellington to the Glenn Miller Orchestra played in its lounge, and the television shows *Maury* and *The People's Court* were filmed inside its ballroom. It also had a prestigious phone number: the PEnnsylvania 6-5000, as mentioned in the song by the Glenn Miller Orchestra.

The hotel was assigned the phone number back in 1919, and it's still being used today, making it the oldest phone number in the United States. The "PE" in Pennsylvania stand for the numbers 7 and 3—which correspond to the letters on a telephone's dial. This means that, including the New York City area code, the phone number for the Hotel Pennsylvania was (and still is) 212-736-5000.

An Oil-American City

It's a tiny town today, but Titusville in northwestern Pennsylvania was the birthplace of one of history's most important economic developments.

Town: Titusville

Location: Crawford County

Founding: 1796

Population (2008): 6,200

Size: 7.5 square miles

County seat: No

What's in a Name?

In 1796, the town began as a single plot of land claimed by a settler named Jonathan Titus.

Claim to Fame:

- Before the 1850s, procuring oil was a much simpler process than it is today. Men simply gathered the oil at seeps (where it seeped out of the ground) and dug narrow holes into the ground near the seeps to find more. But on August 22, 1859, Titusville local Edwin Drake demonstrated that there was a way to get to *all* the oil in the ground: he drilled through the rock to find the source and reinforced the holes with piping, to prevent them from collapsing. Drake was the first person to drill for oil in the United States, and today, the Drake Well Museum sits at the site of that first drilling.

The Birth of "Clean Air"

In October 1948, in a Rust Belt town about 20 miles south of Pittsburgh, a heavy, choking smog settled over the streets and houses. For four days, it suffocated the people living there, but it also led to the first clean-air regulations in the United States.

Donora, Pennsylvania, got its start as a factory town. In 1899, the Union Steel Company (founded by William H. Donner, Andrew and Richard Mellon, and Henry Clay Frick, who also teamed up with Andrew Carnegie) laid out the town and set up shop. The group even named the place after themselves: Donora was a combination of Donner and Nora, Andrew Mellon's wife.

Pollution: A Way of Life

By the late 1940s, Donora had grown to about 14,000 people. The steel company still employed many of them (though it had since changed its name to the American Steel and Wire Plant), and the Donora Zinc Works had opened in 1915. Those two factories, both owned by U.S. Steel, pumped smoke into the air constantly, so smog was a common problem. Some residents tried to do something about it: In 1918, residents sued the Zinc Works, claiming pollution from the factory had made them sick. (They won and the owner had to pay damages.) And in the 1920s, a group of farmers across the river in Webster also complained, saying pollution from the factories was killing their crops. The city started taking samples of the air around town to test the pollution levels, but no one ever did anything about it. The factories were too important to the town's livelihood. According to one resident, "It was a normal way of life."

A Killer Smog

But on October 27, 1948, a weather system moved into the Monongahela Valley and dropped a heavy fog over Donora. The fog trapped the sulfur and other chemicals pumping out of the factories. With nowhere to go, the pollution started filling up the air in town.

Most of the people in Donora weren't worried initially. They figured it was just very bad smog that would pass eventually. Joann Crow, who was 12 years old at the time, said, "Dad couldn't drive us to school because it was so hard to see. He had to walk us . . . with a flashlight, which we thought was fun." As the days wore on, the smog grew thicker. At a high school football game on October 29, people in the crowd couldn't see the players on the field, and the ball kept getting lost in the haze.

Then came a rash of breathing problems. The first victim was a man walking home at night. He started choking, stopped for a moment to rest, and died. Soon, people all over town were choking from the bad air. According to one resident, "The air was yellow and so full of sulfur. It burned my eyes so badly that I had tears. My eyes were burning like fire." The local hospital was overcrowded with patients, firemen were going door-to-door with oxygen tanks, and doctors couldn't examine people fast enough. Ultimately, about 7,000 Donora residents got sick. Twenty of them died in just five days, a horrifying number for a town in which only 30 people had died during the entire previous year. The local funeral home was so overwhelmed that it ran out of caskets.

"Murder from the Mill"

Finally, on October 30, the town council convinced the

superintendent at the Zinc Works to close the plant in hopes of preventing more deadly gases from being pumped into the air. And the next day, the weather changed. A front moved in, pushed the fog out of town, and it began to rain. Almost as quickly as it had come, the smog disappeared.

As the poisonous air cleared, people clamored for some kind of explanation. U.S. Steel called the deaths an "act of God" and blamed them on asthma and other ailments, but a doctor at Donora's Board of Health, William Rongaus, thought differently. He argued that the deaths and sickness were the direct result of air pollution. He said later, "People were dying while I was treating them. I called it murder from the mill."

Even so, the people of Donora were initially unwilling to take on U.S. Steel in a fight for clean air. The company employed thousands of townspeople, and thousands of others ran support businesses that depended on the steelworkers. But the story had made the national news, and it wasn't just up to Donora anymore.

Acting for Clean Air

The deaths in Donora were big news, especially after major newspapers in Pittsburgh and Philadelphia picked up the story and radio personality Walter Winchell discussed it on his broadcasts. Pennsylvania's Department of Health, the U.S. Public Health Service, and Donora's town council launched investigations . . . the first organized inquiries into the effects of air pollution.

Their findings showed that the mills were contributing to the pollution in Donora, but authorities shied away from officially blaming U.S. Steel. Others were bolder—editors at the newspaper in Monessen, just a few miles from Donora, wrote that the damage was "something no scientific investigation is necessary to prove. All you need is a pair of reasonably good eyes." For its part, U.S. Steel—though it admitted no liability—did eventually pay small settlements (between $1,000 and $30,000) to the people who got sick or lost loved ones.

More important, though, the study was the first real recognition that air pollution was a major problem in the United States. Change came slowly, but the events at Donora inspired lawmakers (first on the local and state level, and then nationally) to enact legislation to clean up America's air. The Air Pollution Control Act of 1955 was the first, but the most sweeping was the Clean Air Act of 1970, which put strict restrictions on emissions from automobiles and factories. During the congressional hearings debating the law, Donora came up repeatedly; the danger the town's residents had faced in 1948 was something no one wanted to encounter again. The law was updated in 1990, and today, the air over the United States is much cleaner than it was in 1948—it's estimated to have 98 percent less lead, 41 percent less sulfur dioxide, and 28 percent less carbon monoxide, though environmentalists stress that there's still a long way to go before the air is truly "healthy."

Donora These Days

The decline of the steel industry hit Donora hard, and today, it's a small town of about 5,000 people. The Zinc Works closed in 1957, and the steel plant shut down in 1966. For many years, Donora's older residents saw the 1948 smog as a stain on their town's reputation. According to one city councilman, "The smog in Donora over the years had been looked upon as a black eye. The older folks just didn't want to talk about it because they thought it was bad publicity." But as people moved out (and in) and the hazards of air pollution became more widely known, Donora started to take pride in its history and its place in the environmental movement.

In 1998, on the 50th anniversary of the tragedy, the town erected a historical marker. And in 2008, the Smog Museum opened downtown. It's filled with photographs and artifacts from the five days when smog smothered Donora. The museum's motto: "Clean air started here."

Did You Know?

In 1905, Pittsburgh's John Harris and Harry Davis partitioned off part of their penny arcade, set up a film screen, and charged a nickel for entrance into what Pennsylvanians claim was the first movie theater in the United States. Soon "nickelodeons," a term coined in Pittsburgh, were popping up across the nation.

As the motion picture business grew, storefront nickelodeons gave way to motion picture palaces. And once again Pennsylvanians were at the forefront of the change. In 1908, door-to-door salesman Samuel "Roxy" Rothapfel opened a nickelodeon in the back room of a saloon in Forest City. Thirty years later, Rothapfel owned a chain of theaters that included some of America's largest motion picture palaces, and he managed the country's largest theater: New York's Radio City Music Hall.

You Can't Do *That* Here!

In its history, Pennsylvania has had some pretty dumb laws. Example: Did you know there used to be one that disqualified gubernatorial candidates who had participated in a duel?

Around the House

- No more than 16 women may live together. If they do, their house is be considered a brothel.
- Wives may not hide dirt or dust under a rug in their house.
- Singing in the bathtub is prohibited.

Travel Advisories

- All motorists who drive at night on a country road in Pennsylvania must stop every mile and send up a rocket signal, like the kind that comes in a flare kit. Then they must wait 10 minutes for the road to be cleared of farm animals before resuming their journey.
- If a group of horses approaches a driver on a road, the driver must pull over and cover the vehicle with a blanket or canvas that camouflages it with its surroundings until the horses pass.
- Selling a motorized vehicle on a Sunday is against the law.
- In the city of Tarentum, it's illegal to tie a horse to a parking meter.
- In Pittsburgh, donkeys and mules are banned on trolley cars.

- There's a block in Carlisle that requires all people who park there to pay a $50 annual fee. People must also move their cars every night for street cleaning, even if snow or ice prevents it, or else receive a parking ticket.

No Fun

- It's illegal to buy more than two packages of beer at a time unless they're being purchased from an official beer distributor. (It's unclear whether a "package" means a 6-pack, a 12-pack, a case. . .)
- In Ridley Park, it is against the law to walk backward while eating peanuts in front of the Barnstormers Auditorium while a performance is underway.

Go Fish!

- Fish may not be caught by any part of their body but their mouth.
- The law prohibits catching a fish with your bare hands.
- It is illegal to use dynamite to catch fish.
- You must obtain a hunting license to hunt on your own land, but it is legal to fish on your land without a fishing license.

Did You Know?

The site on which Pittsburgh's National Aviary was built was once a prison and the city's first plant conservatory. Today, it's one of the largest aviaries in the United States and is home to more than 500 birds.

Pen-sylvania

John Updike once said that he and fellow author John O'Hara "could have been nurtured only in Pennsylvania, not in Boston or Brooklyn." Here's how the state shaped them . . . and other famous wordsmiths.

James A. Michener

Hometown: Doylestown, Bucks County

Michener was born in New York City, but he was adopted by a widow from Bucks County, Mabel Michener. He always considered himself a Pennsylvanian and credited his early years in Bucks County with fostering his storytelling abilities. Michener said later,

> My mother read to me when I was a boy. I had all the Dickens and Thackeray and Charles Read and Sinkiewicz and the rest before I was the age of seven or eight. And so I knew about books. And there was a good library in our town, and I read almost everything in there. But primarily, I had very good teachers—teachers who wanted to make kids learn.

Michener went to Swarthmore College on a full academic scholarship and graduated with honors and a degree in English. He then taught at several schools in Pennsylvania. But when World War II broke out, he joined the navy and was sent to the South Pacific. He drew on this experience to write his first novel, *Tales of the South Pacific*, which won the Pulitzer Prize in 1948. He went on to write more than 40 other books. The most famous: *Hawaii*, *Centennial*, *The Source*, *The Bridges of Toko-Ri*, *Chesapeake*, and *Space*.

Keystone Fact: Michener dabbled in Pennsylvania politics. In 1960, he was chairman of the Bucks County Committee to Elect John F. Kennedy, and in 1962, he ran for Congress as a liberal Democrat in predominantly conservative Republican Bucks County. Not surprisingly, he lost.

Pearl S. Buck

Hometown: Perkasie, Bucks County

Pearl Buck grew up in China, where her father worked as a missionary, and Chinese was her first language. She became a Pennsylvanian later in life, when she moved to Bucks County in 1934 and bought a 60-acre farm called Green Springs. Buck spent the last 38 years of her life there, writing . . . and winning awards. Some of the books she wrote at Green Springs: *His Proud Heart*, *The Patriot*, *Today and Forever*, and *The Child Who Never Grew*. But she's best known for the now-classic novel *The Good Earth*, for which she won a Pulitzer Prize in 1932. In 1938, Buck became the first American woman to win a Nobel Prize.

Keystone Fact: Buck's oldest daughter, Carol, was born with severe mental and physical disabilities, and Buck herself was unable to have additional children, though she did adopt. This experience inspired Buck to found the Welcome House Adoption Program in 1949. The organization concentrated on placing biracial children who were, at the time, considered unadoptable. Today, Welcome House is part of the larger Pearl S. Buck International foundation, a humanitarian foundation headquartered at Buck's Green Springs farm in Perkasie.

John Updike

Hometowns: Reading, Shillington, and Plowville

The man who would become one of America's most famous novelists spent his early years in and around Reading, Pennsylvania. When he was 13, he and his family moved to his grandparents' farm in Plowville, where the elders spoke Pennsylvania Dutch almost exclusively. After high school, Updike went to college at Harvard but returned home in the summers to work for the *Reading Eagle*, a local paper. He started out as a copy boy and went on to write features.

Updike published his first book, *The Poorhouse Fair*, in 1959. That story was set in New England, but Pennsylvania played an important role in some of his other works, including *The Centaur*, which won the National Book Award in 1963, and the Rabbit series, five books that tell the story of 1950s Pennsylvania everyman Harry Angstrom. (Two of the "Rabbit" books won Pulitzer Prizes.)

Keystone Fact: Updike has also published many stories in the *New Yorker* that are set in a fictional Pennsylvania town called Ollinger, a stand-in for Plowville.

John O'Hara

Hometown: Pottsville, Schuylkill County

Like Updike, John O'Hara also created a fictional Pennsylvania landscape modeled after the town where he grew up. In 1934's *Appointment in Samarra* (and in several short stories), his characters inhabit a coal-mining town he called "Gibbsville."

O'Hara had a reputation as a drinker and carouser, and most of his stories dealt with depravity and alcoholism. Class struggles also played a role, inspired by O'Hara's own experience of falling into poverty after his father, a prominent doctor, died in 1924 when O'Hara was 19, after which the one-time prep-school student could no longer afford to go to Yale.

Appointment at Samarra was initially criticized for its forthright discussions about sex, and *BUtterfield 8* tells the story of a call girl who poses as a model. (Elizabeth Taylor won an Academy Award for her role in the 1960 film adaptation.)

Keystone Fact: Penn State's Special Collections Library houses an exact reconstruction of O'Hara's study and a collection of his papers.

Edgar Allan Poe

A writer of horror stories and often called the father of the mystery novel, Edgar Allan Poe was born in Massachusetts in 1809. His parents died when he was two, and he lived with a foster mother until she died when he was 20. He spent several years moving from place to place around the East until he landed in Philadelphia in 1838. He lived there for six years and wrote several of his most famous works while in Philadelphia.

Poe rented a house on North Seventh Street, where he lived with his wife Virginia, his mother-in-law, and a beloved cat named Catarina. This was where he wrote "The Tell-Tale Heart," "The Black Cat" (inspired by Catarina), and "The Gold Bug," which won a newspaper-sponsored contest. He also began work on "The Raven" while living in Philadelphia, though the poem—which made him internationally famous— was later published in New York.

Keystone Fact: Poe's home at 532 North Seventh Street is now the Edgar Allan Poe National Historic Site. Self-guided tours lead visitors through the house and the cellar, which looks a lot like the fictional cellar where a murderer kills his wife in "The Black Cat." Recitations of Poe's terrifying tales and spooky candlelight tours take place throughout the year.

Poor Richard

Witty and wise, Benjamin Franklin certainly had a lot to say.

Between 1732 and 1758, Benjamin Franklin published an annual almanac—he took the pseudonym "Poor Richard" and called the publication *Poor Richard's Almanack*. Many of the famous phrases attributed to Franklin came from that work. See how many you recognize.

Speaking Plainly

"Fish and visitors stink after three days."

"God helps them that help themselves."

"The noblest question in the world is: What good can I do in it?"

"A good example is the best sermon."

"They who can give up essential liberty to obtain a little temporary safety deserve neither liberty nor safety."

"There was never a good war or a bad peace."

"He that lieth down with dogs shall rise up with fleas."

"Work as if you were to live a hundred years, pray as if you were to die tomorrow."

"To err is human, to forgive divine; to persist devilish."

"Nothing can be said to be certain, except death and taxes."

"He that is good for making excuses is seldom good for anything else."

"People who are wrapped up in themselves make small packages."

"So convenient a thing it is to be a reasonable creature, since it enables one to find or make a reason for everything one has a mind to do."

"Old boys have their playthings as well as young ones; the difference is only in the price."

"He that teaches himself, hath a fool for his master."

"Three may keep a secret, if two of them are dead."

"Early to bed and early to rise makes a man healthy, wealthy, and wise."

Clever Comebacks

Ben Franklin also made witty remarks off the page:

- When Franklin saw a demonstration of hot-air balloons in France, another spectator asked, "What good is it?" Franklin responded, "What good is a newborn baby?"

- At the signing of the Declaration of Independence, John Hancock urged all present to sign the document, saying, "We must all hang together." "Yes, we must indeed all hang together," Franklin added, "Or most assuredly, we shall all hang separately."

Must-see Muscletown

*Uncle John wondered . . . what Pennsylvania city is older
than New York, but newer than England's (Old) York?*

Town: York

Location: York County

Founding: 1741

Population (2008): 41,000

Size: 5.3 square miles

County seat: Yes

What's in a Name?

Settlers who moved out of Philadelphia started the town and
named it after York, England, where many of them were from
originally.

Claims to Fame:

- The York Peppermint Pattie, now manufactured by Hershey
  (more about that on page 284), was invented in York in 1940.

- The Continental Congress met in York from September 1777
  to June 1778.

- During the Civil War, Penn Park in downtown York was
  the site of the York U.S. Army Hospital. Between July 1862,
  when the hospital opened, and the end of the war in 1865,
  more than 14,000 Union soldiers were treated there, including 2,500 from Gettysburg alone.

- In 1777, George Washington was having little success in his military campaigns. So a group of disgruntled soldiers, led by Brigadier General Thomas Conway, met in York's Golden Plough Tavern and cooked up a plot to oust Washington from his position as the head of the Revolutionary army. (They failed.) The tavern still stands today, and is the oldest building in the city.

- In the early 1900s, the York Motor Car Company built an automobile called the Pullman, a luxury car that cost between $1,500 and $3,000. (A Model T, the most popular car at the time, cost about $500.) The York company went bankrupt in 1917, but not before it launched a publicity campaign to show how durable their automobile was: in 1908, an employee drove a Pullman from York to San Francisco, California, and back. It took him a month.

- York is nicknamed "Muscletown" because, in 1932, body-builder and fitness advocate Bob Hoffman started the York Barbell Corporation there. He went on to become an Olympic weightlifting coach. York is now home to the USA Weightlifting Hall of Fame.

- York's biggest employer: a Harley-Davidson motorcycle plant. Half of all Harley employees work there.

Quote Me

"I thought it might be a good move to get into a beauty contest so I tried for Miss Pennsylvania and won. I think that helped me get noticed, at least by the people of Pennsylvania."

—Sharon Stone

Food, Glorious Food

From fried pork scraps to Tastykakes, Pennsylvania's delicacies are a source of hometown pride.

Shoofly Pie

There's a rumor that shoofly pie is actually a French dish whose top looked like a cauliflower (*cheux-fleur* in French), and eventually the term was shortened to "shoo-fly." But Pennsylvanians don't buy that. They know that Pennsylvania Dutch settlers invented shoofly pie in the early 1900s, when they ran out of fruit one winter and had only flour, molasses, and lard to make a dessert. Those chefs fashioned a sweet, gooey tart that's often topped with a sugary flour crumble.

Despite the French rumor, the sticky treat's name probably comes from the number of flies it attracts as it cools, eliciting cries of "Shoo, fly!" from bakers. Today, shoofly pie comes in two varieties: "wet bottom" (soft filling and a crumb topping) or "dry bottom" (with the crumb topping mixed into the pie).

Scrapple

After the bacon and chops have been cut, what's a frugal farmer to do with the rest of his pig? In the case of German settlers in eastern Pennsylvania, they put the scraps—head, heart, liver, tongue, and skin—into a pot; boiled them; cut off the leftover meat; mixed that with cornmeal, onions, and spices; and created a new dish. Most people eat scrapple at breakfast (with fried eggs), but scrapple sandwiches are also popular. Common condiments: maple syrup, ketchup, apple butter, and mustard.

Red Beet Eggs

The hue of these puckered eggs is more pink than red, but the name comes from the red beets used to color and flavor the eggs, and once again, this culinary delight comes from the Pennsylvania Dutch. Sweet, tart red beet eggs show up at nearly every Pennsylvania picnic.

Recipe: Combine ¼ cup of sugar, ½ cup of vinegar (some people prefer apple cider vinegar), a pound of sliced red beets, and a sliced onion, and boil for 15 minutes. Then pour that mixture over one dozen peeled hard-boiled eggs. Put it all in a sealed container and let it marinate in the refrigerator for three days.

Tastykake

Individually wrapped snack cakes from Philadelphia's Tastykake company have attracted a cultlike following. Devotees live for favorites like Butterscotch Krimpets, Cream-Filled Buttercream Iced Chocolate Cupcakes, and Lemon Pie turnovers. The name comes from cofounder Herbert Morris's wife who, when she tried the bakery's early samples, proclaimed them "tasty."

For years the treats were on sale only in Pennsylvania. But as the company grew, so did its distribution, and today, Tastykake addicts worldwide can order their favorites on the Internet.

Tasty Trivia

- 10 cents: Cost of the first Tastykakes.
- 150 feet: Length of the company's oven.
- 2,000: Number of cakes an actress dressed as Marie Antoinette tossed from the tower of Philadelphia's Eastern State Penitentiary to celebrate Bastille Day in 2008. She

shouted, "Let them eat Tastykake!" as the desserts fell. (The prison closed in 1970 and is now a tourist attraction.)

- 14,080: Number of Tastykake pies that, when laid end-to-end, would stretch for one mile.

- 135,000 pounds: Amount of sugar the company's bakers use every day.

- 4.8 million: Number of treats that Tastykake bakers make daily.

Did You Know?

In the late 1760s, British immigrants established a series of settlements in the West Branch Susquehanna River valley in what is now Lycoming County. But the British government recognized the land as belonging to the local American Indians, so the Crown didn't govern the area—which meant that the settlers essentially had no government. So in 1773, they created their own. Every year, they elected three "fair-play men" to oversee all legal matters and to make sure everyone was treated fairly. The fair-play men's word was the law, and the system worked well. It didn't last long, though: the tiny enclave remained operational only until 1785. After the Revolutionary War, the settlers' land became part of the newly independent United States, and the state of Pennsylvania dissolved the fair-play system.

Pennsylvania Evens

*While we were researching the Keystone State, we ran across
these interesting numbers. (The "odds" are on page 146.)*

Pennsylvania has 2 . . . of the United States' most prestigious
orchestras: the Philadelphia Orchestra and the Pittsburgh
Symphony Orchestra.

Pennsylvania has 4 . . . lighthouses on Lake Erie, but only two
are officially considered "historic," meaning they're on the
National Park Service's "Inventory of Historic Light Stations."
The oldest of the two is the Erie Land (Old Presque Isle) Light,
first lit in 1867.

Pennsylvania has 6 . . . international airports: Lehigh Valley,
Pittsburgh, Philadelphia, Wilkes-Barre/Scranton, Harrisburg,
and Erie.

Pennsylvania has 22 . . . species of snakes.

Pennsylvania has 40 . . . miles of shoreline along Lake Erie.

Pennsylvania has 116 . . . state parks.

Pennsylvania has 130 . . . four-year colleges and universities
that enroll more than 590,000 students.

Pennsylvania has more than 5,100 . . . miles of railway.

Washington's War

*Two decades before the American Revolution, George Washington
lost a battle at a makeshift fort in the Pennsylvania woods
. . . and accidentally started an international incident.*

The Stakes

In the mid-1700s, the French and British were still embroiled
in a dispute over which empire would control the Ohio Valley,
a vast tract of land encompassing modern-day Ohio and parts
of West Virginia, Indiana, and southwest Pennsylvania.
Virginia's lieutenant governor Robert Dinwiddie saw a chance
to make money from furs and real estate in the Ohio Valley.
So in 1749, the English government gave Dinwiddie and his
business partners 200,000 acres of land near present-day
Pittsburgh to settle in the name of Britain and on which to
build a fort to protect the territory. This would give Britain
control of important trade routes through the heart of the new
frontier, and the Virginians would prosper from the new business opportunities. There was only one problem: the French
military. The French had already laid claim to the Ohio
Valley—they'd established trade relations with the American
Indians and built several forts.

But in the winter of 1753, Governor Dinwiddie hired a
young surveyor named George Washington to act as his ensign.
He sent the man to the French fort Le Boeuf (at what is now
Waterford, Pennsylvania) to inform the French commander,
Jacques Legardeur de Saint-Pierre, that the English were
ordering the French to leave the Ohio Valley at once. Saint-
Pierre politely declined, and when Washington returned to

Virginia, he gave Dinwiddie more bad news: Washington had scouted out a strong French military presence in the valley and learned of plans for reinforcements in the spring. Concerned, Dinwiddie sent Washington back to the Ohio Valley, this time with orders to defend British interests.

Shots Fired

On May 24, 1754, Washington and his men were busy building a wagon road from Alexandria, Virginia, through the forest into the Ohio Valley to make it easier for Virginia to send settlers and soldiers into the frontier. They made camp in the Great Meadows, where there was freshwater from streams and enough grass for their animals.

While awaiting reinforcements and supplies, they got a tip from a friendly Seneca chief that hostile French soldiers lurked nearby. Chief Tanaghrisson, whom the British called Half King, wanted the French out of the valley, too—partly because he believed that the British would do more for his people, but mainly because he held the French responsible for the death of his father.

On May 28, Tanaghrisson guided Washington and 40 of his militiamen to what is now known as Jumonville Glen. There, they surprised a sleeping French colonial militia. (It's still debated whether the Frenchmen were a hostile force or only emissaries sent to warn Washington that he was in their territory.) No one knows who fired the first shot, but when the musket smoke cleared, 10 French soldiers were dead and 21 others, including the commanding officer, Ensign Joseph Coulon Sieur de Jumonville, were British prisoners. Then, according to most reports, Tanaghrisson took revenge on the French and scalped Jumonville.

That Little Thing Upon the Meadow

Jumonville had been under Washington's protection as an officer and prisoner of war, though, and Washington expected French reprisals for his death. So in the low-lying, marshy clearing of the Great Meadows, Washington's men hastily constructed Fort Necessity, whose stockade fence was made of white oak posts driven into the ground. Inside the fence were swivel guns—small cannons mounted on posts that could be turned in various directions—along with a shed to hold provisions. Washington notified Dinwiddie about the fort and claimed that it would hold off at least 500 attackers.

Tanaghrisson, however, was unimpressed with Fort Necessity, which he called "that little thing upon the meadow." Ringed in by higher ground and dense forest, the fort seemed vulnerable to attack. So even though Washington got reinforcements from Virginia and South Carolina on June 12, Tanaghrisson and his men refused to defend the fort. Without their Indian allies, the Virginians had less than 400 men to hold off the enemy.

On the morning of July 3, 600 French troops and 100 other American Indians led by Captain Louis Coulon de Villiers—the half-brother of Jumonville—fired on the fort from the cover of trees. Holding the higher ground, the French and their allies were able to take deadly aim on the troops trapped in the meadow. Washington soon knew he'd made a mistake. Even the weather worked against Fort Necessity: heavy rain swamped the Great Meadow, making it nearly impossible for the militiamen to keep their gunpowder dry and their muskets firing.

Lost in Translation

By nightfall, almost a third of Washington's troops were dead or wounded. Others raided the fort's supply of rum and became too drunk for battle. That evening, when the French sent a surrender offer, Washington knew he couldn't refuse. A Dutchman who was fluent in both French and English translated the French terms, and Washington wearily signed the surrender document.

On July 4, 1754, Washington and his men retreated from the Great Meadow and left Fort Necessity to the victorious French, who burned it down. It was a bleak day for Washington, but it would have been worse if he'd known that the Dutchman had missed translating an important clause: that Washington had assassinated Jumonville.

The Jumonville Affair

That charge of assassination haunted Washington, who resigned from the militia before he could be demoted. The French government used the signed surrender as propaganda, and the "Jumonville affair" ignited passions that led to the Seven Years' War in Europe (known as the French and Indian War in North America). The conflict eventually involved all the major powers of Europe—France, Great Britain, Austria, Prussia, the Russian empire, Sweden, Spain, Portugal, and the Netherlands—as well as their colonies. The theaters of the conflict spanned the globe from Virginia and Canada all the way to India. British statesman Horace Walpole later wrote, "The volley fired by a young Virginian in the backwoods of America set the world on fire."

The British won the French and Indian War in 1763, but the conflict still influenced history. The American colonists who'd fought for King George's lands wanted their rights as British citizens. Meanwhile, the king found the defense of the territories to be a drain on the treasury, and imposed high taxes on the colonists to foot the bill. Taxation, of course, eventually helped spark the American Revolution—a conflict largely directed by a more experienced General George Washington, who never surrendered again.

● ●

Did You Know?

Penn State University is one of the largest and most respected universities in the United States. Here are some facts about the school:

- The university's main campus in State College, Pennsylvania, has been a site of higher learning since 1855, when the state general assembly created the first school on the property: an agricultural college called the Farmers' High School of Pennsylvania.

- With more than 40,000 students enrolled, the State College campus is the largest in the Penn State system. But 23 other campuses around the state serve an additional 40,000 students.

- Penn State is ranked among the United States' top-15 universities and is often called one of America's "public Ivies."

- The university's Beaver Stadium—home of the famous Nittany Lions football team—is the second-largest college stadium in the United States, with 107,282 seats. (The University of Michigan's stadium is the largest.)

Good Scares

Here's a tour of some of Pennsylvania's Erie . . . er, eerie spots.

Altoona: The Baker Mansion

The Ghosts: Elias and Anna Baker

The Story: In 1836, Elias Baker and his cousin bought an iron furnace near Altoona, and he moved his wife and two sons there from Lancaster County. His daughter Anna was born a couple of years later, and at first, the family lived in a small home near the furnace. But in 1844, Baker bought his cousin out and kept all the profits from the furnace for himself. Now a wealthy man, he spent the next five years building his family a 28-room mansion. With limestone walls, marble fireplaces, and decorations made from the iron produced at the furnace, the Baker home was lavish.

The family, however, wasn't always happy there. Young Anna Baker wanted to marry a local man whom her father deemed "unsuitable." He forbade the marriage, and even though Anna was angry with her father, she lived in the house until she died in 1914 in her 70s.

Haunted Happenings: Today, the Baker mansion is a museum and the site of the Blair County Historical Society. Employees and visitors have reported a number of mysterious sightings—everything from Elias Baker's ghostly form on the stairs to strange orbs showing up in digital photos. One employee even said that she heard someone whispering her name when she was closing up for the night. But the most dramatic occurrences involve Anna Baker's wedding dress.

When her father forced her to cancel her wedding, Anna

packed up her white wedding dress and hid it away. Years later, the historical society put it on display in a glass case. But according to a report the society keeps of all haunted happenings in the mansion, several people said they've seen the dress case shaking and the dress rocking back and forth.

Cashtown: The Cashtown Inn

The Ghosts: Confederate soldiers and various children

The Story: Peter Marck built the Cashtown Inn, a rest stop for travelers, eight miles outside Gettysburg in 1797. The inn (and later, the town) took their name from the fact that Marck issued no credit and always insisted that patrons pay in gold or silver before he'd give them a room.

In late June 1863, Confederate soldiers under the command of General Ambrose P. Hill took over the inn. Robert E. Lee had gotten word that the Union army was on its way, and he ordered Hill to hold Cashtown, which was situated on one of the Confederacy's supply routes. The inn was the perfect place for the soldiers to stay. It had comfortable rooms, a stable for horses, an oven for baking bread, and a freshwater spring. The inn also served as a Confederate hospital; soldiers wounded at Gettysburg were transported to the inn via carriages and wagons. And about a week later, when the Confederacy was defeated at Gettysburg, the inn acted as a stopping point for the retreating troops.

The Cashtown Inn has changed hands several times over the past 150 years, and at times, it fell into disrepair. (One owner nearly sold the building to a condo developer.) But in 2006, Jack and Maria Paladino bought the place and restored it as a bed-and-breakfast.

Haunted Happenings: Employees and visitors often report

paranormal activity at the inn. One employee claimed that an invisible figure pulled her ponytail. Others mentioned a rocking chair that moved by itself, doors that slammed of their own accord, and a Confederate soldier who roamed the hallways and knocked on the door of room #4. One guest said someone mysteriously packed his suitcase, and others heard the faint voices of children playing. For their part, the owners say that their dog and parrot seem to simultaneously follow invisible things with their eyes.

In December 2007, the Sci-Fi Channel television show *Ghost Hunters* filmed an episode about the Cashtown Inn. The show's investigators visit supposedly haunted places and try to expose frauds or find nonparanormal explanations for strange activity. But they couldn't explain the happenings at the Cashtown Inn. The group stayed overnight there and reported a variety of bizarre occurrences, including a picture frame that turned over on its own and boot steps on the top floor. One of the investigators also noted that, while he was sitting on a sofa, the cushions moved as though an invisible person had sat down next to him.

Bethlehem: Lehigh University's Linderman Library

The Ghosts: An unidentified ghost, possibly Lucy Linderman

The Story: Lucy Packer Linderman died in 1873. In her honor, her wealthy father, Asa Packer, donated $500,000 to Lehigh University to build a library. The original structure went up in 1878, got an addition in 1929, and underwent a renovation between 2005 and 2007.

Haunted Happenings: An unidentified ghost (whom some claim is Lucy Linderman herself) reportedly likes to haunt the library and tease the people who work there. One of the library's assistants, Gayle Nesbeth, told a story of going to the library's basement and finding about 150 magazines pulled off of their shelves and restacked in an artful design. Some suspected a student prankster, but the doors were locked when Nesbeth went into the basement. She said, "The designs were just beautiful, like an architect had done them . . . I would love to know who did it if it wasn't a ghost because it must have taken hours to complete."

Did You Know?

If western Pennsylvanians had gotten their way in the years before the American Revolution, there would have been 14 colonies. Settlers in Pennsylvania's western frontier—and in most of what's now West Virginia, the Maryland panhandle, and parts of eastern Kentucky—didn't think the government in the urban East empathized with their rural needs. So they suggested creating their own colony. In 1775, they petitioned the Second Continental Congress to become a colony called Westsylvania. But with the colonies on the verge of a revolution, the congress decided to ignore them. For the next several years, Westsylvanian supporters refused to be silenced, but in 1782, a Pittsburgh lawyer—and advocate of a strong national government—went to the Pennsylvania general assembly with his own legislation: make it an act of treason for citizens of an existing colony to petition for a new state. It worked; the threat of treason quashed the Westsylvania movement and the areas remained part of their original colonies.

The Weather Prophet

You've seen it on the news and even in that Bill Murray movie: Every year, groundhog Punxsutawney Phil looks for his shadow. If he sees it, we'll have six more weeks of winter. If he doesn't, spring is sure to come early—or so say the people in Punxsatawney.

Groundhog Day traces its roots back to an early European celebration called Candlemas. Literally "candle mass," it was the day when clergy members blessed all their congregation's church candles. Candlemas was held every February 2, right between the winter solstice and the spring equinox, and over the years, the day's weather took on a superstitious component: if the sun shone on Candlemas, winter would supposedly continue. But if the weather was cloudy or rainy, winter was over.

Sometime before the 1800s, the Germans added their own twist to the holiday. They used a hedgehog to predict the weather: If the sun was shining and the hedgehog cast a shadow, winter would continue. But if he was shadowless, spring was on the way. German immigrants who arrived in Pennsylvania in the 19th century brought this tradition with them, but there weren't any hedgehogs there, so they improvised and used groundhogs instead.

The Original Groundhog Day

The first official Groundhog Day was celebrated on February 2, 1886, in the town of Punxsutawney, about 80 miles northeast of Pittsburgh. The local newspaper proclaimed good news: "Up to the time of going to press the beast has not seen its shadow."

The following year, members of the newly created Punxsutawney Groundhog Club gathered at Gobbler's Knob, a small clearing just outside of town. (They chose the spot because it was well populated with groundhogs.) The local newspaper editor was there, too, and he officially proclaimed Punxsutawney the world's weather capital. The group also officially named its groundhog: "Punxsutawney Phil, Seer of Seers, Sage of Sages, Prognosticator of Prognosticators, and Weather Prophet Extraordinaire."

The Legend

Over the years, legends grew up around Punxsutawney Phil:

- The town's folklore claims that there has never been more than one official weather-forecasting groundhog and that Phil is more than 120 years old. (Legend says he stays fit by sipping "groundhog punch," which adds seven years to his life every time he takes a drink.)

- Once Phil decides whether or not spring will come early, he announces his prediction to the Inner Circle's president in a language called Groundhogese. The president translates for the rest of the world.

The Truth

The folklore is fun, but we've also tracked down some of the truths about the life and times of Punxsutawney Phil.

- When he's not predicting the weather, Phil and his female companion, Phyllis, live in a climate-controlled area called the Groundhog Zoo. It's a fiberglass enclosure connected to the Punxsutawney Memorial Library. There, he spends 364 days a year in leisure . . . mostly napping. A group of locals who call themselves the Inner Circle and have prestigious titles like "Stump Warden" and "Fair Weatherman" care for the couple. (The Inner Circle is also the group that crowds around Phil every February 2, wearing top hats and tuxedos as he looks for his shadow.)

- The Inner Circle claims that there's been only one Phil. No one knows for sure how many groundhogs have played the role over the years, but because a groundhog's average lifespan is six to eight years, a fair estimate is that there have been 15 or 20 Phils since 1886.

- The folks in Punxsutawney claim that Phil is always right with his weather predictions. Not so. In fact, according to weather records, he's correct only about 40 percent of the time.

Did You Know?

Want fries and slaw on that? That's how they make sandwiches at Pittsburgh's Primanti Bros. restaurants. Their giant sandwiches start with two thick slices of crusty Italian bread, stuffed with sizzling meat (choices: steak, turkey, sausage, ham, pastrami, chicken, corned beef), cheese, tomato, and fried egg. Then they put hand-cut fries and coleslaw right in the sandwich. The result: a six or seven-inch-thick creation. Don't even think of cutting it with utensils—you'll be laughed out of the place—but you will get a sheet of wax paper to catch whatever falls out.

It Happened in 1787

Pennsylvania officially became America's second state on December 12, 1787, but that wasn't the only important thing that happened that year.

January

Sir Frederick William Herschel, a British astronomer, discovered two of Uranus's moons: Oberon and Titania.

February

The tallest man ever to live in Great Britain was born on February 10. William Bradley weighed 14 pounds at birth and grew to be seven feet, nine inches tall. He still holds the record of "Britain's tallest man."

May

British sea captain Arthur Phillip and the First Fleet (11 ships carrying convicts) set out for the Australia penal colony on May 13.

June

Connecticut statesman Oliver Ellsworth—whom George Washington appointed as the third Chief Justice of the Supreme Court in 1796—proposed that the new country be called the "United States."

July

The U.S. Congress enacted the third Northwest Ordinance,

which laid out rules for how areas in the Northwest Territory (now the Midwest) could enter the Union: territories could apply for statehood when they had populations of 60,000. The ordinance also outlawed slavery in the new states, assured their residents religious freedom, and made provisions for public education.

August

John Fitch launched the first steamboat on the Delaware River. After serving in the Revolutionary War, Fitch settled in Bucks County, Pennsylvania, and got to work building a sailing vessel powered by steam. On August 22, he successfully sailed his 45-foot steamboat for the first time, and he patented the design four years later. (Robert Fulton, who usually gets credit for building the first steamship, didn't launch his first boat until 1801.)

October

Mozart's opera *Don Giovanni*, based on the story of libertine Don Juan, premiered at Prague's Estate Theatre on October 29.

November

Robert Lowth, an English bishop and writer of one of the best-known grammar books in the English language (*A Short Introduction to English Grammar*), died on November 3.

December

Delaware became the first state to ratify the U.S. Constitution on December 7.

Man of Steel, Part II

*By 1892, Andrew Carnegie was a wildly successful steel tycoon
who was trying to forge a reputation as a forward-thinking
businessman. But one bloody workers' strike was about to
change that reputation forever. (Part I is on page 19.)*

Publicly, Andrew Carnegie advocated for more influence
and better conditions for workers, but he did not actually
run his businesses according to those ideals. His profits relied
on keeping costs down. Workers in Carnegie's steel mills were
on the job for 12-hour shifts (often without breaks), seven
days a week, and many earned salaries of about $500 a year,
less than teachers (who made about $650 a year). Carnegie
spent very little on safety measures, so accidents in his factories were common; workers were often disabled and sometimes
killed.

In 1892, with his steel profits declining, Carnegie tried to
cut costs by lowering the wages of workers at his mill in
Homestead, Pennsylvania. That—and the company's history of
poor working conditions—led the Amalgamated Association of
Iron and Steel Workers (AA) to call for a strike there.

Say No to Strikers . . . Round Two

Carnegie was on vacation in Scotland at the time, so he
entrusted the mill's manager, Henry Clay Frick, to handle the
strike. Frick acted decisively: he refused to negotiate with the
union and locked workers out of the plant. He also brought in
guards from a private security firm, the Pinkertons, to keep the
union workers away from the mill and even built a 12-foot-

high fence around the mill, complete with barbed wire and rifle peepholes. But his drastic measures drew an equally drastic response from the miners. As the workers tried to drive the Pinkertons out of Homestead, gunfights broke out. The men set dynamite, dumped oil into the Monongahela River (where the Pinkertons' barges were docked), and set the oil on fire. Ten workers died and hundreds were injured, but they finally got the Pinkertons to leave. As the strike continued, the mill hired nonunion workers to fill the strikers' jobs and called in the Pennsylvania state militia protected them as they traveled to and from the mill.

The strike lasted four months before the workers, destitute and at a stalemate with the Carnegie management, finally gave up and went back to their jobs. For his part, Carnegie remained solidly behind Frick. He wrote to his manager, "We are with you to the end." But by the time Carnegie returned to Pennsylvania, the media and public who had once praised his business ethics now branded him a hypocrite. He was seen as personally responsible for the 10 strikers' deaths and for ruining the lives of the men who had worked so hard to help make his fortune.

Carnegie later called the Homestead strike "the trial of my life . . . Such a foolish step—contrary to my ideals, repugnant to every feeling of my nature." A few years later, perhaps out of remorse, he built a library, swimming pool, concert hall, and bowling alley in Homestead. But still, Carnegie continued to pay his workers low wages, he effectively drove all unions out of Pittsburgh's steel industry, and by 1900, his mills were bringing in annual profits of more than $40 million.

The Deepest Pockets in the World

In 1901, Carnegie sold his steel company to J. P. Morgan for

$480 million. (It became part of the massive U.S. Steel Corporation.) On making the deal, Morgan said, "Congratulations, Mr. Carnegie. You are now the richest man in the world." But Andrew Carnegie had always believed that excess wealth was of no benefit to an individual. He once said, "The man who dies rich, dies disgraced." So after selling his steel company to Morgan, he proceeded to give away 90 percent of his fortune.

That money built more than 2,000 libraries across the United States—$5 million went to the New York City Public Library and established the Carnegie Institution to provide research for American colleges and universities. Carnegie himself created Pittsburgh's Carnegie-Mellon University (then called the Carnegie Institute of Technology) and funded the city's Beaux Arts Complex. He also established a pension fund for Pittsburgh's teachers and created the Carnegie Endowment for International Peace, which, among other things, built a Palace of Peace in The Hague, Netherlands. Today, it's the world's international court. Andrew Carnegie died in 1919 at the age of 83.

Quote Me

"Concentrate your energies, your thoughts, and your capital. The wise man puts all his eggs in one basket and watches the basket."

—Andrew Carnegie

Ex-Stream Architecture

*When you think of architecture, you can't help but think of
Frank Lloyd Wright, and one of his most incredible
creations is right here in Pennsylvania.*

This architectural wonder isn't nestled in the middle of a
large city. In fact, it's not in a convenient location at all—
to find it, visitors have to travel miles of winding roads deep
into Pennsylvania's Allegheny woods. Yet every year, thousands
of people from all over the world make the journey to
Fallingwater.

What makes the house so special? When it was built, it
was an architectural marvel. The three-story home that Wright
designed for businessman Edgar J. Kaufmann and his family,
juts out 30 feet above a waterfall on Bear Run Creek and is
made of reinforced concrete and sandstone. The creek's running water can be heard from every part of the house, the
hearth is constructed out of boulders from the creek, and the
walls are full of windows, affording breathtaking views of the
surrounding forest.

The Architect

In the early 1930s, Frank Lloyd Wright was badly in need of
some income. He'd been one of America's premier architects,
but had caused a scandal when he'd left his second wife for
another woman (his third wife). Since then, his client list had
dwindled, and the Great Depression made the problem worse.
With few prospects in sight, Wright's style of architecture—
called "organic" because it incorporated a building's environ-

ment into the structure's design—was in danger of being lost. Most people felt that Wright, then in his 60s, had already achieved his greatest accomplishments and that his best years were behind him.

But while attending a party at the home of the Kaufmanns—Edgar Sr., who was president of Kaufmann's department store in Pittsburgh, and his wife, Liliane—Wright made a not-so-subtle push for a job when he remarked that the couple's house wasn't "worthy" of them. The insult must have made an impression because, in December 1934, Kaufmann took Wright to a piece of property he owned in the Pennsylvania woods where he planned to replace some aging cabins with a new summer house.

When Kaufmann showed Wright the family's favorite picnic spot—a large, flat rock overlooking a picturesque waterfall on Bear Run Creek—Wright had found what he was looking for: the perfect site for an "organic" house that would seem to grow naturally out of the rocks. As Wright told an interviewer many years later, "The natural thing seemed to be to cantilever the house from that rock bank over the falling water." It was a daring innovation: a house suspended over a waterfall.

Wright quickly came up with the idea, but he didn't put his plans to paper until Kaufmann came to Wright's studio weeks later to see how the Bear Run project was progressing. Wright began to sketch the plans shortly before Kaufmann arrived, and his staff hurried to finish them while Wright and his unsuspecting client had lunch.

The Client

Kaufmann was shocked when he saw Wright's plans for a

three-story house hovering above Bear Run Creek. His request for a view of the waterfall had been ignored, and what was worse, he knew this house—which Wright had started calling "Fallingwater"—would cost about $155,000, a lot more than he'd originally planned to spend. The location wasn't what he'd had in mind, either. Kaufmann said to Wright, "I expected you to build the house beside the falls, not on top of them!"

But Kaufmann had experience as a civic leader and planner of public works buildings, and he realized he was looking at plans for an architectural masterpiece. He knew that Fallingwater would increase his social standing (as Jews, he and his family had been shut out of Pittsburgh's elite society). And on a more idealistic level, Kaufmann felt that good architecture transformed people's lives for the better. So he gave the go-ahead for Fallingwater.

A New Kind of House

Building began in the summer of 1936. Local craftsmen excavated sandstone on the property and incorporated it into the house. Vertical sandstone walls separated horizontal "trays" of reinforced concrete that formed the living and bedroom levels on massive terraces that seemed to float above Bear Run.

But suspending a house over a waterfall posed problems, and engineers disagreed about how to make the house structurally sound and stable. One famous controversy erupted over the four concrete beams that supported the living room. Worried that they would collapse, Kaufmann ordered engineers to double the amount of reinforcing steel inside the concrete. Wright was furious that the changes were made without his being consulted, and he sent an angry note to Kaufmann: "I don't know what kind of architect you are familiar with but it apparently isn't the kind I think I am . . . If I do not have your confidence—to hell with the whole thing!" Kaufmann wrote back this famous reply: "I don't know what kind of client you are familiar with but it apparently isn't the kind I think I am. If I do not have your confidence in the matter—to hell with the whole thing . . . P.S. Now don't you think that we should stop writing letters?"

Other conflicts arose over Wright's plan to cover the building in gold leaf to match the surrounding forest's autumn leaves. Kaufmann chose a less expensive solution: beige paint. But in spite of the complications, building went relatively smoothly. By December 1937, the house was ready for the Kaufmanns to move in.

Fallingwater's organic theme continued indoors. The floor was made of huge slabs of polished and waxed sandstone. The large boulder that had been Kaufmann's favorite picnic spot became the hearth of a massive stone fireplace. The living area was an early example of an "open floor plan"—one great room replaced the usual parlor, dining room, and study. Liliane Kaufmann wrote to Wright that her family spent some of the "happiest weekends" they'd ever known in the completed Fallingwater.

The Power of Fallingwater

The Kaufmanns weren't the only people happy with their new house. About a month after they moved in, *Time* magazine featured a photo of Fallingwater on its cover, proclaiming the house as Wright's "most beautiful job." The Museum of Modern Art published a book about the house, and architectural critics praised it.

As Fallingwater's fame grew, so did Wright's career. Rumor had it that writer Ayn Rand used the Fallingwater project as inspiration for her novel *The Fountainhead* (Gary Cooper played the Wright-esque architect in the film version), and the good press led to a renaissance for Wright's career. He went on to develop many new projects, including the Guggenheim Museum in New York City and the Marin County Civic Center in California. Within his lifetime, Wright became known as "the world's greatest architect."

A Public Treasure

The Kaufmann family held on to Fallingwater until 1963, when Edgar Kaufmann Jr. turned it over to the public through the Western Pennsylvania Conservancy (WPC). By 2005, more than 2.7 million people had toured the house that *Smithsonian* magazine called "one of 28 places to visit before it's too late."

But for all its popularity, the building hasn't aged well. Kaufmann—who once called his beloved home the "seven bucket house" for the leaks in its flat roof and the mold in its damp walls—wouldn't have been surprised. The worrisome cantilevered terrace in the living room seems to have become as much of a problem as Kaufmann feared. Not even the extra steel was enough to keep it from drooping over the years.

In 2001, worried that the main terrace would eventually fall into the creek, the WPC launched an $11.5 million restoration of Fallingwater. Engineers not only strengthened the terrace but also restored corroding steel, waterproofed the building, and made water treatment, sewage, and landscape improvements. Today, with the restoration complete, visitors can again tour the home and see many of its original artwork and furnishings.

Only in PA

Pennsylvania is the only state that . . .

. . . doesn't impose a tax on non-cigarette tobacco products such as cigars and chewing tobacco.

. . . has two Major League Baseball teams in the same league: the Philadelphia Phillies and the Pittsburgh Pirates are both in the National League. All others with two—Florida, Illinois, Missouri, New York, Ohio, and Texas—have one team in the American and one in the National League. (California, the only state with more than two teams—it has five—has two in the American and three in the National League.)

. . . doesn't allow local police departments to use radar to catch speeding drivers. (State police may.)

. . . has made Flag Day (June 14) a legal state holiday.

. . . has a geologic time period named after it. The Pennsylvanian period is a subperiod of the Carboniferous, and runs from roughly 320 to 286 million years ago. The term was first used in the 1800s by geologists studying rocks in the Keystone State. (The Mississippian period is named after the river, not the state.)

. . . has a name that requires all eight fingers (thumbs not included) to type.

. . . gives 100 percent of the proceeds from the state lottery to

programs for the state's older residents. The Pennsylvania
Lottery was established in 1971 and, since then, has contributed more than $18.3 billion to programs for the elderly.

. . . **was an original colony, but lacked** an Atlantic coastline.

. . . **mines anthracite coal,** the hardest, most lustrous, most
pure, and most valuable type.

. . . **by law, requires doctors to notify the state** if a patient is
unfit to drive for any reason.

. . . **does not require that the signing of a will be witnessed**
(although many Pennsylvania counties do).

● ●

Did You Know?

The Amish don't allow bumper stickers on their buggies.
But if they did, they might choose one of these (all of
which we've actually seen on cars in Pennsylvania):

- Neigh if Ye Be Amish.

- I Brake for Barn Raisings.

- What happens in Rumspringa stays in Rumspringa.

- Elect an Amish for President. See how the oil companies
  like that!

Welcome to "Penn State"

East side, west side, and all around the state . . . see if you can find the 20 cities hidden in this Pennsylvania-shaped puzzle.
(Answers on page 298.)

ALLENTOWN	LANCASTER
ALTOONA	PHILADELPHIA
BETHLEHEM	PITTSBURGH
BLUE BALL	POCONOS
BUTLER	RADNOR
CHESTER	READING
ERIE	SCRANTON
HARRISBURG	VILLANOVA
HERSHEY	WILKES-BARRE
JOHNSTOWN	YORK

```
        O
    A R A
D N L V K H L A N C A S T E R Z R K Z
R O R O N D A R J W G R U B S I R R A H
J O H N S T O W N S O N V B V Q E O A H F
K T Z A H G R U B S T T I P U T A Y Z U
A L X L R L P J P O C O N O S Y D E F
S A E L Q E Y E R R A B S E K L I W
G Y A I H P L E D A L I H P L E N U G Y
C Y K V R N O T N A R C S M S L G F U L R
Y E H S R E H N U J P B L U E B A L L C
T R G C P U B Z I B E T H L E H E M
```

Grapes of Wealth

Whether you prefer wine or Welch's, drink up! Pennsylvania grows some of the best grapes in the nation.

The term "wine country" conjures up images of California and France, but parts of Pennsylvania have ideal grape-growing conditions. Rolling hills provide drainage, the growing season is long, and the state gets enough rain each year to provide natural irrigation. As a result, Pennsylvania is home to more than 14,000 acres of grapes, making it the fourth-largest grape producer in the United States. (Only California, Washington, and New York grow more.)

Juice, Yes! Wine, No?

Ninety percent of Pennsylvania's grapes are harvested for juice production. In 1911, the Welch Grape Juice Company built a plant in North East, Pennsylvania, that has become one of the largest grape-processing plants in the world. Today, it covers more than 60 acres and is the largest employer in the area. The plant's 75 tanks can hold 17 million gallons of juice, and it produces about half of Welch's total output.

Winemaking, on the other hand, has a long—but limited—history in the Keystone State. William Penn planted Pennsylvania's first vineyard on his property in 1683, but the first commercial vineyard in the state (and the country) opened in Spring Mills, along the Schuylkill River, in 1793. Called the Vine Company of Pennsylvania, it operated there until 1822. A hundred years later, the wine industry in Pennsylvania had suffered two setbacks: First, when vintners tried to add European vines, they discovered that a tiny indigenous insect—grape phylloxera—fed on the roots of all but the native Concord and Niagara grapevines and destroyed the European varieties. Then, in 1920, Prohibition shut down all commercial wine production in United States.

Back in Business, Finally

Prohibition was repealed in 1933, but Pennsylvania was the last state to lift its ban on commercial wine production. (Pennsylvania's liquor board was especially conservative.) Finally, in 1968, the state allowed small wineries to sell their product directly to the public as long as the wine was made with Pennsylvania-grown grapes. Since then, more than 120 wineries have opened, and today, Pennsylvania wineries are mostly small, family-run operations that produce less than 5,000 gallons of wine each year. The state ranks eighth in wine output, with approximately 920,000 gallons produced in 2007.

Pennsylvania Wine Country

There are seven wine regions in Pennsylvania today: Lake Erie, the Pittsburgh countryside, the Northern Wilds (north-central Pennsylvania), Upper Susquehanna, Lower Susquehanna, Lehigh Valley and Berks County, and the Philadelphia countryside. More than 50 types of grapes are grown for wine production.

Ice, Ice Baby

Most of Pennsylvania's grapes are harvested by early October, but even after the weather gets colder and the first frost hits the vines, there is one last harvest to be made. A few Pennsylvania vineyards produce ice wine, a specialty drink that can be made only from grapes that have frozen on the vine. After most grapes have been picked, vintners leave some of them to dehydrate (and sweeten) for about two more months on the vine.

Then, in December or early January, after the first hard freeze hits, the vintners handpick and press the frozen grapes. They remove the ice crystals inside the skin and leave behind just the highly concentrated pulp, which then ferments for two to three months. The result is a sweet dessert wine.

Because of the special growing conditions, the labor-intensive harvesting, and the fact that it takes four times as many grapes to produce one bottle, ice wine usually comes in small bottles (6 to 12 ounces) with a high price tag (sometimes up to $50 each).

Did You Know?

The wastewater released by Welch's North East grape juice plant contains a small amount of fructose and glucose sugar in it. So an Ohio-based biotechnology firm, NanoLogix, and researchers at Gannon University in Erie came up with a "bioreactor" that feeds this sugar water to millions of bacteria, which then produce hydrogen gas as a waste product. (Hydrogen has been touted as a possible alternative power source.)

The bioreactor hasn't been used on a large scale yet, but the North East plant has already successfully tested the first prototype, and the hydrogen from bacteria produced electricity. NanoLogix's plan is to build a large bioreactor to filter all of Welch's wastewater and harvest hydrogen gas. Then the company wants to install the reactors at bottlers around the country, creating an alternative power source for new types of energy-efficient cars.

"Broad Street Bullies"

*Pennsylvania has two National Hockey League teams, the
Philadelphia Flyers and the Pittsburgh Penguins. Here's the history
of the Flyers. (Penguins fans can skate over to page 198.)*

The Details

Name: The story of how the Flyers got their name goes like
this: The Flyers formed in 1967, the year the NHL expanded
from the original six teams to twelve. A contest was held to
name the new team; 11,000 ballots were submitted, and the
winner was the "Flyers." But according to team lore, owner Ed
Snider's sister Phyllis had already chosen that name, so it was a
foregone conclusion that it would "win." Other names in the
running: Bashers, Blizzards, Bruisers, Huskies, Keystones,
Knights, Lancers, Liberty Bells, Raiders, and Sabres.

Colors: Black, orange, and white. Bill Putnam, one of the team's
owners, thought they were "hot" colors.

Logo: The "Flying P": a winged, black letter P with an orange
dot, representing a hockey puck, in the hole of the P.
Philadelphia graphic artist Sam Ciccone designed the logo and
the team's uniforms with their distinctive stripe running from
the collar down both arms. (The stripe represents wings.)

Through the Years

The Flyers were a good team right from the start, making the
playoffs in their first two seasons. They also became known as
one of the toughest teams in the league, earning the nickname
of "Broad Street Bullies" (after Philadelphia's Broad Street,
home of the Spectrum Arena). By the 1973–74 season, the
Flyers were regarded as the best team in the NHL, and they

proved it by beating Bobby Orr and the Boston Bruins in the Stanley Cup Finals. The next year, they won the Cup again.

In the 1975–76 season, though, the Flyers went back to the finals a third consecutive time . . . and they got clobbered, losing four games to none to the Montreal Canadiens.

The Flyers made the playoffs every year for the next 12 years, making it to the finals three more times but not winning the Stanley Cup. From 1989 to 1995, they didn't make the postseason even once, but since then, they've begun another run—the Flyers have missed the playoffs only once since 1995.

Flyers Facts

- The Flyers have seven players in the NHL Hall of Fame, including legends Bill Barber, Bobby Clarke, and Bernie Parent.
- The team has the record for the most ties in a single season: 24 in 1969–70. The Flyers also hold the record for the longest undefeated streak (ties included), going 35 straight games without a loss in 1979–80.
- The Flyers weren't the first hockey team to play in Philadelphia. In fact, Pittsburgh's first NHL team—the Pirates, who played from 1925 to 1930—were also Philadelphia's first hockey team. The Pirates moved to Philly for the 1930–31 season and were renamed the Philadelphia Quakers, but they were so bad that they folded after a year.
- The most famous Broad Street Bully was defenseman Dave "the Hammer" Schultz. He wasn't huge—just 6' 1" and 185 pounds—but he was a vicious hitter and was famous for getting into fights. Schultz still holds the record for the most penalty minutes in a single season: 472 . . . almost eight full games' worth.

It's a Zoo Out There

There are about 60 mammal species found in the hills, woods, and rivers of Pennsylvania. Here's a rundown of the most common.

Black Bears

Although black bears were once hunted to near-extinction, there are about 15,000 of them in Pennsylvania today. And some of those are among the largest on record: in the last few years, hunters have routinely brought in males that weighed more than 800 pounds. (The largest black bear ever—hunted in North Carolina in 1998—weighed 880 pounds.)

Wild Boars

Hikers in the Pennsylvania wilderness often come across wild boars, pigs with long tusks curling out from their snouts. The boars typically weigh about 300 pounds, but aren't native to North America—they were brought from Europe in the 1500s. Today, about 3,000 of them roam in Pennsylvania.

Coyotes

Most people think of coyotes as an animal common to the western United States, but over the last 30 years, coyote populations have been steadily growing east of the Mississippi River. The first photographic evidence of them in Pennsylvania came in 1930, and today, there may be as many as 30,000 populating the state.

Bobcats

Bobcats, the only wild feline predators in Pennsylvania, average three feet in length, about 15 inches in height, and weigh 30 pounds. They were hunted almost to extinction by the 1960s, but were protected from 1970 until 1999, and today there are an estimated 3,500 bobcats living in the Keystone State.

Eastern Spotted Skunks

Unlike the classic stripped skunk, these skunks have white, broken stripes on their bodies that make them look spotted. They're found almost exclusively in the southwestern part of the state, and are rarely seen even there. Eastern spotted skunks are smaller than other species—adults average just 15 inches in length—but they still carry a powerfully offensive spray.

Whales

Incredibly, whales—most often fin and right whales—sometimes enter the Delaware River, and have been seen as far north as Philadelphia. (Seals, porpoises, and loggerhead sea turtles have also been seen navigating the Delaware.)

For more Pennsylvania animals, turn to page 293.

● ●

Did You Know?

Beavers used to roam in great numbers all over Pennsylvania, but by the late 1800s, they were completely wiped out by trappers. Then, in the 1910s, they were reintroduced and protected and, by the 1930s, were back to healthy numbers. Today there may be as many as 30,000 living in the state, most of them in the northern counties.

An Erie Feeling

. . . in the Erie Triangle.

Town: Erie
Location: Erie County
Founding: 1795
Population (2008): 104,000
Size: 28 square miles
County seat: Yes

What's in a Name?

An American Indian tribe known as the Eriez were the first people to live in the area. When European settlers moved in, they shortened that to Erie and named the region after the tribe.

Claims to Fame:

- *Field and Stream* magazine has called Erie one of the top-20 family fishing spots in the United States.

- In 1784, the U.S. government signed a treaty with the Iroquois Confederacy (with whom the Eriez were associated), handing over some of the Iroquois' land to the United States. Part of it fell on the border between Pennsylvania and New York, and since the border wasn't clearly defined in those days, both states laid claim to it. The land included a 202,000-acre parcel, nicknamed the Triangle Lands or the Erie Triangle, which provided a potential port on Lake Erie. Further complicating things: Massachusetts and Connecticut also claimed the Triangle, citing colonial-era laws called "sea-to-sea" charters that technically allowed them to expand as far west as they wanted. All four states argued their cases to the federal government, but in the end, Pennsylvania got the land. Why? Connecticut, New York, and Massachusetts already had access to Atlantic Ocean ports, but Pennsylvania was landlocked. That didn't mean Pennsylvania got the Erie Triangle outright, though: the federal government sold the state what is now Erie County for $152,000—about 75 cents per acre.

- Erie is part of the Rust Belt, a region that stretches from Michigan to upstate New York—an American manufacturing center until the decline of the steel industry in the 1970s and 1980s. Today, Erie continues to get most of its revenue from manufacturing. Its main industry: plastics, with four of the top 50 U.S. plastics companies located in Erie.

- Famous Erie natives: Tom Ridge (former Pennsylvania governor and congressman, and onetime secretary of the Department of Homeland Security), Pat Monahan (lead singer of the band Train), and Ann B. Davis (Alice on *The Brady Bunch*).

- Erie has two nicknames: Gem City, because of Presque Isle Bay's sparkling water; and Flagship City, because it was the home port of Commodore Oliver Perry's flagship, the *Niagara*, one of nine American ships that defeated the British during the War of 1812's battle of Lake Erie.

The Great Innovator

Everyone's heard the story about Benjamin Franklin flying a kite during a thunderstorm and proving that lightning and electricity were the same. But his discoveries and inventions extended beyond just science to politics, civic improvements, meteorology, and everyday life.

The Biggies

Given how many things Benjamin Franklin invented, it's a wonder he had time to help found a nation. Here's a sampling: He invented bifocals, the lightning rod, and the Franklin stove—a safe, metal-lined furnace that created fewer sparks than old fireplaces, circulated heat, and used less wood. Those are among the most famous, but he also developed a flexible catheter for his brother who suffered from kidney stones, a chair with a reversible seat that could function as a stepladder, an odometer to measure postal routes, a "long arm" mechanical device to pluck books from high shelves, and swim fins. Franklin didn't patent any of them, though. Instead, he put them all in the public domain so that everyone could use them.

Politics

- Franklin also created America's first political cartoon. It was the "Join, or Die" drawing of a cut-up snake that illustrated an editorial in his newspaper, the *Pennsylvania Gazette*. The editorial encouraged the New England colonies to fight together in the French and Indian War. Later, reprints of the cartoon were used as a rallying cry during the American Revolution.

Concerns Around Town

- The first fire department—the Union Fire Company in Philadelphia—and fire insurance to cover "houses" (both businesses and homes) were Franklin's ideas.

- Franklin formed a club of friends and business associates, called the Junto. Together, they developed the first public lending library in America: the Library Company. Franklin and the other Junto members each paid a fee to be members of this library, and the money was used to buy books. The organization (now called the Library Company of Philadelphia) is still around today.

Healthy Living

- Long before people figured out that eating citrus fruit could prevent diseases like scurvy, Franklin was touting the advantages of daily servings of fruit. "An apple a day keeps the doctor away" is one of his most famous sayings, but Franklin also claimed that oranges, limes, and grapefruit were healthy, especially for the gums and skin.

Time and Weather

- Franklin was the first to recognize that most storms on the East Coast came from the southwest, and he was the first to map and describe the Gulf Stream.

- We can thank (or blame) Franklin for Daylight Saving Time. When he was a diplomat in France, Franklin published a whimsical article for the *Journal de Paris*, bemoaning the fact that since no one in France got to work before noon, thousands of pounds of candles were wasted at night. He then listed ways to take advantage of sunlight. One of his suggestions was adjusting the clocks to include more hours of daylight. (He also suggested rationing candles and ringing church bells at dawn, so no one is sure whether or not he was serious.)

Music

- A music lover, Franklin created the glass armonica, an instrument in which a rod held spinning glass bowls of different thicknesses. When a musician rubbed the glass with wet fingers (much like you'd "play" a wine glass), the bowls emitted different notes. Franklin once said, "Of all my inventions, the glass armonica has given me the most satisfaction."

Did You Know?

Pittsburgh boasts the only trio of identical bridges in the United States. They're called the "Three Sisters" and span the city's Sixth, Seventh, and Ninth streets. All three yellow suspension bridges were built between 1924 and 1928 by the American Bridge Company, which still has its headquarters outside Pittsburgh.

The bridges are better known by their commemorative names: the Sixth Street bridge honors Roberto Clemente, Seventh Street is called the Andy Warhol Bridge, and the Ninth Street bridge is named for Rachel Carson.

The Pittsburgh Vaccine

In 1954, Dr. Jonas Salk introduced his polio vaccine to the world, putting the city of Pittsburgh at the forefront of the development and testing of what many people considered a "miracle" medicine.

Polio has been around for thousands of years. Ancient Egyptian art shows children with withered limbs using canes, and many historians believe that Roman emperor Claudius walked with a limp as a result of having polio as a child. The first cases of the virus weren't reported in the United States until 1894, though, when 132 children in Vermont came down with the disease.

Over the next five decades, polio became one of the most feared and mysterious diseases in America. It wasn't the most deadly; many more people died of influenza and pneumonia. But polio seemed to appear without warning and affected mostly children. There was also no cure, and no precautionary measures seemed to ward the disease off completely. By 1952—the height of the polio epidemic in America—58,000 cases were reported, and parents, scientists, and government officials clamored for anything that would relieve the suffering. That's where Jonas Salk and Pittsburgh came in.

"Salk" of the Earth

Jonas Salk was born in New York City in 1914. The child of Russian immigrants, Salk was the first in his family to go to college. He attended the City College of New York and then medical school at New York University, where he got involved with a research group investigating the influenza virus.

Two decades earlier, in 1918, a strain of influenza had killed a staggering 25 million people worldwide, including thousands of American soldiers fighting in World War I. When World War II began in 1939, the U.S. government stepped up efforts to create a flu vaccine to protect its soldiers abroad. Scientists had recently isolated the germ that caused influenza, and Salk worked with microbiologist Thomas Francis Jr. (first at NYU and then at the University of Michigan) to develop a flu vaccine for American soldiers. Their vaccine used killed strains of the flu virus and laid the foundation for much of Salk's later polio research.

Into the Pitt

In 1947, the University of Pittsburgh offered Salk a job: head of the medical school's Virus Research Lab. The goal for Salk and his team (which included Francis and other researchers from around the country) was to develop a safe and effective polio vaccine.

Over the next five years, Salk made some incredible discoveries. First, he managed to isolate the specific germs that caused polio and found that there were actually three strains of the virus. Then he figured out how to create killed forms of each strain and include them in a single vaccine that prevented polio infection. By proving that killed strains of the virus could create the antibodies necessary for immunization, Salk also proved one of his own longstanding theories: that killed virus vaccines could be just as effective as muted live virus vaccines, which contained weakened (but live) germs and ran a risk of infection. This went against the popular opinion of the time, which dictated that only a muted form of a live virus would work.

Salk's team wasn't the only research group looking for a polio vaccine, and they got some outside help from other scientists who made important discoveries of their own. In particular, researchers in Boston discovered how to grow the poliovirus in human tissue. This meant Salk's laboratory tests could be more accurate. (He'd been using monkeys.)

Human Guinea Pigs

By 1952, Salk was satisfied that his vaccine was finished, but so far, it had worked only in the laboratory. It was now time to test it out on humans. His first subjects: his wife and three sons. None showed any ill effects, and none contracted polio.

Next, he expanded the clinical trials to a large group of schoolchildren. Since his goal was to see protective polio antibody levels rise in their blood, Salk also needed a control sample. He found it in a group of children at the D. T. Watson Home, about 12 miles outside of Pittsburgh, who had recovered from polio.

The first children outside of Salk's family to receive the polio vaccine (which Salk called the "Pittsburgh Vaccine") were from the city's Arsenal Elementary School on 40th Street. When the notices went home about the coming vaccine trials, eager parents returned the permission slips in droves.

Over the next year, more than 15,000 children around Pittsburgh took part in the clinical trials. And in 1953, Salk and his colleagues expanded their experiment to 1.8 million children throughout the United States, Canada, and Finland. By 1955, the scientists were satisfied with the vaccine's results: it was 70 percent effective against the first strain of polio and 90 percent effective against the second and third strains.

Immediately, mass immunization campaigns sprang up

across the United States. And by 1957, the number of reported polio cases had dropped by about 85 percent. By 1994, polio had been nearly eradicated in the United States.

No Success Without Controversy

Jonas Salk never patented his vaccine; he wanted the entire world to benefit from his discovery. But Salk wasn't without his critics. He often gets credit for developing the "first" polio vaccine, but in reality, his was just the first to find mainstream success in the United States. In 1950, Hilary Koprowski, a doctor and researcher from Poland who eventually settled in Philadelphia, introduced a live oral vaccine that proved successful in trials. Koprowski had neither the funding nor the backing of a major institution to bring his vaccine to the American public, but he used it in other countries, including Zaire, where a quarter of a million children received the inoculation.

Cures for the Future

Koprowski's efforts also inspired Albert Sabin, a researcher at the University of Cincinnati, to develop his own live oral polio vaccine in 1957. Salk's vaccine worked to prevent the debilitating effects of polio, but it didn't always protect against the initial flulike symptoms. Also, it required booster shots. Sabin's vaccine, on the other hand, prevented the disease altogether and required only one dose. For almost 30 years, Sabin's oral vaccine was the most widely used means of preventing polio. But in 1999, the U.S. Public Health Service recommended that doctors return to using Salk's killed-virus vaccine in order to prevent the handful of polio infections caused by the live-virus version.

In 2005, the University of Pittsburgh hosted a symposium honoring the 50th anniversary of the vaccine's development. The speakers included the university's researchers, polio experts, and even Jonas Salk's son, Peter, who also became a doctor and researcher. He has spent most of his professional career researching vaccines for the HIV and AIDS viruses.

Did You Know?

Pennsylvania women made major strides during the 1930s. Here are three who logged impressive "firsts."

Ann Brancato Wood

Notable for . . . being the first woman elected to the Pennsylvania state legislature (1932).
Hometown: Philadelphia

Helen Richey

Notable for . . . being the first woman to pilot a commercial airliner (1934).
Hometown: McKeesport

Crystal Bird Fauset

Notable for . . . being the first African American woman elected to a state's house of representatives (1938).
Hometown: Fauset was born in Maryland in 1894, but moved to Pennsylvania in 1918. She lived in Philadelphia until she died in 1965.

King of Malls

*It's the largest shopping mall on the East Coast and
the second largest in the United States. But just
how big is the King of Prussia Mall?*

It's so big that . . .

- The amount of soda served every year at the King of Prussia
Mall could fill five Olympic swimming pools.

- There are 13,376 parking spaces available for shoppers and
employees.

- Walking every indoor hallway and aisle would cover a distance of about 13 miles . . . the same as the entire length of
Manhattan.

- There are 11 ATMs, 65 places to get something to eat and
drink, and 386 stores.

- The mall uses more than 500,000 lights for its annual
Christmas display.

- Its interior encompasses about 3 million square feet—as
much as two Louisiana Superdomes.

- All of its electrical wires, if laid end to end, would reach
about 115 miles . . . or from New York City to Hartford,
Connecticut.

What's in a Name?

The King of Prussia Mall was named after the Montgomery
County town it's in, which got *its* name from an 18th-century
tavern. The town's first name was Reesville, for the Rees family

who were among the first settlers to the area and who owned the tavern. Most historians agree that the family named their tavern "King of Prussia" for Frederick the Great (Prussia's king from 1740 to 1786), but no one seems sure why. One theory says it was to honor Prussia's support of the colonists before and during the American Revolution. Another claims the name was a way to attract Prussian soldiers (stationed at Valley Forge) to the business. Either way, the town took its name from the tavern, and the post office made it official in 1850.

Did You Know?

In the 1850s, religious zealots Peter and Hannah Armstrong purchased four square miles of land in the mountains of northeastern Pennsylvania. They advertised in Philadelphia newspapers for people to come and live in the town, which Armstrong called "Celesta"—where they would await the return of Jesus. In the 1860s, the Pennsylvanian government began demanding taxes from the Armstrongs, who owned all the community's land. They refused to pay and, in 1864—in order to avoid prosecution—turned over ownership of the land to "Creator and God of heaven and earth, and to His heirs in Jesus Messiah, for their proper use and behoof forever." Celesta was legally owned by God until Armstrong's death in 1892, when the government confiscated and sold it for back taxes.

Let Freedom Ring

Just how well do you know the Liberty Bell?

In 1751, to celebrate the 50th anniversary of Pennsylvania's constitution, which laid out citizens' rights and freedoms, the Pennsylvania Assembly ordered a 2,000-pound bell from the Whitechapel Foundry in England to hang in the steeple of the State House (now Independence Hall). The assembly had it inscribed with a verse from the Bible's book of Leviticus: "Proclaim Liberty throughout all the Land unto all the inhabitants thereof."

Over the last 250 years, the Liberty Bell's history has been clouded in myth . . . until now. See if you can decipher fact from legend.

1. Fact or legend: The Liberty Bell came to America on a slave ship called the Myrtilla.

2. Fact or legend: The Liberty Bell cracked the first time it was rung on the Fourth of July.

3. Fact or legend: It took three bells to make the Liberty Bell we know today.

4. Fact or legend: The Liberty Bell rang on July 4, 1776, for the reading of the Declaration of Independence.

5. Fact or legend: During the Revolutionary War, the Liberty Bell was hidden so the British troops couldn't capture it.

6. Fact or legend: The Liberty Bell was rung to signal the ratification of the U.S. Constitution.

7. Fact or legend: The Liberty Bell was given its name by patriots during the American Revolution.

8. Fact or legend: The Liberty Bell has been in a train crash.

9. Fact or legend: The Liberty Bell got its famous crack in 1835 when it was rung for Supreme Court Chief Justice John Marshall's funeral.

10. Fact or legend: Taco Bell bought the Liberty Bell to help reduce the national debt.

Answers on page 298.

Did You Know?

Thousands of Americans refused to fight in the Civil War for religious reasons, and most of them were from Pennsylvania. That's because the Keystone State was home to so many people whose faith forbade them to use violence, such as Quakers and Shakers. Both the Union and Confederate armies made provisions for objectors to either serve in a nonmilitary capacity or pay a tax to avoid duty altogether. The number of conscientious objectors from Pennsylvania: about 4,000.

Batter Up!

This is one of our favorite stories, and it's appeared in Uncle John's Bathroom Reader before. But it's so important to Pennsylvania that we couldn't leave it out. If you've ever played Little League baseball (or cheered on someone who has), you have a Pennsylvanian to thank for the game.

Happy Accident

One afternoon in 1938, Carl Stotz went out into his Williamsport, Pennsylvania, yard to play catch with his two nephews. They would have preferred to swing at some balls, but the yard was too small to use a bat. So they just played catch. On one throw, a nephew tossed the ball so far that Stotz "had to move to the neighbors' side of the yard," as he recalled years later. "As I stretched to catch the ball, I stepped into the cut-off stems of a lilac bush that were projecting several inches above the ground. A sharp stub tore through my sock and scraped my ankle. The pain was intense."

As Stotz sat nursing his ankle, he was suddenly reminded that he had played on the same kind of rough turf when he was a kid . . . and he remembered a promise he'd made to himself when he was young. Back then, equipment was scarce—he and his friends hit balls with sticks when they didn't have any bats, and used baseballs until the threads unraveled and the skins came off. Then they patched them up with tape and used them until there wasn't anything left to tape back together. Some of his friends had even played barefoot because they didn't have any shoes. Stotz explained: "I remembered thinking to myself, 'When I grow up, I'm gonna have a baseball team for boys, complete with uniforms and equipment. They'll play on a real field like the big guys, with cheering crowds at every game."

Downsizing

Stotz didn't have any sons of his own, but he decided to fulfill his promise by organizing the neighborhood boys into baseball teams. That way, they could experience the thrill of playing real games on real fields, wearing real uniforms—not just playing stickball in open fields and abandoned lots.

He spent the next few months organizing teams and rounding up sponsors to pay for the equipment. At the same time, he set about "shrinking" the game of baseball so that kids from eight to twelve years old could really play. "When I was nine, nothing was geared to children," Stotz explained in his book *A Promise Kept*. Take bats, for example: "We'd step up to the plate with a bat that was both too heavy and too long. Choking up on the bat merely changed the problem. The handle would then bang us in the stomach when we lunged at the ball. We didn't have the strength or leverage for a smooth, controlled swing."

Trial and Error

Stotz finally found child-sized bats and equipment for his teams, and at every team practice he adjusted the distances between the bases and between the pitcher's mound and home plate, trying to find the ideal size for a field. The goal was to come up with distances that were fair for the outfielders (how far a child could actually throw), and for the runners—how fast could they realistically run to beat the throw. After much experimentation, he settled on 60 feet between bases (as opposed to 90 feet in the big leagues) and 40 feet between the pitcher's mound and home plate (60 feet, 6 inches in the bigs). (The distance from mound to plate later changed to 46 feet and remains that today.)

The only thing Stotz didn't change was the baseball itself. That way, he figured, kids could practice with the balls they already had.

Sponsors

Shrinking the game turned out to be a lot easier than finding sponsors willing to pay for uniforms and equipment for the three teams in the league. Two and a half months after he'd started, Stotz had been turned down by 56 companies. But when he made his 57th sales pitch, he finally landed his first sponsor—the Lycoming Dairy Farm chipped in $30.

Stotz used that money to buy uniforms and set the date of the league's first game for June 6, 1939. He also paid a visit to the offices of *Grit*, Williamsport's Sunday paper, and asked them to mention the league's first game in the paper. Sports editor Bill Kehoe asked Stotz what the league was called, but Stotz didn't have a name yet. He'd considered calling it the Junior Baseball League, but that was too similar to a women's group called the Junior League. Also, because he'd modeled his kids' league after the big leagues, he'd considered calling it either the Little Boys' League or the Little League, but he couldn't decide between the two. He didn't like the sound of "Little Boys' League," but was worried that people would think the "Little League" meant the size of the league, not the size of the boys. In the end, he let Kehoe choose—Little League it was.

For the rest of the story, turn to page 153.

Colonial Philly

The long answers reveal three facts about the early days in the City of Brotherly Love. (Answers on page 302.)

Across

1 Worms, frequently
5 Fed G-
9 Cut a rug
14 Tone down
15 Broccoli ___ (turnip cousin)
16 Neighborhoods
17 City near Provo
18 The ___ *Reader*
19 Photographer's word
20 Philadelphia building that hosted the First Continental Congress
23 Longshoreman, e.g.
24 Sawbuck
25 Pact
28 Not kidding
32 Tiff
33 Director Vittorio de ___
35 Meas. of an economy's income
36 Philadelphia's nickname in colonial times, because of its rich cultural life
40 River, in Reynosa
41 Fox's den
42 Rand of fan dancing fame
43 Capitol figure
46 Julia of *The Bourne Ultimatum*
47 Director Peckinpah
48 Playwright Fugard
50 On-and-off Philadelphia role in Revolutionary days
56 Big shot
57 Cake decorator
58 When repeated, Mork's phrase
59 "And ___ grow on!"
60 Longest river
61 Sandpaper surface
62 Tyra Banks is one
63 Isn't well
64 Shopper's come-on

Down

1 College VIP
2 Kind of glow around one
3 Roman road
4 Pattern used to create documents
5 Solomon of nursery rhyme
6 Photo finish
7 Daisy Mae's love
8 At no time, poetically
9 One of Santa's reindeer
10 Designer Giorgio
11 Moon walker Armstrong
12 "Don't ___ us, we'll . . ."

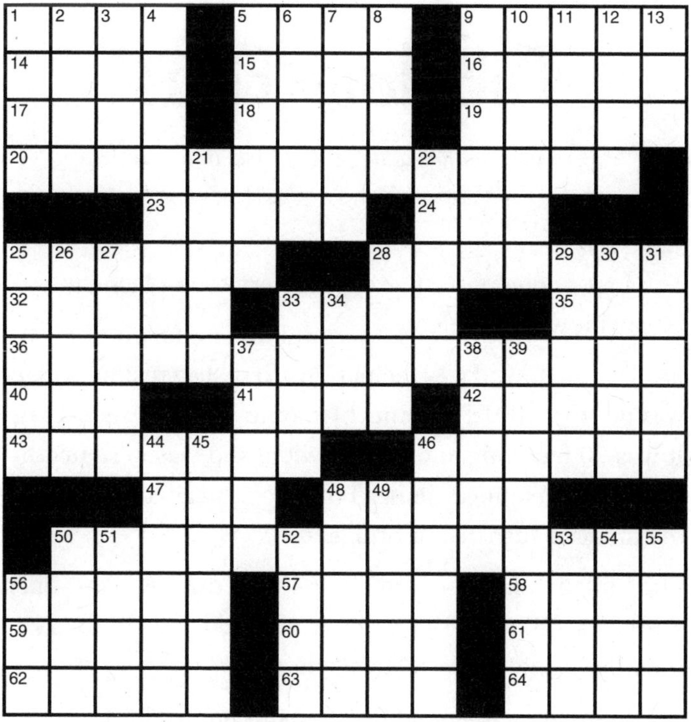
1
2
3
4
5
6
7
8
9
10
11
12
13
14
15
16
17
18
19
20
21
22
23
24
25
26
27
28
29
30
31
32
33
34
35
36
37
38
39
40
41
42
43
44
45
46
47
48
49
50
51
52
53
54
55
56
57
58
59
60
61
62
63
64

13 U-turn from WNW
21 Big name in stationery
22 Word with iron or engine
25 Winter Palace residents
26 Knot again
27 Hawke of *Dead Poets Society*
28 Battle memento
29 *Darby ___ and the Little People* (1959 Sean Connery film)
30 "I give!"
31 Fixes, in a way
33 Glide like a hawk
34 "Don't mind ___ do!"
37 Replay feature, for short
38 Prevent legally
39 Banisters, e.g.
44 Quick on the uptake
45 One skilled in alterations
46 Doesn't hog
48 ___ art (text graphics)
49 Immune system component
50 Dessert, say, to a dieter
51 Gets older
52 Name hidden in caricatures
53 Figure skater Lipinski
54 Blue dye
55 Mandolin cousin
56 Wash, as a floor

Fabulous Firsts

*Pennsylvania has a long list of firsts in the United
States, and even in the world. Here are a few.*

- The first public protest against slavery took place in
  Germantown in 1688.

- Jacob's Creek Bridge—the nation's first suspension bridge—
  was built in 1801 to connect Uniontown and Greensburg.
  It was 70 feet long and 12 feet wide, and was designed by
  Uniontown engineer James Finley, often called the "father of
  the modern suspension bridge."

- The Philadelphia Zoo—the first zoo in the country—opened
  on July 1, 1874. In 1937, the owners added a children's zoo,
  the first in the Western Hemisphere.

- The first concrete-and-steel baseball stadium in the United
  States—Forbes Field—was built for the Pittsburgh Pirates
  in 1909.

- The first gas station in the country opened at Baum
  Boulevard and St. Clair Street in Pittsburgh's East Liberty
  neighborhood in December 1913.

- The first pulltabs on cans were used by the Iron City
  Brewery in Pittsburgh in 1962.

- The first Big Mac was sold in Pittsburgh at the Uniontown
  McDonalds in 1967.

- The first "Mr. Yuk" sticker—the "yucky" face put on con-
  tainers to show that the contents are toxic—was made at the
  Poison Center at Children's Hospital of Pittsburgh in 1971.

(The previously used skull-and-crossbones image proved too attractive to kids, who associated it with pirates and thought it must mean something fun.)

- The first documented use of an emoticon—the smiley face— was at Pittsburgh's Carnegie Mellon University in 1982.

- The first simultaneous heart, liver, and kidney transplant was performed at Presbyterian-University Hospital in Pittsburgh in 1989.

- Timothy Heidler of Duncansville, Pennsylvania, suffered a crushed larynx (voicebox) in a 1978 motorcycle accident. In 1998, he had the first successful larynx transplant in the world (at the Cleveland Clinic in Ohio). After recovering from the operation, he was able to speak normally for the first time in two decades.

- The first license plates displaying a Web site address— www.state.pa.us—were issued in Pennsylvania in 2000.

Did You Know?

From the United States' earliest days, Philadelphia's abolitionists were a thorn in the side of slaveholders. In fact, one famous slave master (none other than George Washington) complained that while he was on a trip to Philadelphia, a Quaker "stole" one of his slaves in order to free him.

Dynasty, Philadelphia Style

Scandals, shipwrecks, affairs—sound like a soap opera? Actually, it's all part of the life of Louisa Lane Drew, who settled in Pennsylvania in the 19th century and made a name for herself . . . first in the theater, and then for raising a show-business dynasty that became known as the Barrymores.

L ouisa Lane Drew wasn't a native Pennsylvanian—she was born in London in 1820—but she moved to Philadelphia with her mother when she was just seven years old. Both quickly got involved in the city's thriving theater community. In 1827, Louisa made her American theatrical debut in *Richard III* at the Walnut Theatre and later performed in Washington, D.C., and New York City, ultimately earning high praise as Little Pickle in the Bowery Theatre's *The Spoiled Child*.

A Traveling Show

In 1830, Louisa and her family formed a traveling theater company. But on a trip to the Caribbean, their ship hit a rock near Santo Domingo in the Dominican Republic, and they all had to jump overboard. In her autobiography, Louisa wrote, "We were 40 miles from any settlement, and the captain and one other would have to go the city of San [Santo] Domingo and obtain a brig to get us off. To haul by land was impossible. We were there six weeks." By the time they were able to set sail again, Louisa's stepfather and her youngest sister had died of yellow fever.

The rest of the family (Louisa, her mother, and two more sisters) returned to the United States briefly, but then joined another traveling troupe. This time they all headed to the Bahamas. When a night storm drove their ship into a sandbar, they found themselves shipwrecked yet again. This time, when rescue came, Louisa's mother decided to take her daughters home to Pennsylvania and leave the high seas to the sailors.

Husbands #1, #2, and #3

When she was 16, Louisa married her first husband, a middle-aged English actor named Henry Blaine Hunt. The couple toured with many U.S. theater companies, including one that starred Junius Brutus Booth (John Wilkes Booth's father). It was during this time that Louisa established a solid reputation as an actress, playing opposite some of the most popular actors of the day—Tyrone Power (great-grandfather of the 20th-century actor) and Edwin Booth (John Wilkes Booth's brother). She also earned $20 a week, the highest salary paid to a leading lady at that time.

After 11 years of marriage, though, the Hunts divorced—a scandalous act for the mid-1800s. Louisa quickly married another actor, George Mossop, but Mossop was a heavy drinker and died just five months later.

Within a year, Louisa was appearing onstage with another actor, John Drew, who was rumored to be smitten with her half-sister, Georgiana. But Louisa won out and married him in 1850.

Pennsylvania, Here We Come!

The Drews settled in Philadelphia, where their three children were born. Like most women of her day, Louisa focused on raising her family; her husband took a job managing the city's

Arch Street Theatre. The Arch had opened in 1828, and by the time John Drew took over, it was one of the city's premier playhouses. Actor Edwin Forrest (often called the "grand tragedian of the American stage") performed in many plays there, and English comedian William Burton had been a former manager.

But John Drew was restless. After just two years of managing the Arch, he left his family and joined a traveling theater troupe that also employed Louisa's younger half-sister, Georgiana. With John Drew gone, the Arch needed a new manager, and Louisa took over in 1861. She was the first woman ever to run the business.

Husband #3, Take Two

John Drew and Georgiana returned to Philadelphia in 1862—with a baby girl named Adine. Louisa and John had never divorced, so Adine's paternity became the object of scandal and rumor. Even though no one ever proved she was John Drew's daughter, people suspected. Still, when Georgiana became too ill to take care of her baby, Louisa took the child in and kept her even after John Drew died in May of that year.

To support the family, Louisa continued to run and perform at the Arch. Under her leadership, the old theater prospered, and Louisa became as well known for her good business sense as for her acting skills. Some of the most celebrated players of the time worked the Arch—even John Wilkes Booth took on the role of Macbeth there, two years before he assassinated Abraham Lincoln.

The Family Ties That Bind

Despite her many marriages (and her occupation), Louisa became a respected member of Philadelphia society; a staunch

Episcopalian, she even had her own pew reserved at St. Stephen's Church. She also raised five children, mostly alone, and cared for her elderly mother.

Louisa's daughter, also named Georgiana, and her son Jack followed their mother into the family business. Jack eventually went to New York, where he took on a role in Edwin Booth's *Hamlet*. Appearing with him was a then-unknown actor named Maurice Barrymore. The two became friends, and when their production ended, Jack brought Barrymore home to Philadelphia, where Georgiana fell in love with him.

But Louisa didn't care for Maurice Barrymore. She felt he was irresponsible and not good enough for her daughter. Still, despite Louisa's objections, the couple married in 1876 and had three children: Lionel, Ethel, and John Sidney Blythe Barrymore . . . who eventually became the grandfather of Drew Barrymore.

Curtain Call

The Barrymores lived in Philadelphia with Louisa, who kept working. In 1880, she took on her most famous role as Mrs. Malaprop in *The Rivals*. Despite being 60 years old, she toured with that production and others for the next decade.

Louisa eventually developed a disease called dropsy— known today as edema—which causes excessive fluid to build up in the body. She died in her sleep on August 31, 1897, and is buried in Philadelphia's Mount Vernon Cemetery.

Ghosts of Business Past

Until the mid-20th century, Pennsylvania was a manufacturing
powerhouse, and Bethlehem Steel was one of the companies
that dominated the state's industrial landscape.

Building Bethlehem

In the early 19th century, Bethlehem Steel was the second-
largest steel producer in the United States. (Pittsburgh-based
U.S. Steel was first.) But it began humbly in 1860 when a
group of businessmen from the Lehigh Valley Railroad bought
a paper company and turned it into an iron manufacturer. The
company's first manager was John Fritz, well known as a
skilled ironmaster and mechanical engineer. It was a good
match—Fritz brought with him a patent for mass-producing
wrought-iron rails that brought the first big money to
Bethlehem Steel (then called the Bethlehem Iron Company). It
also brought the first military contract: the company produced
rails for the Union to replace supply lines that Confederates
destroyed during the Civil War. And Bethlehem produced
65,000 tons of rails for the Trans-Siberian Railroad.

Over the next 40 years, as other companies got into the
rail-making business, Bethlehem was forced to evolve. In the
1880s, it started making warships for the U.S. military and
built the largest defense manufacturing plant in the world.
Then, in 1901, the company's owners sold the business to
Pennsylvania-born businessman Charles M. Schwab (no relation to the Schwab discount brokerage company). At first,
Schwab thought he'd concentrate on shipbuilding, but when
that failed three years later, Schwab decided to turn Bethlehem

into a steel company that would compete with his former employer, U.S. Steel.

Making Its Mark

The first seven decades of the 20th century were successful for Bethlehem Steel. Under Schwab's guidance, the company developed especially strong beams that made it possible to build higher buildings and longer bridges, including the Golden Gate Bridge in San Francisco. Bethlehem also got some important military contracts during Word War I; Russia, Great Britain, and France all contracted with Bethlehem Steel long before the United States got involved in the war. Then, during World War II, Bethlehem was the United States' largest defense contractor, making ships, shells, and other military equipment. Throughout the 1950s, 1960s, and 1970s, Bethlehem continued to prosper, even building a 21-story tower to house the company's corporate headquarters.

In the 1980s, though, Bethlehem began a slow downturn. The market for American-made steel was diminishing as foreign steel prices dropped, and Bethlehem couldn't compete. By 2001, the company had filed for bankruptcy, and a year later, the International Steel Group of Ohio bought the company. Bethlehem Steel was no longer an active company, but its effect on Pennsylvania was undeniable. In its heyday, the company had employed more than 200,000 people, produced 23 million tons of steel annually, and helped make Pennsylvania one of America's most industrialized states.

To read about the Pennsylvania Railroad, turn to page 209.

Five Things You Should Know About Joe Montana

One of football's most celebrated quarterbacks, Joe Montana learned how to throw a tight spiral in the backyard of his Monongahela home. Here's a chance to learn more about his boyhood in the Keystone State.

1. He began his football career under false pretenses.

By the time he was eight years old, Montana wanted to play organized football, but there was a problem: Monongahela's local peewee league didn't allow players to suit up until they were nine. So Joe Sr. lied on his son's registration form and enrolled the boy a year early. Despite being younger—and smaller—than most of his teammates, Montana was named the team's quarterback and quickly impressed his coaches with his confidence and accuracy.

2. His high school football career started on the sidelines.

Montana's high school coach, Chuck Abramski, thought the 165-pound quarterback was too skinny to withstand the physical grind of high school football, and he ordered the young man to hit the weight room. Montana refused because the training would interfere with his other sports—he also played baseball and basketball—so Abramski benched the future Hall of Famer. "He was a fired-up, gung-ho coach, but he never got over the fact that I didn't take part in his summer weight program," Montana recalled. Montana finally cracked the starting lineup during his junior year and was named to *Parade* magazine's All-American team the following season.

3. He nearly became a Tarheel and a basketball star.

Although he's best known for his exploits on the football field, Montana was an accomplished all-around athlete whose first love was basketball. "I could practice basketball all day," he said. By the time he was a high school senior, he was playing guard and leading the Ringgold Rams to the 1973 regional championship. College recruiters were so impressed with Montana's skills that he was offered a basketball scholarship to the University of North Carolina. Montana ultimately turned down that offer in favor of a football scholarship to Notre Dame. But in 1977, he was a member of the championship team in Notre Dame's annual Bookstore Basketball Tournament.

4. He chose Notre Dame because of a fellow Pennsylvanian.

One of the reasons Montana chose to attend the University of Notre Dame: it was the alma mater of his boyhood idol, Terry Hanratty, a Butler, Pennsylvania, native who won two Super Bowl rings as a backup quarterback with the Pittsburgh Steelers. Montana became a fan of Hanratty at an early age and even honed his skills by throwing footballs through a swinging tire in his backyard after hearing that Hanratty had used the same technique.

5. His high school stadium bears his name.

Monongahela's Ringgold High School honored its most famous alumnus at the beginning of the 2006 football season by changing the name of Ringgold Stadium to Joe Montana Stadium. Montana was on hand for the festivities and was later inducted into the school's hall of fame along with Major League Baseball legends Stan Musial and Ken Griffey Sr. and former National Football League kicker Fred Cox.

Career Stats

- Montana played for 15 seasons with two teams: the San Francisco 49ers (1979–92) and the Kansas City Chiefs (1993–94).

- He completed 3,409 passes for 40,551 yards and 273 touchdowns.

- He was selected to the Pro Bowl eight times (1981, 1983, 1984, 1985, 1987, 1989, 1990, 1993).

- He won four Super Bowls and was the Super Bowl MVP three times (1981, 1984, 1989).

- He was inducted into the Pro Football Hall of Fame in 2000.

Did You Know?

One of Pennsylvania's first counties was Bucks County—named after Buckinghamshire in England, where William Penn's family lived.

The Ketchup King

From our archives: here's a story you'll relish. It's about the Pennsylvania man whose name became synonymous with a condiment so popular it's now found in nearly every American fridge.

Young Salesman

Henry John Heinz always had a head for business. Born in Sharpsburg, Pennsylvania, on October 11, 1844, he started selling vegetables from his family's garden when he was eight years old. By the time he was 12, the boy was selling his mother's homemade horseradish sauce door-to-door in his neighborhood.

Thirteen years later, he had a burgeoning condiment business and a partner, Clarence Noble. They bottled their horseradish sauce (and pickles, sauerkraut, vinegar, and so on) under the name Heinz and Noble and delivered their goods by horse-drawn wagon to grocers in and around Pittsburgh. Heinz peddled his wares in clear glass bottles so that his customers could be assured that the products were fresh and were what they advertised. His motto: "Always remember to place yourself in the other person's shoes."

Ketching Up

Business was good until 1873, when a banking panic caused a widespread depression in the United States. Two years later, Heinz and Noble was forced into bankruptcy, but Heinz (with his brother and cousin) bounced back. In 1876, he introduced the product he became known for: Heinz sweet tomato ketchup.

Heinz didn't invent ketchup. The condiment had been

around in some capacity for hundreds of years. The ancient Chinese used the brine from pickled fish as a dipping sauce and called it *ke-tsiap*. From there the sauce made its way to Malaysia, where the name was modified to *kechap*. In the 1680s, Dutch and British explorers brought the concoction back to Europe, where the upper classes spiced it up with pickled mushrooms, anchovies, kidney beans, and walnuts. Eventually, the British bottled that and called it "catsup." By the late 1700s, the recipe found its way to New England, where tomatoes were added to the mix. In the mid-1800s, entrepreneurs exploited the American taste for sweet food and started selling catsup made with tomatoes, vinegar, sugar, cinnamon, cayenne, and salt.

What Heinz did was make ketchup accessible and affordable to the mainstream public. Once an exotic condiment, ketchup became a staple in American households, thanks to Heinz.

The Proof's in the Pickle

Throughout the late 1800s, Heinz expanded his product line to include everything from apple butter to pickled onions to the first sweet pickles (and sweet pickle relish) ever to hit the market. He also expanded his company and, in 1890, opened a new, bigger manufacturing plant in northern Pittsburgh. By then, he was producing more than 60 different products.

Heinz still wanted to increase his customer base, so he employed what turned out to be an ingenious publicity stunt. For the 1893 World's Columbian Exhibition in Chicago, he gave attendees cards that promised them a free pickle-shaped watch charm if they came by his display. The stunt was a huge success. According to a news report of the time, "It has just been discovered that the gallery floor of the Agricultural

Building has sagged where the pickle display of the H. J. Heinz Company stood, owing to the vast crowd which constantly thronged their stand to taste their goods or procure a watch charm."

The charm, of course, clearly bore the name Heinz, and when the attendees headed home with their trinkets, the company got an enormous amount of nationwide advertising. And to make sure that the pickle symbol became synonymous with the company, Heinz used the image on his logo and later commissioned a 40-foot-high pickle (lit up with 1,200 brand-new electric lights) to be put on display on New York City's Fifth Avenue.

Don't Forget the Slogan

What Heinz still needed, though, was a catchy slogan. That came to him during an 1896 trip to New York when he saw an advertisement for "21 styles of shoes" on the side of a train. He liked the idea of many different varieties, and thought the ad conveyed what he wanted for his company: to show that Heinz had so many foodstuffs, customers needn't go elsewhere. He fiddled around with the numbers and eventually settled on 57 varieties, even though the company had more than 60 products. Why 57? Legend has it that five was Heinz's lucky number and seven was his wife's. But some people claim Heinz just liked the way the numbers looked together or that he'd miscounted his products.

No matter. It worked. Heinz put "Heinz 57" on every magazine ad, television commercial, and bottle of ketchup his company sold. Within just a few years, Heinz's "57 varieties" was one of America's most recognizable marketing slogans.

Home Sweet Factory

Besides being a savvy businessman, Heinz was (by all accounts) a generous boss. At a time when long hours, poor working conditions, and low pay were the norm for urban American workers, Heinz believed that they should be treated well on the job. Over the years, the company won many awards for its working conditions, and one union leader even called Heinz's plant a "utopia for working men."

Heinz also liked to give his workers a bit of fun. At one point, after seeing alligators on a trip to Florida, he set up an enormous tank atop one of his buildings and brought in a live, 800-pound alligator just so his workers could see it.

The Beat Goes On

Henry John Heinz died of pneumonia in 1919, but the company and brand he created in Pittsburgh flourished. Today, Heinz is a $10 billion company and employs more than 32,000 people around the world. And never forgetting what first brought it mainstream success, the company continues to sell about 650 million bottles of ketchup a year.

Did You Know?

The Amish have their own way of phrasing common proverbs. See if you recognize these:

- Such as the tree is, such is the fruit.
- Bend the tree while it is young; when it is old it is too late.
- Don't count your eggs before they are laid.

PA on TV

Can CSI: Altoona be far behind?

Everything from Saturday morning cartoons to reality shows have included Pennsylvania in their settings, but most took a "blink and you miss it" approach: Bill Cosby's animated *Fat Albert* took place on the streets of Philadelphia, and the sitcom *Boy Meets World* was set in an unnamed Philadelphia suburb. The characters on Showtime's *Queer as Folk* called Pittsburgh home, and residents of MTV's reality series *The Real World* lived in Philadelphia for the 2004 season. But none of those shows really highlighted their Pennsylvania digs. There are two others, however, that stand out for making Pennsylvania part of the show.

The Office

"There ain't no party like a Scranton party, 'cause a Scranton party don't stop," said Michael Scott (portrayed by Steve Carell) in an episode of *The Office*. And it's thanks to this show that Scranton has become one of America's premier tourist destinations. (*More about Scranton on page 218.*) The American version of *The Office* began in 2005 as a knockoff of a British series of the same name, and it became one of the highest-rated comedies on television.

Scranton Sites

- Dunder Mifflin, the paper company where the characters work, is fictional, but most of the show's local haunts are based on real places in Scranton. In fact, *Office* writers frequently thumb through the Scranton phone book when they need to set a scene outside of the office.

- In one episode, Michael Scott takes his female employees to Victoria's Secret in the Steamtown Mall. Today, that mall sports the show's "Scranton Welcomes You" sign (shown in the opening credits) in its food court.

- The Scrantones (a local band that claims it was voted the "best bar band in Lackawanna County three years running") performs the show's theme song.

Mister Rogers' Neighborhood

Fred McFeely Rogers (aka, Mister Rogers) was born in Latrobe in 1928. Forty years later, he was the host of one of the most popular children's programs in history: *Mister Rogers' Neighborhood*. The show began in 1968 in Pittsburgh and was first broadcast locally; in 1970, PBS picked it up for national distribution. Even as *Mister Rogers' Neighborhood* was beamed into homes all over the United States, it continued to be filmed at WQED studios in Pittsburgh and stayed there for its entire 33-year run. (Reruns still air today.)

Neighborhood Nuggets

- One of the show's best-known segments is "The Land of Make Believe," which was populated with puppets and could be accessed only by a magical trolley. The trolley was based on one in Pittsburgh that Rogers had loved riding while he was growing up.

- Pittsburgh's industrialism is reflected on the show: Mister Rogers often visited local factories for his "How People Make Things" segment.

- The Pittsburgh Children's Museum hosts a permanent

exhibit modeled after the show, complete with a replica of Mister Rogers' house and a life-size, working trolley. In June 2007, the museum also included an exhibit based on the show's "How People Make Things" segment.

- The Idlewild theme park in Ligonier (Pennsylvania's oldest amusement park) features a Mister Rogers attraction: kids can ride the trolley, meet delivery man Mr. McFeely, and cavort with the characters from the Land of Make Believe.

Did You Know?

The Horseshoe Curve, a famous curved section of track owned by the Pennsylvania Railroad (and now a tourist attraction and National Historic Landmark), was once targeted by the Nazis. "The Curve," a section of track that makes a 220-degree U-turn, was used by trains traveling east over the Allegheny Ridge toward Pittsburgh. Because it was the industrial link to the western United States, Horseshoe Curve was one of the intended targets of Nazi saboteurs during World War II. In 1942, eight men infiltrated the United States, but they were never able to gain access to the Curve or destroy it. All eight were eventually caught: two got life sentences because they cooperated with the U.S. government, and the other six were executed.

Pennsylvania-isms, Part II

As any Keystone State local knows, there's a difference between
what Pennsylvanians say. . . and what they mean.

How Others Say It: You (plural)
How They Say It in Western PA: Yins, you'uns, youns, or yunzez
How They Say It in Eastern PA: Youse, yuz, or youze
Example: "I got a new plasma. Youns coming over to watch the Steel Curtain?"

How Others Say It: Rubber band
How Pennsylvanians Say It: Gumband
Example: "That bag's leaking wooder! Put a gumband on it!"

How Others Say It: Bedroom slippers
How Pennsylvanians Say It: Poochies or beddies
Example: "Don't forget to take off your beddies before you go out for groceries."

How Others Say It: Bologna sandwich
How Pennsylvanians Say It: Jumbo
Example: "Bring some jumbos wit you dounnashore."

How Others Say It: A nosy person
How Pennsylvanians Say It: Nebby or neb-nose
Example: "Her mom's such a nebby, always snooping into your business."

How Others Say It: Diagonally across the street
How Pennsylvanians Say It: Cattywumpus
Example: "The nebby who lives cattywumpus is always watching me out her winda."

How Others Say It: Ground squirrel or chipmunk
How Pennsylvanians Say It: Grinnie
Example: "That grinnie's running off wit my hoagie!"

How Others Say It: Have you got any?
How Pennsylvanians Say It: Gotnee?
Example: "Gotnee pop for watching da Pens?"

How Others Say It: Is it going to rain?
How Pennsylvanians Say It: Make down? or Make wet?
Example: "Looks like it's gonna make wet."

How Others Say It: Umbrella
How Pennsylvanians Say It: Bumbershoot
Example: "Well, if it's gonna make wet, I better bring my bumbershoot."

How Others Say It: "Did you eat yet?" "No, did you?" "Not yet."
How Pennsylvanians Say It: "Jeetchet?" "Nojoo?" "Notchet."

For more Pennsylvania-isms, turn to page 17.

The City of Brotherly Love

Some stats and little-known facts about Pennsylvania's largest city.

Town: Philadelphia
Location: Philadelphia County
Founding: 1682
Population (2008): 1,448,394
Size: 135 square miles
County seat? Yes

What's in a name?

William Penn named Philadelphia himself. It comes from two Greek words: *philos*, meaning "love," and *adelphos*, or "brother" —the City of Brotherly Love.

Claims to Fame:

- Philadelphia County includes just the city of Philadelphia.

- Article I, Section 8 of the U.S. Constitution gives the country the right to "coin money," so in 1792, the newly independent United States of America created the country's first mint in Philadelphia. Its first production: 11,178 copper coins that went into circulation the next year.

- The city's Fairmount Park began as a private garden, but in 1843, Philadelphia's City Council bought the space, which was located on a hill above the Schuylkill River. Over the years, the park grew to be the largest landscaped park in the United States. Today, it's an entire complex that includes 63 individual parks and more than 9,000 acres.

- Philadelphia's abolitionist movement began in 1833 when some of the city's most prominent activists organized the Philadelphia Anti-Slavery Society. During its 37-year history, the group worked to end racial and gender discrimination and was one of the first to allow women and minorities to join—ultimately, 42 women became members, nine of them black. The Anti-Slavery Society raised money for abolition, funded integrated schools, and helped escaped slaves to flee the South. The group disbanded in 1870, considering its objective—ending slavery in the United States—"accomplished" after the Confederacy surrendered in 1865.

- Philadelphia is made up of about 12 different neighborhoods. (We say "about" because locals disagree on where exactly the boundaries are.) Some of the best known are South Philly (of *Rocky* and cheesesteak fame), the City Center (where most people visit and work), Chestnut Hill (filled with many historic homes and buildings), and West Philadelphia (home to Drexel University, UPenn, and other colleges).

● ●

Did You Know?

Philadelphia boasts about 2,000 wall murals—more than any other city in the United States.

From Paterno's Playbook

Some wise words from Penn State's most renowned football coach, Joe Paterno.

"The will to win is important, but the will to prepare is vital."

"Publicity is like poison; it doesn't hurt unless you swallow it."

"Success without honor is an unseasoned dish; it will satisfy your hunger, but it won't taste good."

"Besides pride, loyalty, discipline, heart, and mind, confidence is the key to all the locks."

"Losing a game is heartbreaking. Losing your sense of excellence or worth is a tragedy."

"When a team outgrows individual performance and learns team confidence, excellence becomes a reality."

"You have to perform at a consistently higher level than others. That's the mark of a true professional."

"Act like you expect to get into the end zone."

"You need to play with supreme confidence, or else you'll lose again, and then losing becomes a habit."

"Success is never final. Failure is never fatal."

Environmental Crusader

*A lover of the natural world, a published writer at the age of
10, and an ardent opponent of pollution and pesticide use,
Pennsylvania-born Rachel Carson became one of the
world's first and most influential conservationists.*

In 1900, Robert and Maria Carson bought a 64-acre farm in
Springdale, Pennsylvania, about 14 miles from Pittsburgh.
The property included a small clapboard farmhouse—lilacs and
honeysuckle grew near its front porch—two outhouses, a barn,
a springhouse (for fresh water), and a chicken coop. A pear and
apple orchard grew on a hill behind the house. Maria kept a
large vegetable garden, and Robert tended a rose garden.

Rachel, the youngest of the Carsons' three children, was born
on May 27, 1907. From the time she was a toddler, she explored
the woods near the farm. Her mother was college-educated and
well-read in botany and natural history. She introduced her
daughter to the animals, insects, and plants that thrived on their
property and instilled in her children the belief that nature
should be respected and disturbed as little as possible.

In Print

Rachel's brother and sister were almost 10 years older, so she
relied on her dogs for playmates. When she started school, she
developed a talent for writing, and animals became central
characters in her stories. She also looked to her family for
inspiration. At just 10 years old, Rachel published her first
story: "Battle in the Clouds" was about U.S. pilots in World
War I and was inspired by her brother's experiences. The piece

appeared in a popular children's literary magazine of the day: *St. Nicholas*, which focused on work created by children. (F. Scott Fitzgerald, William Faulkner, and e. e. cummings all had stories published in *St. Nicholas* as kids.)

It was the first of several stories young Rachel wrote that made it into print. In 1922, *St. Nicholas* published another piece of hers: "My Favorite Recreation," describing a day spent with her dog. In the story, the pair walks through the Pennsylvania hills, where Rachel takes photographs of birds and their nests. It was her first published nature story and was a forerunner to her later best-selling books.

Shaping a Naturalist's Life

According to Carson biographer Linda Lear, neighbors remembered young Rachel as exceptionally bright and curious about her environment. One oft-repeated story told of her finding a large fossilized shell in a rocky hillside on her family's farm. She read voraciously to find out about the animal that had lived inside it and to discover why a seashell would end up among the rocks near the Allegheny River. She was fascinated to learn that an ocean had once covered the area.

Years later, Carson's interest in evolution and marine science led her to write several books about the ocean. One in particular—*The Sea Around Us*—brought her nationwide attention in 1952 when it won the National Book Award.

Life Off the Farm

Rachel Carson lived in Springdale for 18 years. During that time, the town grew ever more industrialized, and Carson developed a strong dislike for the noise and pollution that came with progress.

In 1925, she left home to attend the Pennsylvania College for Women (now Chatham University) in Pittsburgh. But city life was an adjustment. In those days, Pittsburgh's factories so polluted the area that people often were covered in smoky soot. Living there, Carson appreciated even more the benefits of her rural childhood and became increasingly aware of how fragile the natural world was.

Silent Spring

After four years in Pittsburgh, Carson left Pennsylvania for graduate school at Johns Hopkins University in Maryland, where she studied zoology. Over the next three decades, she worked as a professor, scientist, and researcher, always studying the impact of humans on the natural world. It wasn't until 1962, however, that she published the book that made her famous.

Carson was inspired to write *Silent Spring* after receiving a letter from friends in Massachusetts who were struggling with the effects of aerial pesticide spraying on their rural property. As Carson investigated the use of pesticides in farming, she discovered that they were polluting rivers and threatening wildlife, including the endangered bald eagle. In *Silent Spring*, Carson argued that pesticides could poison the environment, and she called for them to be regulated, particularly DDT, which had come into widespread use on U.S. farms after World War II.

Rachel Carson wasn't the first scientist to notice the harmful effects of DDT and other pesticides, but she was the first to write about them in a way that inspired people to do something about it. In *Silent Spring*, she wrote about a "strange stillness" that fell over an American town after farmers used pesticides:

The few birds seen anywhere were moribund; they trembled violently and could not fly. It was a spring without voices. On the mornings that had once throbbed with the dawn chorus of scores of bird voices, there was now no sound; only silence lay over the fields and woods and marsh.

Controversy and Conservation

The chemical and pesticide industry immediately tried to suppress and discredit *Silent Spring*. But by then, Carson was respected enough as a scientist that all attempts to cover up her findings failed. Instead, the book sparked nationwide interest in pesticide use and prompted President John F. Kennedy to set up a commission to study its consequences.

Rachel Carson died of cancer in 1964, but her book encouraged the creation of the Environmental Protection Agency and the growth of a movement in the United States that worked both to preserve wildlife and habitats, and to change politicians' attitudes about the environment. Her efforts were also, in large part, responsible for DDT finally being banned in the United States in 1972.

Did You Know?

Schuylkill is a Dutch word that means "hidden river." Henry Hudson named Pennsylvania's Schuylkill River in the 1600s when—during an expedition up the Delaware—he passed right by the river's mouth without noticing it. (It was hidden by reeds.)

Seven Things You Should Know About Quakers

If it weren't for the Quakers, there would be no Pennsylvania. Read on to get to know the religious group that founded the commonwealth.

What's in a Name?

"Quaker" is not the official term for the sect: its formal name is The Society of Friends (from John 15:14, in which Jesus says, "You are my friends if you do what I command you").

The origin of the nickname "Quaker" is ambiguous: Some people say it comes from the fact that church members have been known to tremble (or quake) when contemplating God. Others say it comes from a remark by George Fox, the group's founder, who in 1650 told a judge to tremble before the name of God.

The Details . . .

Quakers believe that individuals can have personal relationships with God without priests or ministers. Many Quakers consider the Bible to be an inspirational work, but they don't believe any book is specifically the "word of God." Quakers are generally pacifists, and most are Christian, though some subscribe to other religions or to no specific religion at all.

It's Not Easy Being a Quaker

Quakers are often associated with Pennsylvania—mostly

because William Penn, the state's founder, was a member of the Society of Friends. But the sect was actually founded in the mid-1600s in England, where just being a Quaker was illegal. Early life in the American colonies was no better: Quakers were put to death in Boston in 1659 and 1661. But eventually Quakers became part of colonial life, most notably in Massachusetts and Rhode Island, before Penn founded his colony in 1682.

Sign on the Dotted Line

Quakers formed the colony of Pennsylvania, but they were also present at the creation of the United States of America. Pennsylvania Quaker George Clymer signed both the Declaration of Independence and the Constitution of the United States; fellow Pennsylvanian and Quaker Thomas Mifflin followed suit. Clymer was also a representative to the first U.S. Congress.

Standing Up for Slaves

Early Quakers didn't see any problem with slavery, and many of them (William Penn included) owned slaves. But by the early 1700s, as indentured servants made up more of the population immigrating to Pennsylvania, the attitude toward slavery began to change. It was cheaper for farmers to use indentured servants, but the thinking among Northern whites was also shifting from pro-slavery to abolition. Young Quakers in partic- ular had begun to see slavery as contradictory to their religion's belief that every person contained the "light of God." As a result, American Quakers were at the forefront of the struggle to end slavery, and between about 1750 and 1800, nearly all Quakers in America voluntarily freed their slaves.

Education Matters

Quakers founded many prestigious Pennsylvania colleges, including Swarthmore, Bryn Mawr, and Haverford.

The Fighting Quaker

Although Quakers are usually pacifists, there have been some Friends soldiers in history, most notably Marine Major General Smedley Butler of West Chester, who was nicknamed "the Fighting Quaker." Butler is the last person to have won two medals of honor for separate actions: the first in 1914 during the occupation of Veracruz, and the second in 1915 while fighting in Haiti. Later in life, though, he decried the use of the military for what he considered to be "corporate ends."

● ●

Did You Know?

Boulder Field is a geological curiosity located in the Pocono Mountains' Hickory Run State Park. It's exactly what the name implies: a field of boulders, ranging from basket-ball-sized to massive—some are more than 25 feet across. The field of rocks is approximately 400 feet wide by 1,800 feet long, the rock layer is about 12 feet deep, and though it's surrounded by hardwood forests, there is virtually no vegetation among the rocks. The strange geological forma-tion was caused, geologists say, by the retreat of glaciers during the last Ice Age . . . about 15,000 years ago.

Pennsylvania Odds

Odd numbers, we mean. (Evens are on page 63.)

Pennsylvania has 1 . . . Ivy League university (Penn) and one college that belongs to the Seven Sisters (Bryn Mawr).

Pennsylvania has 3 . . . major rivers: the Delaware, the Susquehanna, and the Ohio.

Pennsylvania has 17 . . . threatened or endangered native plant and animal species, including the bald eagle, the Indiana bat, and the leafy northeastern bulrush (a tall, leafy plant with brown flowers).

Pennsylvania has 33 . . . counties (out of 67) that sit atop bituminous coal beds. The coal beds comprise more than one-fourth of the state's entire area.

Pennsylvania has 2,567 . . . municipalities. That includes all incorporated cities, towns, townships, and boroughs.

Pennsylvania has 44,645 . . . steps (on 712 stairways) in Pittsburgh alone. That's the most of any city in the United States, and more than San Francisco and Cincinnati (which rank second and third) combined. Because of the large number of steps, Ernie Pyle, a famous war correspondent, once joked that Pittsburgh "must have been laid out by a mountain goat."

The Johnstown Flood

*The Johnstown flood was one of the greatest disasters in American
history, but it made heroes of ordinary Pennsylvanians and
was the Red Cross's first attempt at peacetime relief.*

Johnstown, Pennsylvania, in the western Appalachian
Mountains not far from Pittsburgh, was a thriving steel town
in the 1880s. The city had a population of about 30,000 and sat
in a narrow valley at the fork of the Little Conemaugh and
Stony Creek rivers. The townspeople knew that they lived in a
floodplain; it was obvious every spring when heavy rains
poured down the mountain, overran the rivers' banks, and
seeped into nearby buildings and homes. Fourteen miles
upriver—and 450 feet higher in elevation—was the manmade
Lake Conemaugh. Situated on the side of a mountain and held
in place by the South Fork Dam, the lake was two miles long
and home to the exclusive South Fork Fishing and Hunting
Club, where successful Pittsburgh businessmen vacationed. No
one in Johnstown gave much thought to the lake's old, earthen
dam—except to joke about it collapsing someday.

The Deluge
During the night of May 30, 1889, one of the worst rainstorms
in American history dumped 10 inches of rain on Johnstown.
By noon the next day, the South Fork club's engineer took a
nervous look at the rising lake waters and sent a messenger to
telegraph a warning of possible flooding to the Johnstown
authorities. He and the club's president also gathered a work
group and desperately tried to bolster the dam.

They lost the battle. By the afternoon, the lake started to seep over the dam; then, with a roar, the entire dam collapsed. Within 45 minutes, the lake was completely empty, its contents on a disastrous journey downhill. Twenty million tons of water gushed through the narrow valley toward Johnstown at 40 miles an hour, tearing up, crushing, and carrying along everything in its path.

Water, Water Everywhere

The whistles at Johnstown's steel mill sounded just after 4:00 p.m., but people didn't know why (though most historians believe it wouldn't have done any good if they had because it all happened so fast). The first sign of disaster was a deafening roar that grew louder with each second. Some said it sounded like hail, a cyclone, or thunder. One man remembered the crunching sounds of houses torn apart by the water.

At 4:07 p.m., a 60-foot-high wall of water slammed into Johnstown. People on the streets were swept away. Some residents climbed to their rooftops only to be carried off when their houses splintered beneath them. Others floated on rafts of debris and were dashed into buildings or bridges or sucked underwater by whirlpools.

The water moved through the city as one mass until it came to a railroad bridge, where most of the debris started piling up. That slowed the wave down a bit, but the water continued to move through the valley. Survivors who'd been swept toward the bridge clung there or became trapped in the wreckage, which was piled 40 feet high. As night fell, the huge pile of rubble caught fire, and 80 Johnstowners died in the fire.

Triumph Over Tragedy

Amazingly, many Johnstown residents survived the disaster. One was 16-year-old Victor Heiser, who climbed onto the roof of his family's stable. As he watched the wall of water rush toward him, he saw it splinter other structures and expected the same. But instead, the stable was lifted off its foundation and began to roll like a barrel in the water, crashing into other houses in its path. Victor jumped from one piece of house to another, finally landing on a barn roof. He rode it, eventually jumping onto the roof of a brick building. Heiser had looked at his watch when the wild ride began and remembered that it had said 4:20; it wasn't quite 4:30 when it ended. He lost his family in the flood but eventually went on to medical school and developed the first drugs to effectively treat leprosy.

Gertrude Quinn Slattery was just six years old when the flood hit Johnstown. She later told of riding the rolling water atop a mattress and crying out for help. Maxwell McAchren, safe on a rooftop, noticed as she passed by and dove into the water to help. He went under and came up . . . and went under and came up . . . several times before finally reaching the little girl. The two floated along together until they saw a group of men safe on top of another building. McAchren threw Gertrude to them, and both survived.

Helping Hams

In all, 2,209 people—almost 10 percent of Johnstown's population—died in the flood. Four square miles of the town were obliterated, and 1,600 homes were destroyed. Hundreds of missing people were never found, and the last victim wasn't identified until 22 years later.

Donations of money, food, and clothing poured into Johnstown. The citizens of Cincinnati sent 20,000 hams; prisoners in Pittsburgh baked and sent bread. Standard Oil donated a carload of kerosene for light and heat. Emergency shelters, tents, and prefab houses were erected. More than $3 million in donations poured in from around the world. And the American Red Cross, led by Clara Barton herself, carried out its first major peacetime relief operation.

Thanks to the outside help and the resilience of the surviving residents, one of the town's iron companies reopened on June 6, and by July 1, most of the stores on Main Street were open for business as usual. Within just five years, Johnstown's manufacturing centers had recovered.

Commemoration

The South Fork Dam was never replaced, and today, the Johnstown Flood National Memorial preserves the ruins of the dam, part of the old lake bed, and some of the buildings of the South Fork Fishing and Hunting Club. The visitor center regularly shows a film that re-creates the flood. Every May 31, a ceremony is held in remembrance of the victims of the Johnstown flood, and people light 2,209 candles on the remains of the South Fork Dam.

Did You Know?

The first piano built in the United States was constructed in Philadelphia in 1775.

Pretzel City

Happy reading . . . er, redding, er . . .

Town: Reading

Location: Berks County

Founding: 1748

Population (2008): 81,000

Size: 10.1 square miles

County seat: Yes

What's in a Name?

The town was mapped out in 1743 by Richard and Thomas Penn, sons of Pennsylvania's founder, William Penn. The Penn brothers named it Reading after their hometown of Reading, England.

Claims to Fame:

- The iron industry developed in Reading in the 1750s, and by the time of the American Revolution, local factories produced more iron products than manufacturers in all of England. Reading's factories were a major supplier of weaponry and ammunition to the Continental Army.

- Reading is one of the few American cities to have once had a socialist government. Socialist J. Henry Stump was Reading's mayor from 1927 to 1931, 1935 to 1939, and 1943 to 1947. During Stump's first term, every elected city official was a socialist.

- Its nickname is the Pretzel City because in the early 20th century, dozens of pretzel bakeries and packagers made their home in Reading.

- The Reading Railroad opened here in 1838 and was one of the major railways of the Industrial Revolution, shipping coal from the mining regions of western Pennsylvania throughout the northeastern United States. The railroad has been defunct since the mid-1970s, but it lives on as one of the properties on the Monopoly board game.

Quote Me

"Avoid popularity; it has many snares, and no real benefit."

"Humility and knowledge in poor clothes excel pride and ignorance in costly attire."

"Knowledge is the treasure, but judgment is the treasurer of the one who is wise."

"A true friend . . . advises justly, assists readily, adventures boldly, takes all patiently, defends courageously, and continues a friend unchangeably."

"Right is right, even if everyone is against it, and wrong is wrong, even if everyone is for it."

—**William Penn**

Batter Up, Part II

On page 111, we introduced Carl Stotz and Little League baseball. Here's the rest of the story.

Out of the Park

In 1946, there were still only 12 local Little Leagues in the United States—all in Pennsylvania. But big changes came in 1947. Two years after the end of World War II, America's fighting men were back home, settled into their new lives, and finally had time to participate with their sons in Little League.

That year, Little League included 17 independent leagues, and it held its first "World Series." (The Williamsport team took the first title.) The Associated Press and other wire services covered the event, and when stories and photographs of the game appeared in newspapers, Little League's headquarters was deluged with letters from all over the country. People wanted to know how to set up their own leagues.

Making Noise

With Little League's growth came a problem: adults were taking the competition more seriously than the children did. In 1947, parents and other spectators began to routinely boo players and officials during games. Stotz wrote:

> Some of them seemed unable to see the games as simply little boys having fun in a structured . . . athletic program. After all, many of the eight- to twelve-year-old boys had played baseball less than a year. There was certainly no valid excuse for such adult criticism. And it was becoming quite discouraging to some of the boys.

Stotz and other Little League officials complained, and

newspaper editorials condemned the conduct. Within a year, the booing faded.

Little League, Inc.

By the late 1940s, Little League had grown to more than 300 local leagues all over the United States. By 1951, it had more than doubled in size to 776 leagues; there were even leagues in Panama, the first outside the United States. The organization had grown so much that it could no longer be managed effectively by part-time volunteers. So in 1951, Little League incorporated and hired a paid, full-time staff. Carl Stotz was appointed president and commissioner of the league, but his Little League days were numbered.

And Now, a Word From Our Sponsor

In 1948, the U.S. Rubber Corporation became Little League's first national sponsor. In return, the company wanted to help determine the direction of the organization—so U.S. Rubber executives approached Stotz to discuss it. "Essentially," Stotz wrote, U.S. Rubber "proposed a national body that would have total control of the leagues that evolved from it. That body would own every Little League playing field and every Little Leaguer would be a paying member."

U.S. Rubber's plan was exactly the opposite of Stotz's vision; he favored autonomous local leagues, joined in a national organization run by representatives elected from the ranks of the local leagues. The discussions broke off without any change in the direction of Little League, and things seemed amicable. But, as Stotz later wrote, "In retrospect, though, I can see that it was the beginning of a deep philosophical conflict."

The Little Schism

By the early 1950s, Little League was doubling in size every couple of years. It was an enormous success, but Stotz was concerned about the increasing commercialism that accompanied its rise. Another concern was the prominence placed on the Little League World Series, which was played every year in Williamsport. U.S. Rubber and the Little League board of directors wanted to maximize the publicity value of the event, but Stotz wanted to de-emphasize the series. He feared that teams trying to "win their way to Williamsport" would encourage cheating at the expense of good sportsmanship and fair play. The lure of the national spotlight, he worried, would encourage teams to recruit players who were ineligible because they were either too old or lived outside their league's territorial boundaries.

Yet another controversy erupted when Stotz tried to invite legendary pitcher Cy Young, then in his 80s, to come to the 1951 Little League World Series. Two board members thought Young "was an old man who probably couldn't control his bladder, and would embarrass Little League." Stotz invited Young anyway (the event went smoothly), but his differences with Little League, Inc. continued to fester.

You're Out!

In 1952, Stotz stepped down as the president of Little League, but remained as commissioner. A U.S. Rubber executive named Peter McGovern replaced him as president. Then, in 1954, the board of directors adopted a new set of bylaws that stripped the commissioner of much of his power and gave it to McGovern. A year later, McGovern fired Stotz's secretary while Stotz was out of town and replaced her with one of his own aides.

In 1956, Stotz resigned as commissioner and filed suit against McGovern, alleging that he was ignoring Little League volunteers. When Stotz lost the suit, he cut all ties to Little League. A few teams left with him to form the unaffiliated Original Little League, which played their games in a field not far from where Stotz had founded Little League in 1939. Stotz boycotted every Little League World Series game until 1989, when, at age 79, he attended a game to honor the 50th anniversary of the founding of Little League. He died in 1992.

Keep on Swinging

In the years since Stotz left the league, several of his fears have come true. Many leagues and players have been cited for unsportsmanlike conduct and cheating. One of the most publicized events was the case of Bronx pitcher Danny Almonte, who led his team to a third-place finish in the 2001 Little League World Series before officials discovered that he was actually two years older than the rules allowed.

But scandals aside, Little League and the Little League World Series have become positive fixtures in the lives of the millions of kids who participate in them. According to one player who went to Williamsport in 2008, "It's been the best days of my life, pretty much . . . It's unbelievable."

Did You Know?
At 3,823 feet long, the Rockville Bridge in Harrisburg is the world's longest stone arch railroad bridge.

Counter Culture

*The diner industry has taken a hit from the rise of fast food, but
diners remain a fixture in Pennsylvania's culinary culture.*

A Movable Feast

Diners evolved from early lunch wagons, which first began
popping up in New England during the 1800s to offer low-cost
meals to urban workers. Restaurant owners set up shop in
mobile, retired trolley cars, street cars, or railroad cars and
started serving food where workers congregated.

At the turn of the century, there were so many lunch
wagons roaming the streets that cities started requiring operating permits and restricted their hours of business. To bypass
these rules, some owners started settling down in permanent
locations where rent was cheap.

Around 1923, people started calling these stationary lunch
wagons "diners." By then, manufacturers had begun building
them with restrooms and more counter and table seating. In
the 1930s, they got another makeover when longer, sleeker,
stainless steel models came on the scene. After World War II,
the diner business was booming thanks to postwar prosperity.

Although the diner business was born in New England,
much of the industry had shifted slightly south by the 1940s.
Most of the manufacturers were in New York and New Jersey,
and Pennsylvania's close proximity to them was a main reason
that diners became so popular there. It's also why there are a
lot more diners in the southeastern part of the state than there
are in the west.

Pennsylvania Diners 101

There are hundreds of diners in Pennsylvania today. Some things (like food and lingo) are standard from diner to diner, but others depend on the individual establishment.

Geography: The Philadelphia area is home to the most diners in the state. That doesn't mean diners don't exist in western Pennsylvania, however. Most of the area's diner business is concentrated around Pittsburgh and Erie (which makes sense, since those were industrial hubs and provided a customer base). Although no one seems to know why, diners in and around Erie often use the spelling "dinor" instead of "diner."

Diner Dating: The part of town a diner is in can sometimes suggest how long it's been around. For example, diners in the middle of a town tend to be older because they once catered to local customers, before people commuted in cars. On the other hand, diners located close to highways are more likely to have come along later, after the growth and expansion of America's highway system.

Eats: Throughout Pennsylvania, there are certain diner menu standards: meat loaf, milk shakes, triple-decker club sandwiches, chipped beef, French fries with gravy, sticky buns, and homemade pies. Naturally, though, different areas offer some variety—diners in Pennsylvania Dutch country also feature regional specialties like chicken and waffles, pork and sauerkraut, schnitz and knepp (ham and dried apples with dumplings), shoofly pie, and chowchow—a mustard-flavored relish made with corn, beans, onions, pickles, and other vegetables.

Lingo: There was a time when diner owners and patrons spoke a language all their own. The terms are heard less often today, but here are some bits of old-school diner lingo you still might hear floating around the counter:

- Hockey puck: A well-done hamburger
- Burn one: To put a hamburger on the grill
- On the hoof: Meat served rare
- Rabbit food: Lettuce
- Whistleberries: Baked beans
- Wreck 'em: Scrambled eggs
- White cow: A vanilla milk shake
- Bucket of cold mud: Chocolate ice cream
- Sinkers and suds: Doughnuts and coffee
- Blowout patches: Pancakes
- Wax: American cheese
- Pin a rose on it: Add an onion

The Pennsylvania Diner Hall of Fame

Most Original Name: The Yakkity-Yak Diner in North Apollo. Order its namesake from the menu, and you'll get a fried bologna sandwich.

Most Famous: The Downingtown Diner—currently called Chef's Diner and once called the Cadillac Diner—appeared in the 1958 Steve McQueen movie *The Blob.*

Most Political: The American Dream Diner on Herr Street in Harrisburg is a favorite spot of Pennsylvania politicians; state legislation has even been signed at its tables.

Oldest: Kay's Italian Restaurant in Daleville opened in 1920.

Most Successful: German immigrant Richard Kubach opened the Melrose Diner in Philadelphia in 1935 and, according to Brian Butko, author of *Diners in Pennsylvania*, turned the run-down, abandoned business with just 19 stools into the most popular diner in the city in just one year. The diner's jingle: "Everybody who knows goes to Melrose."

Did You Know?

Philadelphia-born Albert Barnes made a fortune in the early 1900s as the inventor and manufacturer of an antiseptic called Argyrol. By the time he died in 1951, Barnes was worth about $3 billion. He was also an eccentric, a philanthropist, and an art lover. In 1922, he combined these interests when he opened the Barnes Foundation in Merion Township. The foundation offered art classes and hosted a museum filled with artwork from Barnes's personal collection—mostly Impressionist and post-Impressionist paintings. The classes were open to the public, but the museum was by invitation only . . . and whether you got an invitation seemed to depend entirely on Barnes's mood. Legend says that writer James Michener was refused entry and that people who wrote asking to make appointments were sometimes turned down in letters "signed" by Barnes's dog.

Jim Thorpe

The place, not the guy.

Town: Jim Thorpe
Location: Carbon County
Founding: 1818
Population (2008): 4,800
Size: 14.8 square miles
County seat: Yes

What's in a Name?

In the early 20th century, athlete Jim Thorpe was one of the most famous people in the world. He won the decathlon at the 1912 Olympics in Stockholm, played professional football, and is frequently named as one of the greatest athletes of all time. Thorpe wasn't from Pennsylvania; he was born in Oklahoma in 1888. In fact, he never visited the town that came to bear his name.

Jim Thorpe died in 1953, and his body was placed in a vault, pending the State of Oklahoma's approval and financial backing for a memorial site in Tulsa. But in the end, the Oklahoma state legislature rejected the plan.

This is where the Pennsylvania town of Mauch Chunk comes in. In the 1950s, officials in the small city of Mauch Chunk (an American Indian name that meant "Bear Mountain") were looking for a way to bring tourists and money to their town, and they needed a hook. So they asked

Thorpe's family if they could build a memorial in Pennsylvania and inter his body there. To sweeten the deal, they'd rename the town Jim Thorpe.

The Thorpe family consented, the town voted, and in 1953, Mauch Chunk became Jim Thorpe. Ever since, the body of Thorpe has lain in a park called the Jim Thorpe Memorial. His marble tomb is etched with pictures depicting him playing various sports.

Claims to Fame

- Mauch Chunk's opera house opened in 1882 and was originally built as a combination bazaar and concert hall. In the early 20th century, musicians from Al Jolson to John Philip Sousa performed there before it became a movie theater in 1927. Over the years, the building fell into disrepair, but eventually, the town's historical society bought it and renovated it. Today, the old opera house is again a performing arts theater.

- Mauch Chunk's Switchback Railroad is often called one of America's first roller coasters. The railroad began in the 1820s as a means for miners to get coal from a nearby mountain to the town below. Powered only by gravity, the train barreled unrestrained down a mile-long track. (Mules pulled it back up.) In 1873, the train started carrying thrill-seeking passengers instead. That year alone, about 35,000 people rode on the Switchback. It closed in 1929, but the track's path remained. Today, bikers and hikers can travel the railroad's 18-mile route.

Prank-More College

This year, we decided to give Uncle John's "Best Hijinks" award to Swarthmore College. These kids really know how to let loose.

Swarthmore College is one of America's finest small liberal arts colleges. Its students have a reputation for being smart, intense, and bookish—a reputation that they cultivate carefully. But Swarthmore students also know how to have fun, and they have a long history of pranks and silly traditions. Here are some of the most memorable.

The Crum Regatta

The Saturday morning of Parents' Weekend is the time for the Crum Regatta. Students compete on nearby Crum Creek in boats they build themselves out of "found" materials. Boats can be made out of almost anything: one student used trays from the cafeteria, and in 2007, a student waded down the creek while pulling five girls on a wooden plank. (He came in third.) Nearly everyone wins a prize—first, last, most creative, etc.

Dash for Cash

Once each semester, members of the men's and women's rugby teams run through the school's main administration building, Parrish Hall, grabbing fistfuls of dollars from the hands of eager spectators. The catch? All the runners are naked. The tradition got started in 1990 (or 1989—no one seems completely sure) when a group of players on the men's rugby team streaked through one of the women's dormitories. The women wanted the men to do it again, and they agreed under one condition: the women had to give them some cash. It's all for a good cause, though. The money collected these days goes to buy supplies for the teams. (Rumor has it that members of the faculty have been offered cash *not* to participate.)

The McCabe Mile

One night in the spring of 1970, Dave Johnson and Peter Gould, two Swarthmore "sewer rats" (students who liked to study in the basement of the school's McCabe Library), decided that they needed to let off some steam. The library had just been redecorated with new orange carpeting, and the two figured out that it would take 18 laps around the orange carpet to make a one-mile run. So when the library closed for the night, they put on their running shoes and did it.

Word of their race got around, and the next spring, 18 Swatties (as Swarthmore students are known) showed up for the run. Eventually, it became one of the school's most cherished traditions. In 1974, students even started handing out a "trophy" . . . a single roll of Scott toilet paper to honor Thomas McCabe, the library's namesake and a former chairman of the board at the Scott Paper Company.

A Unique Start

- With so many students participating in such a small space, a position at the head of the line is highly desirable, so the organizers devised a competition. Before the start of the race, someone reads a quotation. The first Swattie to identify the source and shout out the book's title gets to go to the front of the line.

- The race begins when the book from which the quotation was read is slammed shut.

The Department of Men's Studies

One of Swarthmore's most ingenious pranks of all time took place at the start of the fall 2007 semester. Seniors Ben Blander, Nathan La Porte, and Mike Rosenberg formed an entire fictitious department . . . the Department of Men's Studies. The three printed an "addendum" (formatted to look just like a real catalog) and handed it out to all incoming freshmen. The addendum explained that "due to a printing error, one department was left out of the College Bulletin." Offerings in the Department of Men's Studies included classes such as Demolition, Beer and Malt Liquor, and Study a Broad. The school's registrar, Martin Warner, even allowed the pranksters to staff a table at the Departmental Advising Fair. Warner said that he found the parody of the course catalog "cute."

● ●

Did You Know?

Nearby Haverford College has its own traditions. According to many people on campus, there are three things that every Haverford student must accomplish (outside the classroom) before graduation:

1. Swim in the duck pond.

2. Run the Naked Mile, a tradition that began at the University of Michigan, where students run naked through campus on the last day of classes each spring. It seemed like so much fun that other schools, including Haverford, took up it up.

3. Spend a full night in Magill Library cramming.

On the Radio

KDKA of Pittsburgh has many things to be proud of. Here's one: it's the oldest commercial radio station in the United States.

Thank Frank

In 1890, 16-year-old Frank Conrad got a job at the Westinghouse Electric and Manufacturing Company of Pittsburgh. He would eventually spend his entire working life (51 years) there and, early on, began experimenting with the new medium of radio. In 1919, he set up a crude radio station in his garage, trading messages with just a few listeners. But one night when he ran out of things to say, Conrad played music. The people who heard it wanted more, so he did it again . . . and again. As more listeners picked up his broadcasts, he developed a following.

A local music store was the first business to take notice; it supplied records for Conrad to play in return for on-air advertising. Next, a department store started selling ready-made radios so that people could listen to Conrad's show. Previously, most people had made their own radios, but that took time and the public didn't want to wait to hear Conrad's music. Finally, Westinghouse started paying attention.

Radio, the Early Days

Back then, radio stations were mostly low-key operations, headed by individuals (like Conrad) or small businesses, who used them to communicate with each other—very few people saw radio as an entertainment or profit-making medium. But because Conrad had so much success playing music, Westinghouse came to believe that entertainment was radio's future.

On November 2, 1920, the company debuted its own station, KDKA, which would include programs aimed at creating a solid listener base and would make money from advertising. The first broadcast? Results from that year's presidential race between Warren G. Harding and James M. Cox. KDKA became the first commercial (for-profit) radio station in U.S. history.

In 1992, KDKA switched to an all-talk format, which it still uses today. The last song played? Don McLean's "American Pie," about "the day the music died."

The Name Game

If you're wondering where KDKA got its call letters, here's the story: Before 1920, radio was mostly used for communication—between ships and shore, for example. That radio network grew out of earlier telegraph stations, which had been assigned identifying call letters, and radio operators used them, too. Different countries had different call letters; U.S. stations all began with K, W, or N. When Westinghouse applied for its license, the letters KDKA were the next available on the government's list.

Innovation

Being the United States' first commercial station was quite an accomplishment for KDKA, but the station racked up other firsts, too:

1921: In January, it hired the first full-time radio announcer, Harold W. Arlin, who provided the first play-by-play coverage of a Major League baseball game: the Pittsburgh Pirates versus the Philadelphia Phillies. (Pittsburgh won.) That year, KDKA was also the first to broadcast a presidential inaugural address, a heavyweight championship bout (Jack Dempsey beat Georges Carpentier), and a football game—between the victorious University of Pittsburgh and West Virginia University.

1922: KDKA hosted comedian Will Rogers in his first radio broadcast.

1924: The station took part in the first transcontinental radio broadcast. A New York City station broadcast a program from the Waldorf-Astoria ballroom; KDKA picked it up by short-wave radio and sent it to a station in Hastings, Nebraska, which sent it on to San Francisco.

1927: KDKA became part of NBC's Blue Network, a chain of stations across the country that broadcast simultaneously. It was the progenitor of the national radio and television networks we know today.

1951: *Ed and Wendy King's Party Line*, the first radio talk show, debuted and ran for 21 years.

1954: Rege Cordic and his talk show *Cordic and Company* set a new standard for morning talk shows. Instead of sober, straight journalism, *Cordic and Company*—with regular guests Louie the Garbageman and Omicron the Alien—featured zany humor.

1982: KDKA was the first AM station to broadcast in stereo.

Did You Know?

In 1958, State College Area High School, near Penn State University, became the first in the country to offer driver's education.

The Pittsburgh Pirates Quiz

*Think you know the history of Pennsylvania's
oldest Major League Baseball team? Let's
find out. (Answers on page 302.)*

1. When did the organization that became the Pittsburgh Pirates start playing ball?

    A.   1862

    B.   1872

    C.   1882

    D.   1892

2. What was the earliest name of the team that became the Pirates?

    A.   Alleghenys

    B.   Grays

    C.   Spiders

    D.   Parkers

3. When did the team play its first actual game in Pittsburgh?

    A.   1892

    B.   1896

    C.   1901

    D.   1908

4. Why did the team become the Pirates?

A. The nearby coastline was once famous for piracy.

B. They stole a player from another team.

C. Their team logo resembled a skull and crossbones.

D. Their owner's favorite novel was *Kidnapped*.

5. What is the fewest number of wins recorded by the team in one season?

A. 15

B. 23

C. 42

D. 51

6. How many times have the Pirates won the National League pennant, but *not* the World Series?

A. 1

B. 2

C. 3

D. 4

● ●

Did You Know?

In 1999, M. Night Shyamalan's film *The Sixth Sense* earned seven Oscar nominations. Since then, Shyamalan, who grew up in the Philadelphia suburb of Penn Valley, has based his production company in Conshohocken, giving the Commonwealth its first major film production company since the collapse of Lubin Films in 1914.

Philadelphia Triple Feature

Wishing for a night of movies with the word "Philadelphia" in them? Here you go!

Philadelphia (1993)

What It's About: A hotshot lawyer (Tom Hanks) gets fired by his Philadelphia law firm when the senior partners discover he has AIDS. He sues and is represented in his fight by an attorney (Denzel Washington) who has to overcome his own homophobia to try the case.

Uncle John's Ranking: Four cheesesteaks out of four. Philadelphia plays a big part in the movie, which was filmed in the city. Featured landmarks include City Hall, the Furness Building at the University of Pennsylvania, and the Wachovia Spectrum.

Philadelphia was the first major Hollywood film to deal with the subject of AIDS. It was also the film that won Tom Hanks the first of his two back-to-back Best Actor Oscars. (The second was for *Forrest Gump*.) In his acceptance speech, Hanks called Philly the place where "wise, tolerant men" founded the United States. The film won a second Oscar for the Bruce Springsteen song "The Streets of Philadelphia."

Philly Fact: In the film, Denzel Washington's character mentions that he hopes the Phillies will win the pennant. The year the film was released, they did.

The Philadelphia Story (1940)

What It's About: High society fixture Tracy Lord (Katharine Hepburn) is getting married for a second time, and the first husband, C. K. Dexter Haven (Cary Grant) crashes the festivities with a sardonic journalist (Jimmy Stewart) in tow. Is he there to see his old wife off—or to get her back?

Uncle John's Ranking: Three cheesesteaks out of four. This film is a classic, but we gave it only three cheesesteaks because, even though the city of Philadelphia shows up in the movie, its role is minor. Portions of the film focus on the lives of people living in Philly's ritzy "Main Line" western suburbs, which were at one time Pennsylvania's equivalent to Beverly Hills or the Upper East Side of Manhattan.

The Philadelphia Story won four Oscars, including Best Actor (Jimmy Stewart) and Best Screenplay (screenwriter Donald Ogden Stewart, who said that the original play he adapted was so well written that writing the film was the easiest job he'd ever had).

Philly Fact: The name "Main Line" refers to the Pennsylvania Main Line railroad, which ran from Philadelphia through wealthy Chester County.

The Philadelphia Experiment (1984)

What It's about: Two sailors in 1943 are on a navy ship in a Philadelphia shipyard, taking part in an experiment to render the boat invisible to radar, when something goes horribly wrong and they find themselves sent forward in time and space to 1984 Nevada. They spend the movie trying to get back to their own era and wondering what will be there when they do.

Uncle John's Ranking: One cheesesteak out of four. Philadelphia makes a very minor appearance in the film. Shipyards in

South Carolina stand in for the Philadelphia shipyards, and the rest of the movie was filmed in Nevada. Plus the movie's stars (Michael Paré and Nancy Allen) aren't well known, and the most prestigious accolade this film garnered was a science fiction–oriented "Saturn Award" Best Actress nomination for Allen (who lost to Daryl Hannah for *Splash*). But as far as '80s B-movie science fiction goes, it's not bad.

Philly Fact: The film is based on the "Philadelphia Experiment" urban legend. The story goes like this: In 1943, a destroyer named the USS *Eldridge* allegedly disappeared from a Philadelphia shipyard after the crew conducted a science experiment on it. The ship appeared in Virginia waters, disappeared, and reappeared in Philadelphia . . . minus a few sailors, who were never found. (The U.S. Navy, of course, claims that it's all fiction.)

● ●

Did You Know?

There's a statue of a kneeling Lenni Lanape warrior hidden in Philadelphia's Fairmont Park. American sculptor John Massey Rhind carved the marble statue in 1902 as a memorial to the Indians who used to live and fish in the area—legend even says that the spot where the warrior sits was a place where the Lenni Lanape once held tribal councils. Finding the statue has become a rite of passage in Philadelphia. To track it down, look on Rex Drive near the stone bridge over Wissahickon Creek.

U.S. Steel: Then and Now

In The Godfather, Part II, *gangster Hyman Roth says, "We're bigger than U.S. Steel." Well, maybe . . . but not many things are. This Pittsburgh-based company started strong and hasn't faltered.*

Then: The United States Steel Corporation officially got its start in February 1901 when 10 smaller companies (including Carnegie Steel, the American Steel and Wire Company, and the American Bridge Company) merged. The combined assets were more than $1.4 billion, making U.S. Steel the country's first billion-dollar company and its largest steel producer.

Now: In 2008, U.S. Steel posted profits of $919 million and is still the United States' largest steel producer.

Then: The company's founders named it United States (or U.S.) Steel because it was a combination of those 10 major American companies.

Now: U.S. Steel became the USX Corporation in 1986 because its shareholders decided there was more to the company than just steel. (It had also become an energy producer after buying the Marathon Oil Company.) But in 2001, it went back to its original name when the steel side of the business spun off from the larger corporation and became its own publicly traded company. The energy side did the same and once again became the Marathon Oil Corporation.

Then: The peak of U.S. Steel's employment was during World War II—in 1943, the company had more than 300,000 people on its payroll.

Now: U.S. Steel employs about 49,000 people worldwide.

Then: When U.S. Steel first consolidated in 1901, business powerhouses Elbert H. Gary (for whom the steel town of Gary, Indiana, is named) and Charles M. Schwab shared control: Schwab was president, and Gary was chairman of the board. By 1903, however, the two proved that they couldn't work together. Schwab resigned and went on to open Bethlehem Steel (*more about that on page 122*), and Gary continued at his post until he died in 1927.

Now: The company's chairman and CEO is John P. Surma Jr., a Pittsburgh native and Penn State graduate.

Did You Know?

Today, Penn State's athletic teams are known for their blue and white uniforms, but in 1887, students actually voted for black and pink to be the school's colors. After a few weeks of wearing black and pink uniforms, the athletes started noticing that the colors faded in the sun and had become blue and white. Rather than fight a losing battle with nature, the school officially changed its colors in 1890.

The Little Team that Could

Villanova's victory over seemingly unbeatable Georgetown in the 1985 NCAA Men's Basketball Championship is considered one of the greatest upsets in sports history. How did the unheralded Wildcats sneak into the Hoyas' den and come away with a trophy?

Try, Try Again

Over the course of the 1984–85 basketball season, the Villanova Wildcats encountered Big East Conference foe and defending national champions Georgetown Hoyas twice. The Hoyas, led by all-American Patrick Ewing and coached by the equally imposing John Thompson, defeated the Wildcats 52–50 in overtime on January 11, 1985, and again by a score of 57–50 on February 11. After being ousted in the Big East Conference Tournament by St. John's, the Wildcats (with their 19–10 record) could only wait and hope until the NCAA announced which teams would be playing in that year's tournament.

Fortunately for the Philadelphia school, the tournament had been expanded from 48 to 64 teams that year, and this meant that more of the "bubble teams"—those that were unsure if they would be selected—made it. Villanova barely squeezed into the tournament as an eighth seed largely on the basis of its tough regular-season schedule and the fact that it was one of the few teams to lose to Georgetown by a slim margin.

Before the Wildcats could even think about defeating the Hoyas, though, they would need to improve the consistency of their play. In particular, the Wildcats' top players—center Ed

Pinckney, forward Dwayne McClain, and guard Gary McLain—
would need to embrace Coach Rollie Massimino's philosophy
of being patient and focusing on one game at a time. The team
didn't have superstars or a dominating center like Patrick
Ewing, but it did have a lot of smart players. If they could
become a cohesive team like Massimino wanted them to,
they'd have a chance.

The Long Road to the Top

During the tournament, Villanova's players put their mediocre
regular season behind them and produced victories over
Dayton, Michigan, Maryland, and North Carolina. Suddenly,
Dwayne McClain was on the cover of *Sports Illustrated* along
with Georgetown's Ewing and St. John's Chris Mullin. At the
time, most sports fans and journalists viewed the Wildcats as
an anomaly, a team that had put together a great run but whose
time was almost up. Villanova, though, remained undaunted.

Next came the semifinal. Villanova played Memphis State,
which was considered a superior offensive team. In the end,
though, Villanova came out ahead; the Wildcats' defense shut
down the Tigers, 52–45. There was just one game left: on
April 1, Villanova would play top-ranked Georgetown for the
national championship.

Big and Nasty

Many fans of college basketball consider the Georgetown teams
of that era to be among the most dominant in history. They
had reached the NCAA championship game twice, and won in
1984. The 1984–85 team spent most of the season ranked #1,
and entered the tournament as the favorite to win it all again.
Ewing, a seven-foot center who worked tirelessly on both

offense and defense led the team. The Hoyas' opponents that season had shot less than 40 percent from the field (not including free throws) and were held to under 60 points in 21 of 38 games. The Hoyas employed a full-court press— aggressively defending the other team's ball handler over the entire length of the floor—for almost the entire game. They were not afraid to deliver hard fouls and played with an intimidating demeanor. Few thought the Wildcats had a chance.

The (Shot) Clock Strikes Midnight

A 45-second shot clock had been used throughout the 1984–85 regular season on an experimental basis, but for the tournament, the NCAA ruled that teams would play under the old rules, without a shot clock. (Today, the shot clock is standard.) For Villanova, this was a boon: they could milk the clock, holding and passing the ball patiently while waiting for high-percentage shot opportunities to open up. Against Georgetown in the first half, they did just that, making 13 of 18 shots from the field and 11 of 13 free throws. When forward Harold Pressley converted a basket just before halftime to give Villanova a 29–28 lead, fans across the country were stunned. There were 20 minutes left to play, though. Surely Georgetown would come out of its funk.

After falling behind by six points early in the second half, Georgetown slowly chipped away at Villanova's lead and was ahead 54–53 with just under five minutes to play. With the pressure mounting, the Wildcats refused to deviate from their plan. After lulling the Georgetown defenders by passing the ball around the perimeter, the Wildcats put the ball in the hands of backup guard Harold Jensen, who sank a wide-open jumper to reclaim the lead for Villanova, 55–54.

In the last two minutes, the Wildcats converted 11 of 14 free throws to keep the title just out of the Hoyas' reach. As a team, Villanova made 9 out of 10 second-half shots to finish with a shooting percentage of 79 percent for the game, a tournament record that stands to this day. When McClain dove after a loose ball in the closing seconds and held it tight to his chest with one fist in the air, the once-mighty Hoyas' season ticked away.

The Sweet Smell of Victory

On the podium, Gary McLain held the trophy above his head and Ed Pinckney shouted, "Look at the scoreboard . . . Everybody said Georgetown would win. Everybody! But it's us!"

And what of the Hoyas? After a season spent tormenting opponents with their physical play, they watched the Wildcats receive their commemorative gold watches in the postgame ceremony.

Did You Know?

In 1885, York doctor George Holtzapple used oxygen to treat a patient suffering from pneumonia and then published his findings. He wasn't the first doctor to administer an oxygen treatment, but he was the first to write about it so that others could follow the example.

A Penn-y for Your Thoughts

The words below all have a special association with Pennsylvania.
See how many you can find. (Answer on page 304.)

ALCOA

AMISH

BEN FRANKLIN

BUBBLE GUM

CHEESESTEAK

CHRISTMAS TREES

COAL

CONSTITUTION

EAGLES

GETTYSBURG

GROUNDHOG

HEINZ

HERSHEY

HEX SIGNS

KEYSTONE STATE

KOBE BRYANT

LIBERTY BELL

MACK TRUCKS

MUSHROOMS

PENNSYLVANIA DUTCH

PHILLIES

PINK

POTATO CHIPS

PRETZELS

QUAKER STATE

ROCKY

ROLLING ROCK

ROOT BEER

SAUSAGE

SCRAPPLE

SHOOFLY

SLINKY

TURNPIKE

VALLEY FORGE

ZIPPO

ZOO

```
G I E T A T S R E K A U Q K C E A Q P O
H B U B B L E G U M U S H R O O M S H Y
I S I U X J P U I Q N Q G M T A D N F N
O L H O Q A I S E G R O F Y E L L A V R
Y E H S R E H L I B E R T Y B E L L K C
V Z V P E N N S Y L V A N I A D U T C H
A T L K K H X I U V U B R E E B T O O R
P E J N G E T T Y S B U R G H H H S R I
C R I J H L Y U N D A L C O A A E S G S
O P E E Z I Z S Q L E U K J C L E J N T
N Z B V X R W P T A Z K S C G K Z Y I M
S P I H C O T A T O P O Y A Q U Y L L A
T T Y E Z I P P O C N B E K G H P F L S
I Z W K A E T S E S E E H C N E H O O T
T L H I A L X D C O P B S J E I I O R R
U V Q P G O H D N U O R G T M N L H K E
T J P N A Y Y L Y K K Y H J A Z L S U E
I Z Z R C L C E L P P A R C S T I U W S
O R O U V T N N I L K N A R F N E B U U
N H P T Z Z Z M A C K T R U C K S N P C
```

Revolutionary Documents: The Declaration of Independence

The piece of paper that started it all was written, approved, and even printed in Philadelphia.

Life in Philadelphia in 1776 was chaotic. The Revolutionary War had begun the year before, but even in 1776, many people still hoped for reconciliation with England. By May, though, rebels who wanted a complete break from King George had ousted the loyalists and moderates from Pennsylvania's government. Not everyone agreed, but most of the other colonies had followed suit. When delegates from each state gathered at the Continental Congress in Philadelphia, their collective goal had turned from reconciliation to complete independence from England.

Many of the delegates—men like John Adams and Thomas Jefferson—had read Thomas Paine's pamphlet *Common Sense* (*see page 38*), which presented a strong case for independence. Adams urged the Continental Congress to draw up a formal declaration of independence. The purpose: to make their goals known, let the English government (and the colonists) know what their grievances were, and explain why the colonies needed to be their own nation.

When in Doubt, Appoint a Committee

On June 10, the Continental Congress appointed five men—

John Adams, Thomas Jefferson, Benjamin Franklin, Roger Sherman, and Robert Livingston—to draft the Declaration of Independence. Adams and Jefferson were expected to write the document; Franklin, who was 71 years old and in poor health, lent respectability to the committee; and Sherman was a respected New England politician who supported Adams. Only Livingston seemed an odd choice. He represented New York, a colony still against independence, but he might have been included to appease the colonists who feared a break with England.

Ultimately, the committee chose Jefferson to do the actual writing, though others could have done the job. John Adams was qualified, but most people thought his writing was dull. Even Adams himself told Jefferson, "You can write ten times better than I can." As for Franklin, a proven author, many were concerned that if the wry and witty Franklin wrote the declaration, he'd hide a joke in it.

In the end, Jefferson was chosen because he was an eloquent author and had already put his thoughts about the colonies' rights on paper. Before the meeting in Philadelphia, Jefferson had drafted an article called "A Summary View of the Rights of British America," which laid out his ideas about self-governance and offered justification for the Revolution. The article had made its way to Philadelphia ahead of him, and the other delegates had read and admired it.

Make Haste!

From the day the committee formed to the day Jefferson finished the declaration's first draft took just 17 days. Jefferson wrote mostly in the suite of rooms he'd rented in a Philadelphia home. No diaries or minutes exist to describe his composition process, but scholars are certain that Jefferson drew many of his ideas from a constitution he'd written for Virginia, listing his grievances against the king of England. He also borrowed from John Locke's *Second Treatise on Government*, which theorized that the people had rights and should rebel if their government didn't uphold them. Finally, he took ideas from other writers of the Enlightenment Era, who proposed that freedom and equality were mankind's inherent entitlements.

Jefferson gave Franklin and Adams a rough version on June 28, and they made some editorial suggestions. (When describing King George's attitude toward the colonies, for example, Franklin changed Jefferson's phrase "arbitrary power" to the more severe "absolute despotism.") Jefferson incorporated their changes into a new copy and presented it to the Continental Congress on July 2.

Getting It Passed

For the most part, the delegates made few changes to the Declaration of Independence. They condensed some long paragraphs (like the one explaining why the king was a tyrant) into one or two sentences. But one passage led to debate: Jefferson's original version condemned the slave trade. Even though he owned slaves himself, Jefferson blamed England and King George for the practice, which he called a "cruel war against human nature." But many of the colonies were slaveholding states, and other free states were sympathetic to the practice. The delegates refused to allow the condemnation of the slave trade to stand. Led by Georgia and South Carolina, a group of attendees voted out the paragraph.

Even with that argument settled, a unanimous vote eluded the Congress because New York refused to approve the declaration. New York was still divided on the issue of independence, so the New York delegates abstained from the vote on July 4. All the other colonies voted in favor, though, and the declaration passed. The United States had asserted itself as a separate, independent country.

Hot Off the Press

That same day, the Continental Congress sent the document to a printer so that copies could be rushed to all of the colonies and to General George Washington on the battlefield. On July 8, Colonel John Nixon of the Pennsylvania militia read the declaration to a crowd gathered in front of the State House in Philadelphia.

On July 19, Congress ordered an engrossed copy of the Declaration of Independence. Engrossed documents were written on parchment in a very large script, so they could be posted and read easily, and partly so they could be preserved for the ages. On August 2, John Hancock, the secretary of the Continental Congress, signed the engrossed copy with a grand flourish—followed by most of the other delegates. Even the New Yorkers who had been absent from the vote put their names to it. That engrossed, signed copy is now kept in the National Archives in Washington, D.C.

To read about the U.S. Constitution, turn to page 258.

Pretzel-vania

We always knew Pennsylvanians loved their pretzels. Now we know why.

A Helpful Hobo

According to legend, a hobo approached Lititz, Pennsylvania, baker Julius Sturgis in 1850 looking for work and something to eat. Sturgis didn't have a job to offer, but he did invite the man to dinner with his family. After the meal, the hobo gave the baker a pretzel recipe as a thank-you. Sturgis had never baked pretzels before, but he tried out the recipe on his family, who liked them so much that the baker started selling the new snack around town.

By 1861, Sturgis's pretzels were so popular that he stopped selling bread altogether and opened the Sturgis Pretzel House—the first commercial pretzel bakery in the United States. In 1936, the Sturgis family opened another pretzel bakery—the Tom Sturgis Pretzel Bakery in nearby Reading. Both are still around today, and both are still operated by the Sturgis family.

Pretzel Facts

- The first documented evidence of pretzel-making dates to the 12th century in what is now southern Germany. Back then, the snack was baked in long sticks and was known as a *brezl*, a term that most etymologists believe derives from the Latin *bracchium*, meaning "arm."
- It makes sense that Pennsylvania—particularly the southeast of the state—would be the place that pretzel-making first flourished in the United States. That's where thousands of immigrants from southern Germany settled starting in the

1700s. Along with many other traditions, they brought their
pretzel-making recipes with them.

- Pennsylvania is famous for both the soft pretzels that came
to the New World with German immigrants and the hard
pretzels that developed later. However, the soft variety—
twisted, chewy, and often served warm with mustard—are
what the state is especially famous for.
- How popular are pretzels in Pennsylvania? The average
American consumes about two pounds of pretzels a year; in
Philadelphia, it's about 24 pounds a year.
- In 1983, Representative Robert Walker of Pennsylvania
stood in Congress and extolled the virtues of pretzels. He
announced that from then on (unofficially), April 26 would
be known as "National Pretzel Day." It is still celebrated by
pretzel enthusiasts all over the country, especially in
Pennsylvania.
- In case you're reading this in Beijing, China, and hankering
for a Pennsylvania pretzel, Lancaster-based pretzel maker
Auntie Anne's opened a store in Beijing in 2008. It's just one
of 940 stores the chain operates worldwide.
- In 2003, Shuey's Pretzels, near the town of Cleona in
Lebanon County, made a two-foot-wide, ten-pound pretzel.
It was dropped from the tower of Cleona's fire station at
midnight on New Year's Day, mimicking the ball drop in
New York's Times Square.
- On January 13, 2002, President George W. Bush fainted, fell,
and bruised his face while watching a football game in the
White House—after choking on a pretzel. (White House
officials would not confirm what kind of pretzel it was—or
if it was made in Pennsylvania.)

The Gettysburg Cyclorama

*The desperate fury of the 1863 Battle of Gettysburg still
exists today . . . in a century-old painting in the round.*

What's a cyclorama? It's a large oil painting displayed on a circular wall, a popular form of entertainment during the 19th century. Viewers would stand in the center of it and turn to see the painting all around them, as though they were at the center of the scene. Like movies today, they told stories (usually from the Bible, literature, or history) that transported people to another time. Most cycloramas were more than 40 feet tall and nearly 380 feet in circumference. They were usually accompanied by a props or tangible artifacts, and included music or narration to heighten the effect. By the 1880s, most large cities in Europe and the United States had a building made especially for viewing cycloramas, and one of the most famous and profitable ones created in the United States was the *Gettysburg Cyclorama*.

Charge!

In 1882, 36-year-old Paul Philippoteaux arrived in Gettysburg from France. He was already an acclaimed artist who had made sketches for books by Alexandre Dumas and Jules Verne and worked on military cycloramas in France. Philippoteaux came to the United States because Chicago businessman Charles L. Willoughby—looking to make some money from the public's interest in Civil War history—hired him to paint the final moments of Pickett's Charge during the 1863 Battle of Gettysburg.

The charge occurred on July 3, 1863, when about 13,000 Confederate soldiers marched through open fields and enemy fire to a short hill called Cemetery Ridge in an effort to break through the Union line. It turned out to be a disaster for the Southern army, and a low stone wall (called the "Angle") where the armies met was the farthest point in Union territory that the invading Confederate forces managed to penetrate. It was also one of the bloodiest battles of the Civil War—and its turning point, the moment when the Union army held its line and forced a Confederate retreat.

Making It Look Real

Philippoteaux wanted his cyclorama to be as close to the real thing as possible, so in preparation for painting, he spent weeks researching the battlefield in southern Pennsylvania. He built a 30-foot tower near the Angle so that he'd have a panoramic view of the entire battlefield, made hundreds of sketches of the terrain, and hired a local man named William Tipton to take photographs. Tipton's pictures swept the horizon, covering Cemetery Ridge, the rocky hill called Little Round Top, and the fields below.

In addition to making sure he got the landscape right, Philippoteaux also interviewed Civil War veterans who had survived Gettysburg. No records exist of what the men said, but historians know that their memories of what happened on the battlefield helped Philippoteaux create detailed sketches of the conflict.

Back in the Studio

His research done, it was time to paint. Philippoteaux returned to his studio in France and pasted the photos of Gettysburg together to make a mini-cyclorama. Then, he started painting.

It normally took one painter several years to fill in such a huge canvas, so Philippoteaux hired a crew of about 20 workers to help him.

Each assistant had a specialized task. Some were adept at painting landscapes, others at painting horses, and still others at portraits. For a year and a half, the team put oil to canvas, often standing on scaffolding to reach the high points. Philippoteaux even put his "signature" on the cyclorama by including a portrait of himself holding a sword and leaning against a tree as the war raged around him.

Opening Night

The group finished the painting in 1883, and the work was loaded onto a ship and sent to Chicago, where it would make its debut. It wasn't quite finished, though. After it arrived, workers placed the painting on the walls and added dioramas to make the scene more real. The painted wagon ruts on the canvas extended into actual wagon rut depressions in the packed-earth floor. Stone and wooden structures blended into painted ones to give viewers the illusion that they were actually standing behind Union troops on Cemetery Ridge and facing 13,000 storming Confederates.

The cyclorama opened to the public on October 22, 1883. Ticket buyers climbed a stairway onto a platform and found themselves surrounded by the chaotic moment when the Confederates charged the Union line. Over the next 50 years, the cyclorama spent time in Chicago and made a tour of eight cities around the country. More than half a million people eventually went to see it, and admirers even included war heroes like General John Gibbon, who had commanded the Union army's Second Division at Gettysburg and faced the brunt of the attack from Pickett's men.

A Traveling Show

The Gettysburg cyclorama did so well in Chicago that Philippoteaux made a copy of the painting for display in Boston. It took about a year to create and was again such a success that Philippoteaux churned out two more copies: one for New York City and another for Philadelphia.

The painting in Boston remained on display until 1892, when workmen packed it away in a crate. Then in 1910, businessman Albert J. Hahne bought the Boston cyclorama. It wasn't in great shape; water and fire had damaged it over the years. But Hahne put sections of it on display in his department store in New Jersey anyway. He later sold the painting and it changed hands several times . . . eventually arriving in Gettysburg. The National Park Service (NPS) bought it in 1942, and in 1944, the U.S. Congress designated the cyclorama a National Historic Object. The NPS partially restored the cyclorama in 1959 and, in 1962, put it on display in Gettysburg National Military Park.

A Star Is Reborn

By 2003, the Boston cyclorama had been damaged and cut up so many times that it was nearly half its original size, so the NPS sent it out to be restored. The project was the largest restoration of a painting ever undertaken in North America. Experts from Virginia and Texas cleaned 1.4 million square inches of canvas, bringing the dulled painting back to its original bright clarity. The restorers strengthened and supported the sagging canvas, repaired its unstable parts, and corrected the damage from fire, water, and years of neglect. The painting was also restored to its original dimensions (42 feet by 377 feet). With its new backing and hanging system, it weighed 12.5 tons.

In 2008, a new visitors' center opened at the Gettysburg National Military Park, and the restored cyclorama became a highlight. Today, it hangs in the park's auditorium, and its diorama includes rifles, boots, saddles, knapsacks, and even a full-size cannon donated by Civil War reenactors. To take in the display, visitors ascend to a platform that puts them at the center of Pickett's Charge. Strobe lights and sound effects mimic artillery fire.

But What About the Other Three?

The cyclorama on display at Gettysburg is the copy Philippoteaux made for the exhibit in Boston. The original in Chicago was last exhibited at the 1933 World's Fair there . . . and then it disappeared. In 1965, artist Joseph King found it rolled up and stored behind a smoke-stained wall in a burned Chicago warehouse. King brought the painting to his home in North Carolina, but it was so gigantic he could only unroll it on a football field. (He even had to remove the goalposts at either end because the painting was 76 feet longer than the field.) When he died in 1996, King willed the painting to Wake Forest University, which then sold it to a group of investors. Today, the group is trying to find a buyer who will restore it.

The third Gettysburg cyclorama ended up on a Shoshone Indian reservation, where it was used to make tents. The fate of the fourth painting is unknown.

Did You Know?

Fifty-one percent of all commercial mushrooms in the United States are grown in Chester County, Pennsylvania.

Capital One

*Between 1790 and 1800, Philadelphia was the capital of
the newly independent United States. It was a title for which
Philadelphians lobbied hard and won, though briefly. Here
are the reasons Philly got the honor . . . and then lost it.*

In the Running

In the late 18th century, Philadelphia was among the most
sophisticated cities in the world. At a time when many cities
just had dusty dirt roads, Philadelphia's streets were paved with
cobblestone, sidewalks were brick, and public squares boasted
multistory buildings. The High Street Market—filled with stalls
that sold fresh produce, meat, and dairy products—extended
for an entire mile, and many wealthy people (like Robert
Morris, who owned one of the most profitable trading companies in the United States) lived in Philadelphia. Art and culture
also thrived there, and the City Tavern on Second Street was
one of the fanciest restaurant/hotels in the new nation.

Philadelphia was also home to three continental congresses
before and during the Revolutionary War. The Declaration of
Independence was signed and the Constitution drafted at the
city's state house (now called Independence Hall). Given its
prominence in the Revolution, it seemed logical to Philadelphians that their city would become the new country's capital.

But in 1783, Congress left Philadelphia after 250 soldiers
stormed the state house, demanding back pay. The government
didn't have the money, and Philadelphians sympathized with
the soldiers. So Congress moved—to New Jersey and Maryland, finally settling in New York City.

Ten-Year Stint

Philadelphia wanted the "capital" title back—being a nation's capital would bring prestige and business to the area. But in 1790, the U.S. government decided that instead of assigning the capital to an existing city, it would create a new city that would be independent from any single state. The city would be carved out of a swamp along the Potomac River between Virginia and Maryland. At the time, there were no structures there and it would take at least a decade to build an entire city, so the country needed a temporary capital. Philadelphia got that job for a term of 10 years.

Philadelphians saw it as an opportunity, and they remained optimistic that they could entice the government out of the swamp and back into their city if they just provided satisfactory accommodations. So the two-story brick county courthouse (now Congress Hall) became the home of the U.S. Congress. The House of Representatives met on the first floor, and the Senate met on the second—in a room whose floor was covered with a carpet that bore an American eagle encircled by the seals of the 13 original states.

The city also built President George Washington an immense mansion that had a glass cupola, ornate windows, and a marble staircase. Washington never actually lived there, though. Instead, he rented a house on High Street from Robert Morris, a wealthy Philadelphian who had financed much of the Revolution. The President's House, as the High Street home became known, had a public office on the third floor where Washington conducted presidential business and had room for him to host state dinners.

The Impossible Dream

Despite the fine accommodations, the government did move

the capital out of Philadelphia in 1800. There were many reasons, but the main ones were money, slavery, and disease.

- Building a brand-new capital city meant the federal government would be in complete control of the city's tax revenue, rather than having to answer to the bureaucracy of an existing town. (Some of Pennsylvania's rural counties also backed this because they didn't want to pay higher taxes to support the capital.)

- For his part, George Washington didn't want the capital to be in Philadelphia. He was a slaveholder, and Pennsylvania was a free state. Though he came to Philadelphia to do business, he never officially moved from Virginia.

- And finally, five yellow fever epidemics in the 1790s frightened people away from Philadelphia. During the first one in 1793, Washington and his cabinet left until it was over. And Abigail Adams (whose husband John was president from 1797 to 1801) stayed out of Philadelphia mainly because she feared yellow fever.

Did You Know?

In an effort to convince the U.S. government to keep the nation's capital in Philadelphia, the city wooed the executive and legislative branches. But the members of the U.S. Supreme Court didn't get as much attention—or respect. They met on the first floor of what is now Philadelphia's Old City Hall, where they shared the space with the mayor's court. On days when the mayor was trying city cases, the Supreme Court had to move upstairs.

Prison to Peeps

There's something for everyone in Lancaster.

Town: Lancaster
Location: Lancaster County
Founding: 1729
Population (2008): 55,381
Size: 7.4 square miles
County seat: Yes

What's in a Name?

It was originally called Hickory Town, but in 1729, John Wright, one of the area's wealthiest residents, named the town Lancaster, after Lancaster, England, where he once lived.

Claims to Fame

- The first people to settle Lancaster were the Pennsylvania Dutch. Their name comes from the word *Deutsch*, which means "German" in German.

- The Lancaster County Prison opened in Lancaster in 1775, but the prison standing today—modeled after a medieval castle in Lancashire, England—was built in 1851.

- Between 1799 and 1812, Lancaster was the capital of Pennsylvania.

- Lancaster is home to many firsts: Conestoga wagons, which carried pioneers and goods west, were first manufactured in Lancaster in the 18th century. (They were named for the nearby Conestoga River.) Martin Meylin, a gunsmith from Switzerland, built the first Pennsylvania rifle there; the gun was more accurate than rifles that came before. And the Hamilton Watch Company manufactured the first battery-powered watches in the 1950s.

- At a time when most roads were rough and unpaved, the Philadelphia and Lancaster Turnpike was a transportation marvel. The 62-mile-long road opened in 1795, after just three years of construction, was paved with gravel and stone, and was called the "finest highway in its day." It was also the first major toll road in the United States.

- Lancaster's Rodda Candy Company started making marsh-mallow Peeps by hand in the early 20th century. When Sam Born bought the company in 1953 (and incorporated it into Just Born, his Bethlehem-based candy company), he auto-mated the process. Today, the company produces more than 1.2 million Peeps a year. (That's enough to circle the world twice.)

- Frank W. Woolworth opened his second store in Lancaster in 1879. (The first, in New York, failed after its first year.) It became his first successful five-and-dime and the progenitor of the F. W. Woolworth Company department store chain.

Did You Know?

Pennsylvania has two counties with no traffic lights: Perry County near Harrisburg, and Forest County in the northeastern part of the state.

March of the Penguins

*We told you about hockey's Philadelphia Flyers on page
93. Here's the history of the Pittsburgh Penguins.*

Like the Flyers, the Penguins became a team in 1967, the
year the NHL expanded from the original six teams to
twelve. Owners Peter Block and Jack McGregor held a naming
contest in a local newspaper as a way to drum up support for
the new team. "Penguins" won, and it was a good thing
because the name had actually already been chosen. McGregor
later said that the name must have been leaked to the paper for
inclusion on the list of contenders.

Colors: The team's original colors were blue and white, but in
1980, the managers changed them to black, gold, and white—
the same as the Pittsburgh Steelers football team.

Logo: Pittsburgh freelance artist Bob Gessner designed the
original Penguins' logo: a skating penguin with a scarf tied
around its neck in front of an inverted triangle, which represents the "Golden Triangle," a nickname for downtown
Pittsburgh.

Through the Years

The Penguins were pretty good from the start, making the
playoffs six times in the 1970s. Then times got hard . . . really
hard. From 1982 to 1984, they were the worst team in the
NHL. In fact, they were so bad—and had so few fans—that it
looked like they wouldn't survive. But the last-place team gets
to pick first in the draft, and in 1984, the Penguins picked an
18-year-old from Quebec who would go on to become one of
professional hockey's greatest players: Mario Lemieux.

(Lemieux scored a goal in his first game, on his first shift . . . on his first shot.)

It took some time, but the Penguins finally made it back to the playoffs in 1989. Two years later, they made it again, this time with another hockey superstar, Czech Jaromir Jagr. And this time, they went all the way to the Stanley Cup Finals—where they beat the Minnesota North Stars four games to two. They did it again in 1992, this time sweeping the Chicago Blackhawks four games to none.

After that, the Penguins went on a long Stanley Cup drought. Then in 2005, they made their second blockbuster draft pick, getting 18-year-old phenom Sidney Crosby. The team made it back to the playoffs in 2007. In 2008, they made it all the way to the Stanley Cup Finals but lost to the Detroit Red Wings, four games to two.

Penguin Particulars

- The Penguins weren't the first NHL team in Pittsburgh. The Pittsburgh Pirates (not to be confused with the baseball team) were founded in 1925. After a good first year, they went downhill and finally moved to Philadelphia in 1930, where they folded after one more season.

- Pittsburgh's first general manager, Jack Riley, hated the name Penguins and, for the first season, refused to let it appear on the team's uniforms.

- Pittsburgh has nine players in the NHL Hall of Fame, including Mario Lemieux, Paul Coffey, and Ron Francis.

- The Penguins hold the record for the longest NHL winning streak, winning the first 17 games of the 1992–93 season.

- During the 1992 season, Mario Lemieux announced that he

had been diagnosed with Hodgkin's lymphoma. Aggressive radiation treatments kept him off the ice for two months, but he returned—and still won the Art Ross Trophy for most points scored during the season.

- Lemieux retired in 1997—and bought the nearly bankrupt Penguins in 1998. He returned the team to financial success (especially by getting Sidney Crosby in 2005) and un-retired in 2000. He played until 2006, when he was 41 years old. He's still ranked as the seventh-highest scorer in NHL history.

- On December 23, 2002, radio host Mark Madden said he would donate $6,600 to the Mario Lemieux Foundation if Lemieux ever scored a goal directly from a faceoff. That night, against the Buffalo Sabres, Lemieux scored a goal . . . directly from a faceoff.

Did You Know?

Every member of a hockey team that wins the Stanley Cup gets to take it home for one day. After the 1991–92 Penguins win, defenseman Phil Bourque got it . . . and heard rattling inside the base. He took the bottom off and found a loose nut inside. He also found some names engraved inside the base. (They'd been added by a repair crew decades earlier.) Bourque got a screwdriver and scratched his name in there, too, writing "Enjoy it, Phil Bubba Bourque, '91 Penguins." He remains the only player with his name on the outside *and* the inside of the Stanley Cup.

Dumb Crooks

One of the state's slogans is "You've got a friend in Pennsylvania."
But we don't recommend making friends with these guys.

What's Your Cell Phone Worth?

Dim-Witted Criminal: Randy-Jay Adolphos Jones (a.k.a. Baby Boy) of Columbia, Pennsylvania

Dumb Move: Answering the phone

The Crime: In October 2007, an unnamed woman was sitting in her car in Lancaster when "Baby Boy" allegedly got in the car, grabbed, and fondled her. She fought back and got away, but as she escaped, he snatched her handbag, which had her cell phone inside.

Shortly after the attack, Officer Jeff Gerhart arrived at the scene and asked the victim to call her phone. Jones answered and demanded a $185,000 ransom for the phone's safe return. The woman refused but haggled him down to $200. They agreed to meet at Franklin and Marshall College to make the trade. Officers apprehended Baby Boy (and the cell phone) there. The handbag was also nearby.

The Punishment: Jones was booked for robbery and indecent assault on $100,000 bail and is awaiting trial.

One-of-a-Kind Getaway Car

Dim-Witted Criminals: Robert Coulson Lavery and Robert Steven Miller of Fairview Township, Pennsylvania

Dumb Move: Leaving a trail

The Crime: Two things were wrong with this pair's plan to rob the New Cumberland Federal Credit Union in Fairview Township in November 2006. For one, Lavery smeared chalky drywall compound (also known as joint compound) on his face before entering the bank. It worked well as a disguise but left a trail wherever he went. Second, Lavery's getaway driver, Miller, did a poor job of going incognito. He drove a black Chevy Malibu with a souvenir Rusty Wallace NASCAR plate on the front. In a city with less than 15,000 people, it was the only one of its kind.

When police asked for help in identifying the vehicle, a local resident easily recognized the car and led them to Miller. The robber immediately ratted out his accomplice, who was hiding at Miller's house with $3,775 of the stolen $7,910 . . . and the clothes and car smeared with drywall compound.

The Punishment: Both were convicted of robbery and theft.

Taking Out the Trash

Dim-Witted Criminal: Malcolm Kysor of Albion, Pennsylvania

Dumb Move: Bragging

The Crime: Fifty-four-year-old Kysor escaped from a medium-security prison in Albion in November 2007. He'd been serving a life sentence for beating an Erie County man to death with a golf club in 1981, but one day, he simply climbed into a trash can meant for food scraps and rode out of prison in a garbage truck. (Workers neglected to inspect the truck before it departed, resulting in the prison's superintendent later being removed from her position.)

Kysor evaded capture for four months, but then, while he was living in a park in Bakersfield, California, his story was featured on the TV show *America's Most Wanted*. Kysor couldn't help bragging about this to his fellow transients, and a law-abiding citizen overheard and reported him immediately. When questioned, Kysor gave police an alias . . . one he'd used before and that was already in a national database.

The Punishment: He was extradited to Pennsylvania to serve the rest of his life sentence, plus whatever time he'll receive for the felony escape charge, which carries a maximum of seven years. And since his trash-can maneuver was caught on a prison surveillance tape, it is unlikely that he'll dodge that charge.

Did You Know?

One of the most prominent environmentalists in U.S. history got his start in Pennsylvania. Richard Pough was born in New York, but moved to Pennsylvania in the 1930s to attend Haverford College. He became a photographer and opened a camera shop in Philadelphia. While living there, Pough learned that the state paid hunters $5 for every hawk they killed. (Hawks and other raptors threatened farm animals.) Pough also learned about Hawk Mountain, an area in Berks County where hawks were being killed by the dozens daily. Camera in hand, he went to investigate and was appalled to find hundreds of dead hawks. The pictures he took of the slaughter were published in a local paper and inspired a philanthropist named Rosalie Edge to buy the property and turn it into the Hawk Mountain Sanctuary, a safe haven for birds of prey. Pough also continued his environmental activism: he wrote books for the National Audubon Society and became the first president of the Nature Conservancy.

The Pitts

Welcome to Mister Rogers' neighborhood and one of the cleanest cities in the United States. (Yes, really!)

Town: Pittsburgh

Location: Allegheny County

Founding: 1758

Population (2008): 313,000

Size: 58.3 square miles

County seat: Yes

What's in a Name?

Settler John Forbes, a general in the English army, named the new settlement Pittsburgh after British statesman Sir William Pitt. However, Forbes was actually Scottish, so he may have intended for the city's name to be pronounced "Pitts-burrah," like the Scottish city of Edinburgh.

Claims to Fame:

- Downtown Pittsburgh is triangle shaped, formed by the convergence of three rivers: the Allegheny, the Monongahela, and the Ohio.

- Venice, Italy, is known as the "City of Bridges," but Pittsburgh actually has more: 446.

- Though it never caught on, AT&T debuted its Picturephone (video phone) service in Pittsburgh in 1970. The image was choppy and the screen was small. Fewer than 100 Pittsburghians signed up.

- In 2006, Pittsburgh elected Luke Ravenstahl as mayor. He was just 26, the youngest mayor of a major American city in history.

- Pulitzer Prize–winning novelist Michael Chabon was raised in Pittsburgh and has set many of his novels there, including *Wonder Boys* and *The Mysteries of Pittsburgh*.

- Oldest structure in Pittsburgh: the Fort Pitt Blockhouse, which was built in 1764.

- Despite Pittsburgh's stereotypical image as a polluted steel town, the city has cleaned up its act since the 1970s, when the steel industry waned and many of the local mills closed. Without the mills (and thanks to a concerted effort by the city to get rid of the industry's debris), there's less pollution in Pittsburgh today than in many other American cities. In 2007, *Forbes* magazine rated Pittsburgh the 10th-cleanest city in the United States, and *Places Rated Almanac* calls it the country's "most livable city."

- One of the city's most prestigious colleges, Carnegie Mellon University, is a major American center for robotics research.

- Pittsburgh is home to one of America's most influential public television stations, WQED. That's where native son Fred Rogers (a.k.a. Mister Rogers) began his career in 1954.

- St. Anthony's Chapel contains more than 5,000 religious relics, including those related to Mary Magdalene, St. John the Baptist, and (purportedly) a piece of the cross on which Jesus Christ was crucified. It's the largest collection of Catholic relics outside of the Vatican.

- Some famous Pittsburghians: Gene Kelly, Martha Graham, Dennis Miller, and Gertrude Stein.

Native Son:
A Mario Lanza Quiz

Raised around opera music in his South Philadelphia home, this Keystone Stater went on to become one of the most celebrated singers in the United States.

I talian conductor Arturo Toscanini once described Mario Lanza as having "the greatest voice of the 20th century," and entertainment columnist Hedda Hopper wrote that he was the only person she'd heard who could "double for Caruso." But since his sudden death in 1959 at the age of 38, Lanza has faded from the limelight. At one time, though, the Pennsylvanian was a rising movie star. Test what you know abut him with this true or false quiz.

Mario Lanza was his birth name.

False. Lanza was born January 31, 1921, in Philadelphia as Alfredo Arnold Cocozza. He spent his first 20 years known as "Freddie." The stage name came later, when studio heads thought he needed a name that was easier to spell and pronounce. "Mario Lanza" is a masculinization of his mother's maiden name, Maria Lanza.

MGM studio head Louis B. Mayer "discovered" Lanza when he was performing at the Hollywood Bowl in Los Angeles.

True. Lanza spent a few years in the army during World War II, and after he was discharged, he moved to New York to focus on his musical career. There he performed on a CBS radio show called *Great Moments in Music* and eventually set off on a concert tour. In 1947, at a performance at the Hollywood Bowl in Los Angeles, Lanza caught the eye of Mayer, who signed the singer to a seven-year film contract. Lanza's first film: 1949's *That Midnight Kiss*, which was set in Philadelphia. The movie also featured Kathryn Grayson—who had been sitting with Mayer the night he discovered Lanza. (Rumor has it that, even though they made a couple of films together, Grayson and Lanza never got along; she considered him a hothead and a drunk.)

Lanza was fired from a film role because he had become too heavy to fit into the movie's costumes.

False. Lanza started to find fame in the early 1950s after he played opera singer Enrico Caruso in 1951's *The Great Caruso*, but on the set of the film *The Student Prince*, he ran into trouble. According to biographer Armando Cesari, Lanza and director Curtis Bernhardt butted heads on the very first day of rehearsals: Bernhardt wanted Lanza to restrain his emotional delivery, and Lanza stated that he "had no intention of following such ridiculous orders" and left the set. Lanza demanded that Bernhardt be replaced, but the film's producers balked and Lanza responded by not showing up to work the next day. That got him fired (though tabloids speculated that it was because he'd gotten chubby). Eventually Lanza worked out a deal where he sang the movie's songs, which another actor lip-synched.

The mafia ordered Lanza killed in 1959.

False. Lanza's last American movie, *Serenade*, wasn't as successful as his earlier films, so he left the United States for Europe, where he performed in several concerts and made his last two films: *Seven Hills of Rome* and *For the First Time*. But Lanza's health had been declining for years, likely the result of heavy drinking. On October 7, 1959, when he was just 38 years old, he had a heart attack and died in Rome. Rumors at the time suggested that Lanza's heart attack had been fabricated and he'd actually been assassinated for refusing to perform for mob boss Lucky Luciano. But Lanza's family always denied it.

Did You Know?

Lots of movies have been filmed in or around Philadelphia. Here are 11 of the most famous:

- *Signs* (2002)
- *Unbreakable* (2000)
- *The Sixth Sense* (1998)
- *12 Monkeys* (1995)
- *Philadelphia* (1993)
- *Dead Poets Society* (1989)
- *Trading Places* (1983)
- *Atlantic City* (1980)
- *David and Lisa* (1963)
- *The Young Philadelphians* (1959)
- *Kitty Foyle* (1940)

Ghosts of Business Past, Part II

On page 122, we introduced Bethlehem Steel, one of the most dominant (and now defunct) companies in Pennsylvania's history. Here's another giant company that went boom—and then bust.

The Pennsylvania Railroad

Claim to Fame: Revolutionizing rail travel throughout Pennsylvania and the United States

Business Giant: For much of the 20th century, this railroad (called "the Pennsy") made more money than any other American railway—and was the largest publicly traded company in the world. At one point, its budget was larger than that of the U.S. government.

Ride the Rails

The massive Pennsylvania Railroad started out modestly in 1849 with a short line between Harrisburg and Lewiston, but its founders (led by chief engineer J. Edgar Thompson) envisioned a railway between Philadelphia and Pittsburgh. By horse, it took at least three days to make the 350-mile trip, but a railroad could cut that time by a third—a windfall for manufacturers in western Pennsylvania who needed to transport their products to Philadelphia for export. It took five years, but in 1854, the Pennsy ran its first train from Pittsburgh to Philadelphia. The trip took just 13 hours.

At stops between the two cities, the railroad constructed hotels and train stations to accommodate travelers. The Logan

House in Altoona was among the most luxurious. It was four stories high and included a barbershop, three lounges, and a large dining room where an employee banged a gong to let travelers know when trains were departing.

After the success of the Pittsburgh–Philadelphia line, the railroad kept growing. The company bought or leased lines to Chicago, New York, Washington, D.C., and St. Louis. By the 1920s, the Pennsylvania Railroad ran more than 6,500 trains every day over 28,000 miles of track.

Controversy

The relationship between laborers and management at the Pennsy was notoriously poor, and the company's leaders ran into many problems with strikers and unions. A walkout in 1877 (called the Great Railroad Strike because it included workers from several states) turned violent in Pittsburgh when a mob of angry workers clashed with the state militia; 45 people were killed and one of the railroad's stations burned down. Yet the Pennsylvania Railroad also had a reputation for being one of the safest companies in the country. Its trains used air brakes (which allowed an operator in the train's cab to control the brake, rather than an external brakeman), its signals were electric, and the company created an entire testing division to check its equipment.

End of the Line

The Pennsylvania Railroad remained a titan of transportation until 1968, when it merged with the New York Railroad. That new company didn't last long—just 870 days later, it declared bankruptcy. But Amtrak bought many of the Pennsy's trains and rail lines, and it still runs some of the same routes.

Oh, the Symbolism

How well do you know Pennsylvania's state symbols?

1. The Pennsylvania Department of Conservation and Natural Resources calls the state animal "undoubtedly one of the most influential species of wildlife in Pennsylvania." What is it?

  A. White-tailed deer

  B. Groundhog

  C. Red fox

2. Milk is Pennsylvania's state drink, and dairies in the Keystone State produce more than a billion gallons of milk every year. Where does Pennsylvania rank in milk production compared to the other U.S. states?

  A. First

  B. Fifth

  C. Seventh

3. What's the state bird?

  A. Riffled grouse

  B. Ruffed grouse

  C. Ruffled goose

4. The state fish is also Pennsylvania's only native species of trout. What is it?

  A. Blueback trout

  B. Cutthroat trout

  C. Brook trout

5. Governor Gifford Pinchot chose the mountain laurel as the state flower in 1933. What color are its petals?

A. Blue and white

B. Pink and white

C. Pink and blue

6. Pennsylvania's state fossil is the trilobite, a group of ancient creatures that included some of the first-known animals to have what sense?

A. Vision

B. Hearing

C. Taste

7. Fireflies are Pennsylvania's state insects. For what purpose do the animals use their bioluminescence?

A. Lighting their way

B. Finding food

C. Attracting mates

8. Pennsylvania adopted its state song in 1990. What's it called?

A. "Pennsylvania"

B. "Long Live PA"

C. "The Great Keystone State"

9. As a tribute to its railroad history, Pennsylvania has a state train: the K4s steam locomotive. When did those trains first take to the track?

A. 1865

B. 1880

C. 1914

10. Nineteenth-century American landscaper A. J. Downing called Pennsylvania's state tree the "most picturesque and beautiful of the world's evergreens." What is the tree's name?

A. Douglas fir

B. Eastern hemlock

C. Jack pine

Answers on page 304.

Did You Know?

Quarry owner William Abbot Witman Sr. built a 72-foot-tall red-and-gold pagoda in Reading in 1908 to hide the scarred hills of Mount Penn (where his quarry was located). Witman hoped that the pagoda would eventually become a luxury hotel, but there were no good roads leading to it in the early 1900s and his application for a liquor license was turned down. (No luxury hotel in the years before Prohibition could be successful without selling liquor.) So the structure sat empty. In 1910, Witman sold the building to a businessman who gave it to the city of Reading the next year. Over the years, the city used it as an office, snack bar, art gallery, and, before radio communication became common, even a news transmitter—lights on the top tier flashed different colors to signal winners of presidential elections or other events. Today, the pagoda is a tourist attraction and, in 2008, underwent a renovation.

The Phillies By the Numbers

Baseball is a game of numbers, and nowhere is that more apparent than in the City of Brotherly Love, where the Phillies have been racking up super stats since 1883.

2

Times the Phillies have won the World Series: 1980 and 2008.

3

Official team names in the franchise's history: Quakers (1883–89), Phillies (1890–1942, 1945–present), Blue Jays (1943–44).

4

Number of times Phillies pitcher Steve Carlton won the National League Cy Young Award: 1972, 1977, 1980, and 1982.

5

Stadiums the Phillies have called home: Recreation Park (1883–86), Baker Bowl (1887–38), Connie Mack Stadium (1938–70), Veterans Stadium (1971–2003), Citizens Bank Park (2004–present).

9

Number of no-hitters that Phillies pitchers have thrown to date: 1885 (Charlie Ferguson), 1898 (Red Donahue), 1903 (Chick Fraser), 1906 (Johnny Lush), 1964 (Jim Bunning),

1971 (Rick Wise), 1990 (Terry Mulholland), 1991 (Tommy Greene), and 2003 (Kevin Millwood).

33

Years it took before the Phillies reached their first World Series (1915). They lost to the Boston Red Sox, four games to one.

35

Number of pounds the costume of the team's beloved mascot, Phillie Phanatic, weighs. The tall, birdlike creature made his debut on April 25, 1978, in a game against the Chicago Cubs. The New York design and merchandising firm of Harrison/ Erickson created the Phanatic as an attraction to rival the San Diego Padres' popular Chicken mascot. The Phillies were offered the costume and copyright ownership for $5,200, but in a cost-cutting move, they chose to purchase only the costume for a discount: $3,900. Big mistake. The Phanatic was so popular that five years later, the team had to pay Harrison/ Erickson $250,000 for the copyright. The Phillie Phanatic has since been voted "Best Mascot Ever" by *Sports Illustrated* and was enshrined in the Mascot Hall of Fame in 2005.

38

Number of wins earned by pitcher Kid Gleason in 1890. It's still a franchise record.

58

Home runs hit by first baseman Ryan Howard in 2006—also the most in franchise history.

216

Number of home runs hit by the Philadelphia Phillies during the 2006 season—a Major League record.

716

Record number of official at-bats registered by Phillies shortstop Jimmy Rollins in 2007. Rollins's stellar all-around play earned him the 2007 National League Most Valuable Player Award.

$1,000 (and two players)

Amount the Phillies paid the Pittsburgh Alleghenies to get out-fielder Billy Sunday in 1890. Sunday was a great athlete, known for stealing bases and making incredible catches in the days before fielders wore gloves. Sunday was acquired by Philadelphia to improve the team's chances of capturing the National League pennant and had already played eight years in the major leagues at the time.

But as it turned out, baseball wasn't his true calling— Sunday requested a release from his contract in 1891 to accept the position of secretary of the religious department at the Chicago YMCA. The position paid considerably less than his baseball contract, but it offered the potential to do ministerial work. He later went on to become a world-famous evangelist.

1,199

Runs surrendered by Phillies pitchers during the 1930 season. The mark remains an all-time major league record. (Ouch.)

1915

The first year the Phillies won the National League pennant.

(They also won it five more times: 1950, 1980, 1983, 1993, and 2008.)

43,647

Seating capacity of Citizens Bank Park.

3,206,532

Number of fans who attended Philadelphia Phillies home games in 2004, a franchise record.

Did You Know?

Philadelphia's Mummers Parade has been an official New Year's tradition since the city started sponsoring it in 1901. But its roots go all the way back to the 1600s and Pennsylvania's earliest immigrants.

In medieval England, "mummers" were entertainers who traveled around the countryside performing folklore plays. As Europeans immigrated to Pennsylvania, they brought the mummer practice with them. Philadelphia's first Mummers Parade was an informal neighborhood gathering in the 1870s. People from all over the city showed up on South Philly's "Two Street" (Second Avenue) in costumes to celebrate New Year's Day. Today, the parade attracts more than 10,000 entrants who compete for cash prizes in four categories: Comic (spoofing modern politics), Fancy (dressing in elaborate costumes), Fancy Brigade (dressing in elaborate costumes and performing skits), and String Band (dressing in elaborate costumes while playing in a marching band).

Steamtown

This onetime iron-smelting city in northeastern Pennsylvania is now the proud home of Dunder Mifflin—the world's best-known fictional paper company.

Town: Scranton

Location: Lackawanna County

Founding: 1856

Population (2008): 76,000

Size: 25.4 square miles

County seat: Yes

What's in a Name?

Before it was incorporated as a city, Scranton was a settlement called Capouse, a variation on the spelling of Chief Capoose, who headed the local Munsee tribe. In 1840, businessmen George and Selden Scranton arrived, bought what's now the downtown area for $8,000, and opened an iron-smelting company. Before it officially became Scranton, though, the city had various other names: Slocum Hollow, Armstrong, and Scrantonia.

Claims to Fame:

- The city's nickname of "Steamtown" comes from Scranton's iron-smelting past. Between the mid-1800s until the end of World War II, iron mining and smelting were the city's major industries.

- Scranton has one of the lowest murder rates in the country, averaging about one per year over the last decade. There were none in 2006.

- Scranton's Steamtown Marathon, held every October, attracts about 1,500 runners annually.

- The NBC sitcom *The Office* is set in Scranton. (*See page 131.*) The show is filmed on a set in California, but the scenes of Scranton in the opening credits are real, shot by star John Krasinski. The city itself welcomes the Hollywood association and even displays banners with the name Dunder Mifflin (the paper company depicted on the show) on downtown lampposts. And each fall, venues around the city (including the Steamtown Mall) host a convention for *Office* fans.

- Scranton is the birthplace of Vice President Joe Biden.

- Early 20th-century illusionist and escape artist Harry Houdini had no connection to Scranton (he was born in Hungary and is buried in New York), but the city is home to the Harry Houdini Museum. It's full of personal effects and exhibits detailing the magician's famous stunts. One annual event: a Halloween séance held in an attempt to contact Houdini. (So far, he hasn't answered.)

● ●

Did You Know?

Every year, the White Thorn Lodge in western Pennsylvania hosts a nude volleyball tournament. But don't get any ideas: only members of the lodge (a private nudist club) can participate.

The Lattimer Massacre

In the late 19th century, the tiny coal town of Lattimer was the site of one of the most violent labor strikes in American history. For the strikers, the result was deadly, but for the larger coal mining community, it actually brought some positive changes.

In 1897, Lattimer was a mining town just outside of Hazleton in coal-rich Luzerne County. The Lehigh and Wilkes-Barre Coal Company, which ran several mines in the area, had built Lattimer about 30 years earlier to support its mine there. By the late 1890s, a few hundred people lived and worked in Lattimer.

A Hard-Knock Life

Like many mining communities, Lattimer was a "company" town. The workers lived in company-owned homes, shopped at the company-owned store (a requirement to keep their jobs), and if they were sick, they saw the mine's doctor. Typically, they paid for these things on credit, and when payday came, the mine deducted the expenses before handing over their pay-checks. In many cases, the men came out behind and were constantly in debt to the company.

The miners' financial problems got worse in 1897, when the Pennsylvania General Assembly enacted the "alien" tax in an effort to raise money. The tax required employers to pay three cents per day for each immigrant on their payrolls. (American citizens were exempt.) The mine owners passed the cost on to the workers, deducting it from each man's already dwindling paycheck.

The mine bosses, fearing the growing influence of labor unions, typically hired immigrants who spoke little or no English and had no common language among them. Their reasoning was that if its labor force were made up mostly of men who couldn't communicate with each other, let alone the larger labor movement, they would be less likely to organize. That proved to be a miscalculation.

The Union Comes to Town

By 1897, mine workers in Luzerne County had already started talking with representatives from the United Mine Workers of America (UMWA). The union had been founded in Ohio just a few years earlier and had quickly become a dominant force in the mining industry.

With the support of UMWA, strike talks started brewing at mines throughout Luzerne County. In August, a 350-man workers' march swelled to 3,000 men in just one day, and on September 1, workers at all the Lehigh and Wilkes-Barre Coal Company mines in the region agreed to go on strike. Within days, 10,000 workers at mines all over the region had walked off the job.

The Sheriff and His Posse

While all this was brewing, the Luzerne County sheriff, James Martin, was on vacation in Atlantic City, New Jersey. Once the strikers took to the streets, the mine company bosses ordered Martin to return to Pennsylvania and do something about the unrest. His solution? Form a posse of 87 men who had ties to the coal company, outfit them with Winchester rifles, and break the strike one mine at a time. His first stop: Lattimer.

Confrontation

On September 10, about 400 strikers gathered outside the town of Hazleton, intending to march through it on their way to the Lattimer mine. They were unarmed; UMWA leaders had advised them not to carry weapons. At around 2:00 p.m., led by a worker carrying an American flag, the strikers headed for the mine.

Sheriff Martin and his posse were ready for them outside of Hazleton. The two groups faced off, the sheriff raised his pistol, and he ordered the workers to disperse. When they refused, one of Martin's men grabbed the strikers' flag and destroyed it, igniting a brawl. Martin initially managed to restore order by telling the strikers they could continue if they walked around Hazleton, rather than through it. They agreed and kept marching.

But Martin and his men had no intention of allowing the strike to continue. Instead, they boarded trolleys to intercept the workers at Lattimer. En route, angry townspeople and local police joined the posse, which soon grew to about 150 armed men. Their mood turned ugly—many boasted that they would kill the strikers when they got to the mine. According to one witness, a posse member said he'd "drop six of them."

"A Miniature War"

Around 3:45 p.m., Martin and his men caught up with the strikers just outside of Lattimer. Again, Martin raised his gun and ordered the workers to leave. Again, they refused. But this time, Martin intended to put an end to it.

He shot the flag bearer first. More posse members fired their guns, and the strikers began to run—many were shot as they did. According to witness Dominic Marsello, who was 13 years old at the time, the strikers had been "on the roadway walking with their coats on their arms and that sheriff gave orders to shoot. The men fell like rats—a pity sight. I saw them lying in among the briars near a gum berry tree. It was a miniature war." When it was over, 19 strikers lay dead and 36 more had been wounded. Fearing reprisals, most of Martin's posse scattered and went into hiding after the shooting.

Aftermath

The next day, Pennsylvania's governor sent the state militia to Lattimer and Hazleton with orders to keep the peace. But the expected retaliations never materialized. One group of miners set fire to one of the boss's homes, but otherwise, the townspeople didn't lash out. And the funerals they held for the fallen strikers attracted thousands of sympathetic people from all over the region.

For their part, national newspapers condemned the violence. The *New York Tribune* ran the headline "Strikers March to Death." Most papers also acknowledged the racial component that had led to the massacre. One editorial said, "If the strikers in the Hazleton region were of the English-speaking class there would have been no bloodshed."

Justice Doesn't Come Easy

Sheriff Martin and many of the posse members were tried for their role in the killings, but they were all acquitted. But justice, of sorts, came for the Lattimer miners in the form of a renewed commitment among laborers to demand fair and equal treatment. Publicity of the massacre also helped the nation's workers recognize that immigrant workers, as well as American citizens, needed to be a part of labor reform.

After the Lattimer massacre, immigrant workers continued to join the UMWA—in many cases, in higher numbers than natural-born citizens. The larger voting base helped to bolster the union's power, helping the UMWA gain significant concessions over the next few years. In 1898, it lobbied successfully for an eight-hour workday for coal miners (down from 12 hours). In 1933, it won collective bargaining rights (the legal right to organize and join unions). And in 1946, UMWA workers were among the first in the mining industry to receive health and retirement benefits.

Did You Know?

The Crayola Factory in Easton isn't actually a factory anymore. The original factory also housed a museum, but the building was always crowded with tourists, had a waiting list to visit the museum, and didn't allow children under six because of safety concerns. So in 1996, Crayola's management decided to split the two: the actual factory moved to another site in Easton, and the museum re-opened bigger and more colorful than it had been before. Some highlights: a pane of two-sided glass that kids can decorate, a station for painting with melted crayon wax, and demonstrations of how the company's crayons and markers are made.

There are some interesting demonstrations at the Crayola Factory these days. In particular, employees willingly "prove" the museum's assertion that eating crayons isn't dangerous. One worker says, "You can eat 3,500 crayons a day, and they are not as toxic as one glass of city drinking water." (But we don't recommend that.)

The Joy of Sects: A Pop Quiz

We're speaking, of course, about religious sects, which have always thrived in Pennsylvania. How to tell them apart? Well, to start with, the Pennsylvania Dutch aren't Dutch, but German. Once you get your mind around that, the rest is easy. (Answers on page 305.)

1. You see a group of girls in old-fashioned clothes. They're probably . . .

A. Mennonites

B. Quakers

C. Amish

D. Moravians

2. On the weekend, you notice men moving benches into a home with dark green window shades. You should . . .

A. Call the police to report a bizarre case of burglary, in which thieves are putting furniture *into* the house.

B. Check the entertainment guide in the local paper to see if a concert is scheduled.

C. Realize it's basketball season, buy some pretzels and beer, knock on the door, and ask if you can watch the game.

D. Ignore the whole thing, unless you're Amish.

3. You're invited to a "Love Feast" at the local Moravian church. You should . . .

A. Bring all your souvenir buttons from Woodstock.

B. Practice your musical scales.

C. Bake a pie.

D. Make sure the iPod is charged up because there's likely to be a long, boring sermon.

4. Imagine an all-day religious service with sermons lasting several hours. The preachers do not pause, not even when the listeners get up to eat. At the end of it all, people pair off and wash each other's feet. Who does this?

A. Quakers

B. Amish

C. Catholics

D. Moravians

5. A Mennonite, a Quaker, an Amish, and a Moravian walk into a bar. Which one orders tea?

• •

Did You Know?

Pennsylvania was the first state to . . .

- Manufacture Cracker Jacks (1894).
- Cover balls of chewing gum with hard candy to make gumballs (1900).
- Serve a banana split (1904).
- Sell hoagies (1920) and the Klondike ice cream bar (1929).
- Issue vanity license plates (1931).

Meet Me in Coupon

Comical, unpronounceable: How did Pennsylvania come up with these crazy town names?

Bird-in-Hand

In colonial times, towns often sprang up around an area's tavern and took on the tavern's name. Bird-in-Hand is named for a tavern that had a swinging sign that included a hand holding a bird and the motto "A bird in the hand is worth two in the bush." (The sign may have been the innkeeper's not-so-subtle warning about the accommodations farther down the road.)

Burnt Cabins

In 1750, when squatters were encroaching on Indian lands, their cabins were burned by order of the colonial government.

Coupon

This was a coal town whose center was its general store, which also served as a post office. In 1893, the coal company began using coupons instead of cash to pay workers, but the coupons could be redeemed only at the coal company's store. This so infuriated the postmaster, who also ran the (noncompany) general store, that he pushed the town to change its name from Delaney to the derogatory Coupon as a slam against the coal company. The town complied in 1893.

Eighty-four

The exact origin of this name is disputed, but there are three theories: the name commemorates either the 1884 election of Grover Cleveland, the fact that the post office opened in 1884, or the town's position as the #84 mail drop on the rail line.

Forty Fort

Forty settlers came and built a fort, and then named the town after that founding fact.

Glen Campbell

Glen is a Scottish word for "valley"; Cornelius Campbell was the owner of the town's Glenwood Coal Company in the 1880s. (The name has nothing to do with the country singer, although local lore says he did visit once.)

Intercourse

Intercourse was named in 1814 when the word meant "meeting socially at a crossroads." The town's name either derives from its being at the intersection of the Old Kings Highway and the Washington-Erie Road, or from being near the entrance to a racecourse, the Entercourse.

Nanty Glo

In Welsh, this means a "stream of coal," and indeed, around the turn of the 20th century, coal mining was the area's major industry.

Panic

This town owes its name to a brand of chewing tobacco, the Panic Plug, which itself was named for the hard economic times that followed the Civil War.

Paoli

General Pasquale Paoli liberated the island of Corsica in the late 18th century, and Pennsylvania colonists seeking independence from Great Britain sympathized with him and his cause. The first thing named in Paoli's honor was a tavern, reputed to be a meeting place for American revolutionaries. The town followed suit in 1769.

Scalp Level

Around 1794, the settlers here had a brush-clearing "frolic," at which time they passed around a whiskey jug. With the lumberjacks operating axes under the influence, one of them yelled, "Scalp 'em level, boys," meaning cut the tree trunks level to the ground.

Wilkes-Barre

John Wilkes and Isaac Barre were members of the British Parliament who championed the cause of the American Revolution. This town honored them by taking their names in 1769. (Interesting: John Wilkes Booth was named after John Wilkes.)

Did You Know?

Pennsylvania's nickname the "Keystone State" comes from the fact that during the colonial era, there were six colonies north and six south of Pennsylvania, making it the new country's central link—like a keystone in an arch.

All Aboard!

By the 1850s, Philadelphia was one of the busiest hubs of the Underground Railroad. And by many accounts, 19 out of 20 slaves who made it to Philadelphia were fed and housed by one man—William Still. His dedication to the cause earned him the nickname "The father of the Underground Railroad."

A Run for Freedom

William Still knew first-hand the plight of the runaway slave—his own mother, Sidney, had once been a fugitive. In the early 1800s, Sidney and her husband, Levin Steel, were slaves in Maryland. But when Levin bought his freedom and moved to New Jersey, Sidney took their four young children and ran away to join him.

The family hid during the day and spent their nights tramping through woods and swampland until slave catchers caught them and shipped Sidney and the children back to their master. Sidney tried again, but on that second attempt, she managed to take only her two daughters; sons Levin Jr. and Peter stayed behind with their grandmother. Sidney intended to return for the boys when she had enough money to rescue or buy them, but they were sold before she could do it and the family lost track of them.

Sidney and Levin made a good life for themselves in the North, but they were still in hiding—bounty hunters and slave catchers roamed the area looking for fugitive slaves. The couple moved to a farm in southern New Jersey, and to stay undercover, Sidney changed her name to Charity; the family name became Still. Born in 1821, William was the youngest of Charity and Levin's 18 children. But the tragedy of the two lost boys clouded the family's happiness, and those memories helped make William a dedicated abolitionist.

Philadelphia Freedom

William Still moved to Philadelphia in 1844, when he was 23 years old. He arrived with just three dollars and the clothes he was wearing. At first, he took jobs doing manual labor, but he later taught himself to read and write in order to find better employment. In 1847 he landed a position in the office of the Pennsylvania Anti-Slavery Society where, along with janitorial work, his duties included being a mail clerk.

Still moved up quickly. Soon he was helping the society's Vigilance Committee, which maintained "lines" on the Underground Railroad and housed runaway slaves. By 1851, William Still was the committee's chairman; his responsibilities included finding safe housing, food, and clothing for hundreds of former slaves who were coming to the city from as far south as Georgia. He was part of a committee that interviewed the runaways, taking down their biographies and records of family left behind.

He also kept a lookout for suspicious "packages" . . . trunks or boxes that might contain living human beings. Some slaves were so determined to escape that they hid in parcels and shipped themselves north.

Still also housed fugitives in his own home, where they would rest and gather their strength before hiking a difficult, dangerous trail over the Appalachian Mountains to New York and then Canada. The runaways couldn't stay in Philadelphia because the Fugitive Slave Law of 1850 permitted bounty hunters to track slaves down—even in free states—and return them to their masters. To find real freedom, they had to cross into Canada.

Despite the law, Still's operation continually frustrated slave catchers. He was arrested only once, for allegedly kidnapping a woman named Jane Johnson and her two children. The trio had come to Philadelphia with J. H. Wheeler, their wealthy master, and when Still escorted them to a safe house, Wheeler accused him of kidnapping. Johnson ultimately testified at Still's trial as a surprise witness for the defense, and Still was acquitted of all charges. (Johnson was arrested at the trial, but she managed to escape again.)

Band of Brothers

Over the years, hundreds of people came to William Still for help, but one man who came to see him in 1850 became particularly important. Peter Friedman wasn't a fugitive; he'd already bought his freedom. But he had traveled 1,500 miles from Alabama to Philadelphia hoping to find some word of his mother. Her name was Sidney, he said, and he hadn't seen her since he was six years old when she left him to go north to find his father. William later wrote that as he listened to Peter, "My feelings were unutterable. I could see in the face of my newfound brother, the likeness of my mother."

Levin Sr. had died a few years before, but Sidney was still alive. William took Peter home to introduce him to their mother and siblings. Peter told them his story: After Sidney's former master sold him and his brother, Peter and Levin Jr. were resold again and again. Levin Jr. died in his early 30s from a beating he'd received. Peter had taken the name "Friedman" from a pair of Jewish brothers who helped him buy his freedom, but he'd had to leave his wife and children in the South. After an attempt to free his family failed, Peter spent years saving money until he finally purchased them in 1854 for $5,000—an incredible sum at the time.

Notes from a Secret World

William Still ran his line of the Underground Railroad until 1861, when the Civil War began. The fighting halted many slaves' escape attempts, and President Lincoln's 1863 Emancipation Proclamation officially freed them. Thus began the next phase of Still's life; he bought a coal yard and sold coal to the Union army during the Civil War. After the war, he continued his coal business and used some of its profits to buy real estate.

He also spent time going over records from his days with the Vigilance Committee. Since finding his brother, Still had been especially careful to keep records of his interviews with fugitives, in case their families later came looking for them. But because he'd essentially been running a criminal operation and was often in danger of arrest, he'd kept his records well hidden inside a basement wall.

In the years after the Civil War, though, William Still pulled out those records and compiled them in a book called *The Underground Rail Road: A Record of Facts, Authentic Narratives, Letters, etc.* It was published in 1872 and was an immediate best seller. The 780-page collection included letters, biographies, and interviews with fugitive slaves. Among them were the story of one of President Tyler's slaves, who left the presidential caravan in Philadelphia, and that of Ellen Craft, a light-skinned woman who escaped with her husband William, who had darker skin. Ellen pretended to be a young white man, and William masqueraded as her butler.

At the time, biographies and interviews were new to most people, and few Americans knew anything about the details of life on the Underground Railroad. Both factors helped make Still's book enormously popular. He went on to publish three editions and exhibited the volume at the 1876 Philadelphia Centennial Exposition.

A Full Life

Slavery had come to an end, but William Still continued to champion civil rights. He led a successful campaign to integrate local railway cars in the 1860s. He founded the Mission School (a church-sponsored school for African American children) in North Philadelphia, organized the first African American YMCA, and helped manage homes for the aged, destitute, and orphaned. He spent most of the rest of his life in Philadelphia (with a brief foray to New Jersey) and died there in 1902.

Did You Know?

At 1,244 square miles, Lycoming is Pennsylvania's largest county . . . even bigger than the state of Rhode Island. But Lycoming used to be even larger than it is now. When it was founded in 1795, Lycoming encompassed most of north-central Pennsylvania, and 16 modern-day counties— including Tioga, Forest, and Jefferson—were once part of the original Lycoming county.

The Sixers By the Numbers

One of the NBA's top teams since their opening tip-off in 1963, the Philadelphia 76ers have won 8 division titles and 2 championships. Find out more about this dynamic franchise from the Quaker City.

1

Ranking of the 1966–67 squad, arguably the best Sixers team of all time. In fact, in a poll conducted as part of the NBA's 35th anniversary celebration in 1980, the '66–'67 Sixers were considered the best of their era. That season's squad included Wilt Chamberlain, Hal Greer, Chet Walker, and Luke Jackson.

2

Number of backboards shattered by center Darryl Dawkins during the 1979–80 season. Dawkins, who liked to name his dunks. Examples: Go-Rilla, Yo-Mama, and In-Your-Face-Disgrace. He called his first backboard-breaking slam the "Chocolate-Thunder-Flying, Glass-Flying, Robinzine-Crying, Babies-Crying, Glass-Still-Flying, Cats-Crying, Rump-Roasting, Bun-Toasting, Thank You-Wham-Bam-I-Am-Jam." After the game, Dawkins told reporters, "I didn't mean to destroy [the backboard]. It was the power, the Chocolate Thunder [his nickname for himself]. I could feel it surging through my body, fighting to get out. I had no control over it."

4

Players who received the league's Most Valuable Player Award:

Wilt Chamberlain, Julius Erving, Moses Malone, and Allen Iverson.

5
Conference titles the 76ers have won: 1976–77, 1979–80, 1981–82, 1982–83, 2000–01.

7 feet 6 inches
Height of former 76ers center Shawn Bradley.

12
Number of different uniform designs used by the team since 1963.

33.5
Wilt Chamberlain's scoring average during the 1965–66 season—the highest in franchise history.

34
Jersey number of Charles Barkley. The 6'5" "Round Mound of Rebound" averaged 22.1 points and 11.7 rebounds per game over 16 NBA seasons.

36
Number of consecutive home wins from January 14, 1966, to January 20, 1967, a franchise record.

68
Number of regular-season victories during the 1966–67 season. Philadelphia went on to capture the NBA crown for that season by defeating San Francisco in the finals, four games to two.

500

Number of fans who submitted suggestions to name
Philadelphia's team after they moved there from Syracuse in
1963. The winning entry was submitted by the late Walt
Stahlberg of West Collingswood, New Jersey, in honor of
Philadelphia's revolutionary heritage.

1,122

Games played by Hal Greer, the most of any 76er.

1983

The second (and last) year the 76ers won the NBA
championship.

21,600

Seating capacity of the Wachovia Center, Philadelphia's current
home arena.

842,976

Record home attendance during the 76ers' 2001–02 season.

Did You Know?

Between 1947 and 1969, the U.S. military sponsored
Project Blue Book—a secret operation to investigate UFO
activity in the United States. Over 22 years, project officials
looked into 12,618 reports of UFO sightings. Most of those
were discounted as hoaxes or natural events (like stars or
lightning). But 701 reports remain unexplained—16 of them
in Pennsylvania.

Getting in Toon

This town is always ahead of the curve.

Town: Altoona

Location: Blair County

Founding: 1849

Population (2008): 49,500

Size: 9.8 square miles

County seat: No

What's in a Name?

Local Cherokee Indians called the area *Allatoona,* meaning "high lands of great worth" because the city is situated high in the Allegheny Mountains. However, the name may also come from the German city of Altona. (Many Germans settled in the area.)

Claims to Fame:

- Altoona was laid out in 1849 by employees of the Pennsylvania Railroad. The site was originally a switching point and maintenance stop before trains climbed into the mountains. The town's economy is still largely train-based, with rail yards and train repair facilities.

- It's home to the minor league baseball team the Altoona Curve, who don't take themselves too seriously. Some of their promotions have included Erik Estrada Night, Awful Night (featuring onion bobbing and a gallbladder giveaway), and "A Salute to Quitters."

The Fight for the Wyoming Valley

During the days of the American Revolution, the states often battled each other for territory. Case in point: the 18th-century fight between Pennsylvania and Connecticut for the Wyoming Valley, a conflict known as the Pennamite-Yankee War.

Yours, Mine, or Ours?

The problems began in the 17th century, when King Charles II of England gave two groups the same plot of land. In 1662, he granted the founders of the Connecticut colony an area between the 41st and 42nd parallels, going indefinitely west from the coast (since no one back then knew how far inland the new colonies would stretch). Nineteen years later, in 1681, he gave William Penn a plot that included the one he'd given to Connecticut. And within the borders of this doubly gifted plot was the Wyoming Valley, a fertile arch-shaped area about 20 miles long in what is now northeastern Pennsylvania.

Farmers from both colonies soon flocked to the region. The first Connecticut settlement was near modern-day Wilkes-Barre. Pennsylvania, however, felt that the land lay inside its borders. Neither colony was happy about the other moving in on its territory, but for about 70 years, there seemed to be enough land for everyone. And by 1754, the two states were distracted by other things: in particular, the French and Indian War.

Fight!

In the meantime, rich deposits of coal were found in the

Wyoming Valley, making the place even more appealing to both sides. When a new group of Connecticut settlers arrived in 1769, the local Pennsylvania sheriff, determined to stake a claim for his colony, arrested them for trespassing. The newcomers left, but returned the following year with a militia and built a fort. So the sheriff assembled a larger group and drove them off again.

This just made the Connecticut settlers even more determined to occupy the Wyoming Valley. They contacted a group of ruthless frontiersmen who were promised land for their help and asked for their protection. With those men as bodyguards, the Connecticut "Yankees" (as New Englanders were called in those days) took over the Wyoming Valley, built forts, and dug in. They renamed the place Westmoreland and declared that it was part of Connecticut.

The battle continued, but dissipated a little when the American Revolution began. Some men continued fighting in the Wyoming Valley, but many others (both Yankees and Pennsylvanians, also known as Pennamites) joined General George Washington to fight the British. Pennsylvania's governor, John Penn, the grandson of William Penn, remained loyal to King George III, which only increased the animosity between Pennsylvania and Connecticut.

Battle of the Butlers

In 1778, Major John Butler, a British loyalist stationed at New York State's Fort Niagara, led a group of 400 British soldiers into the Wyoming Valley to clear the region of Connecticut settlers. He also added several hundred warriors from the Iroquois Confederacy to strengthen his numbers.

On the other side, Colonel Zebulon Butler—no relation to

John—of Washington's Continental Army happened to be at home in the Wyoming Valley on furlough. He saw the approaching army and raised his own militia of 300 men to march on John Butler's force. On July 3, 1778, Zebulon Butler met his enemy on open ground, forming a thin line to defend the valley. But because the invading enemy was much larger than his group, this proved to be a fatal mistake.

Wyoming Valley Massacre

Zebulon Butler's group fired just three volleys before they were flanked by John Butler's American Indian allies and over-whelmed. The battle lasted less than an hour and resulted in 200 of Zebulon Butler's men being taken captive. (The rest escaped.)

John Butler let the Indians take control of the prisoners. Whether he knew what would happen to them or not is debatable, but during the night, all but two of the prisoners were killed. The two who escaped spread the story that British and Indian troops had massacred the men of the Wyoming Valley.

The End

This was unwelcome news for the American colonists, already angry at the British and distrustful of their Indian neighbors. American poets wrote memorials to the men, which made the feud and the valley famous. And after hearing of the massacre, George Washington sent soldiers to destroy Iroquois villages.

After the Revolutionary War ended, a 1782 Congressional commission ruled that the Wyoming Valley belonged to Pennsylvania. (Because the commission met in secret and kept no notes, the reasons for choosing Pennsylvania over Connecticut remain a mystery.) Bolstered by Congress's decision, the State of Pennsylvania sent troops to evict the Connecticut settlers. In turn, the angry Yankees declared that neither Pennsylvania nor Connecticut had any authority over Westmoreland—it was an independent state.

Of course, that didn't work, either, and the back-and-forth bickering lasted another few years. Both sides eventually came to an agreement in 1788: per the Congress's decision, Pennsylvania would keep the land but agreed to let the Connecticut farmers stay and to recognize their property rights. Pennsylvania separated the Wyoming Valley into a new county—Luzerne.

Did You Know?

Pennsylvania is the only state that was once home to two Catholic saints. (Only four Americans have been canonized by the Catholic church.) The first was Saint John Neumann, who was Bishop of Philadelphia and opened the first parochial school in the United States in 1852. The second was Saint Katherine Drexel.

Drexel was born in Philadelphia in 1858 and came from a wealthy, philanthropic family—her father founded Drexel University in 1891. She decided early on to devote her life to helping other people and concentrated her efforts on educational opportunities for American Indians and African Americans. Over the course of her life, Drexel opened more than 60 schools, including a mission school in New Mexico and Xavier University in Louisiana, the only black Catholic college in the United States at the time. (Today, the college admits non-Catholics and people of other races.)

Bandstand Boogie!

Before MTV and music videos, there was American Bandstand. *In its 37 years on the air, the show racked up some fascinating numbers.*

1st

Record played on the national show: "Whole Lotta Shakin' Goin' On" by Jerry Lee Lewis.

3

The number of new songs reviewed during each show's "Rate-a-Record" segment. Three teenagers from the studio's audience would rate the new tunes, and the kids also coined the oft-repeated "It's got a good beat and you can dance to it" if they liked it. This part of the show was vitally important to record producers: A good score on "Rate-a-Record" meant the viewing audience would rush out and buy the record, almost always sending it to the Top-10 charts. But a bad rating didn't always spell disaster—in 1963, the then-unknown Beatles got a low Rate-a-Record rating for their song "She Loves You."

4

Hosts in *Bandstand's* history. Bob Horn was the first—he was the one who invited teenagers to come to the studio and dance with the music. In 1956, after Horn was arrested for drunk driving, the studio fired him and hired Tony Mammarella. Soon after, though, Dick Clark took his place. Then in 1989, for the show's final season, David Hirsch took over for Clark.

6

The Philadelphia TV channel (originally WFIL, now WPVI-TV) on which *American Bandstand* premiered in 1952. First called just *Bandstand*, it ran from 3 p.m. to 4:30 p.m., Monday through Friday, when teenagers were getting home from school. The show went national in 1957 and changed its name to *American Bandstand*. It aired on ABC, and by the end of its first year, 64 stations around the country carried the show.

14 years

The minimum age for dancers on the show; 18 was the maximum. They were all local kids from around Philadelphia, and about 60 of them were part of the "Committee"—regulars who appeared on every show during the 1960s and became role models for American teenagers. Becoming a regular was fairly easy: anyone who appeared on the show and received fan mail could be one.

35

Number of songs featured on each program.

69 cents

The average cost of a 45-rpm record in Philadelphia in the 1950s. The fact that records were so inexpensive was one reason for the show's success. In the 1950s, teenagers had more disposable income than ever before (a result of the economic prosperity that followed World War II), and by spending a lot of their money on 45s (which had one song on each side), they became the dominant consumers in the music industry.

500

The number of fan letters received by Arlene Sullivan and

Kenny Rossi, one of the show's most popular couples, during an average week. Sullivan was always surprised by her appeal. She said, "I danced on a TV show. Nothing I did was different than what kids were doing in their basements."

1959

The year Congress began investigating what became known as the "payola scandal." Payola was an illegal practice whereby record companies paid disc jockeys to play their songs on the air. *American Bandstand* and Dick Clark were investigated because both were so prominent in the field. In the end, Clark had to give up his financial interests in the recording business and stop accepting gifts from record companies. (He'd once accepted a fur stole and expensive jewelry from a record company president.)

1964

Year ABC moved production of the show from Philadelphia to Los Angeles. Dick Clark actually facilitated the move; he wanted more time to work on other projects and to be closer to the center of the entertainment industry in Hollywood. After- ward, *American Bandstand* began airing only one day a week.

1989

Year *American Bandstand* went off the air.

Bandstand Bits

- Philadelphia-based singers Fabian, Frankie Avalon, and Bobby Rydell all got their big breaks on *American Bandstand*. They often filled in for acts that dropped out at the last minute, and the exposure gave their careers a tremendous boost.

- Before Dick Clark took over as host in 1956, *American Bandstand* allowed only white teenagers in its audience and on its stage. One of the first changes Clark made was to integrate the show. He insisted that it was only logical, since so many of the artists who appeared on the show were African Americans.

- Only one performer didn't lip-synch during his appearance on the show: B. B. King on January 3, 1970.

- Today, the Top-10 countdown is a common feature on radio and music television stations, but *American Bandstand* was the first to use it.

- The show's theme song was called "Bandstand Boogie."

- Between 2002 and 2005, NBC ran a prime-time drama called *American Dreams*. Set in the early 1960s, it told the story of Philadelphia's Pryor family. The main character—16-year-old Meg Pryor—was a regular on *American Bandstand*. The show's producer: Dick Clark Productions.

Did You Know?

As mentioned on page 93, when it came time to choose the name of Philadelphia's hockey team in 1967, the managers held a newspaper contest; Flyers won, but they wanted an "official winner." So all the ballots that had picked that name were put into a box, and one was drawn. The winner: nine-year old Alec Stockard—except he had misspelled it as "Fliers."

James Buchanan Gets No Respect

So maybe he wasn't the greatest U.S. president.
But he was the only one from Pennsylvania.

James Buchanan, who served as the 15th president of the
United States from 1857 to 1861, had the misfortune of presiding over the dissolution of the country as it careened into
civil war. As a result, history has not judged him kindly—he's
generally ranked in the bottom tier of presidents, and some
consider him *the* worst president. But that doesn't mean he's
not interesting.

The Early Years

Buchanan was born on April 23, 1791, in Franklin County,
near in a place called Cove Gap. Buchanan attended Dickinson
College in Carlisle, Pennsylvania, where he was once expelled
for "bad behavior" (he often disrupted class). He begged to be
readmitted, promised his teachers he'd shape up, and ultimately graduated with honors in 1809.

Buchanan Builds a Résumé

Although he was most famous as president, Buchanan served in
a number of other positions on his way up the political ladder.
He was elected a state representative in 1814 and, beginning in
1821, served five terms as a U.S. representative. He also was
Andrew Jackson's minister to Russia and the Secretary of State
during James Polk's administration. (Polk wanted to nominate

him to the Supreme Court, but Buchanan refused.) Franklin
Pierce appointed him as minister to Great Britain in 1853.

A Reluctant Nominee

Buchanan had hoped to be nominated for president in 1844
and again in the next two elections, but the Democratic Party
passed him over each time. His nomination for president
finally came in 1856 after delegates went through 17 rounds of
nominations before agreeing on him. One of Buchanan's major
selling points was that, because he'd been out of the country as
the minister to Great Britain, he wasn't tainted by America's
major controversy of the time: slavery. Still, as much as he
wanted to be president, he was reluctant to accept the 1856
nomination, writing, "Before many years, the abolitionists will
bring war upon this land. It may come during the next presidential term." Despite that concern, he took the nomination
and won the presidency.

It's Not Easy Being Doughy

Buchanan was known as a "doughface"—a term that meant a
man from the North who was sympathetic to the South—and
in fact, he blamed most of the nation's troubles with slavery on
Northern abolitionists causing trouble. At the start of his
administration, Buchanan learned that the Supreme Court was
about to hand down a proslavery verdict in the case of Dred
Scott, a slave who sued to have the court free him. Instead, the
court (led by Justice Robert Taney) sided with Scott's owner
and declared that because Scott was black and thus not a U.S.
citizen (neither freed blacks nor slaves were allowed citizenship at the time), he couldn't sue anyway.

Buchanan hoped the Dred Scott decision would settle the

slavery issue . . . but of course, it didn't. Instead, it ignited even further controversy (most notably, whether Kansas should be admitted to the Union as a free or a slave state) and threw Buchanan into a battle with his own party. This split the Democratic Party by the election of 1860, when two Democrats ran for president: Buchanan had bowed out, and the two who remained were Stephen Douglas from the North and John C. Breckenridge from the South. The party's split all but assured victory for the Republican candidate, Abraham Lincoln.

Worst Presidential Blunder Ever

By the end of Buchanan's term, it was clear that a number of Southern states were planning to secede, and as president, he needed to do something. So, on December 3, 1860, he announced to Congress that even though it was his opinion that states could not legally secede from the Union, the federal government couldn't stop them, either.

Less than three weeks later, South Carolina withdrew from the Union, and by February 1861—a month before Buchanan's term ended—six more states had withdrawn and formed the Confederate States of America. The first shots of the Civil War, at South Carolina's Fort Sumter, were fired on Buchanan's watch on January 9, 1861.

How important was Buchanan's choice not to take action? In 2006, a group of historians assembled by the University of Louisville called his refusal to do more to halt the dissolution of the Union as the single biggest presidential blunder in history.

Passing the Buck

Buchanan, who had accepted the presidency with reservations, seemed delighted to pass it on to Lincoln in March 1861, telling the 16th president, "If you are as happy in entering the White House as I shall feel [leaving it], you are a happy man." By that time, Buchanan was already so unpopular that the Senate drafted a resolution condemning him. His presidential portrait was removed from the Capitol rotunda for fear it might be vandalized.

Member of the Bachelor Party

Aside from being regarded one of the worst presidents in history, Buchanan is notable for another reason: he's the only U.S. president who never married. Buchanan had been engaged in his late 20s to Anne C. Coleman, a daughter of a wealthy Philadelphia family, but the engagement was broken off (historians still argue by whom). Coleman died soon after, and even though it was never proven, many people speculated she committed suicide. During his presidency, Buchanan's "first lady" was his niece Harriet Lane.

Did You Know?

Martin Guitars has been headquartered in Nazareth, Pennsylvania, since 1838 when C. F. Martin—a German immigrant—moved there with his family. Martin had originally set up shop in New York City, but he grew homesick for Germany. When a friend told him about the large German population in Pennsylvania and that the climate and terrain were similar to the old country, Martin wasted no time, closed his guitar-building business in New York, and reinvented it in the Keystone State.

The Fire that Won't Die

What's unusual about the eastern Pennsylvania town of Centralia?
Nothing . . . except that it has been on fire since 1962.

Centralia sits atop one of the United States' largest veins of anthracite coal, a rare and valuable fuel source with an especially high carbon content. At the turn of the 20th century, Centralia was a booming mining town, and in 1981, more than 1,000 people still lived there. But by 2007, only nine residents remained.

Today, most of the town has been razed. Driveways turn off empty streets into grass lots, and the few houses still standing are propped up by stone or wooden supports. In 1992, the State of Pennsylvania took control of the town, and the post office revoked Centralia's ZIP code in 2002. What turned Centralia into a ghost town? A fire that has burned for almost half a century.

A Wild and Woolly History

Centralia was originally called Bull's Head, named for a tavern of the same name that opened in 1841 and was the town's first business. By 1860, the name had been changed—first to Centreville and then Centralia—and coal had been discovered there. People looking to make their fortunes poured into the area, but the wealth of the coal mines came at a price: one man died for every 35,164 tons of coal mined, a fatality rate three times higher than that of most other mining areas.

Crime was also a problem. Arson and murder were common. And the Molly Maguires, a secret group of organized criminals, even murdered the town's founder in 1868. But despite its rough reputation, Centralia was a booming mining town at the turn of the 20th century.

Stripped

Over the next 50 years, though, as underground mining became less profitable, strip miners bought up Centralia's mineral rights. This inexpensive—but ecologically devastating—method scraped coal from the surface, leaving behind deep gashes in the earth. Over the years, the coal deposits were further depleted, and the strip miners also moved away. Between 1950 and 1960, the number of miners in Centralia dropped by 93 percent.

In May 1962, one of the abandoned strip mines was being used as the town dump, and just before Memorial Day, the dump caught fire. This was not big news—former mining towns often used old mining pits as dumps, and fires were common. Dump fires sometimes ignited (and were quickly extinguished) as often as once a week. Some smoldered longer, but were generally considered just a part of the landscape in the coal region. One mine fire in Laurel Run, Pennsylvania, has been burning since 1915.

But Centralia's fire was different—it burned through the clay layers added to the dump as fire retardants and ignited the coal below. Once the coal seam ignited, the blaze had plenty of fuel and oxygen to keep burning. The only way to put the fire out was to dig up the seam completely and quickly, but two months went by before Centralia officials asked the state for help in putting out the fire. By then, the cost was $30,000, and government funding, hampered by a Congress-imposed spending cap on mine reclamation projects, just wasn't there. The townspeople finally got some of the money three months after the fire began, and they started excavating.

The Money Pit

Digging actually caused more trouble when the newly opened trench exposed the coal seam's surfaces to the air, allowing in more oxygen to fuel the fire. Two months after the digging began, the blaze swept past the trench and progressed along two fronts of the underground coal seam, burrowing slowly toward downtown Centralia. Plumes of steam rose through cracks in the ground.

By 1969, the fire was still burning, and the cost of digging it out had jumped to $4.5 million. Looking for a cheaper solution, officials decided to inject the old mine shaft with ash, hoping to smother the blaze. It was a good idea, but they ran out of money before completing the project. In 1978, the federal government proposed digging a $500,000 trench to stop the fire. It would have to go through the center of town, though, and would destroy two populated streets. Residents vetoed the idea.

As everyone debated, the estimated cost kept rising. When it reached $9 million, government officials started to question whether spending any more money in Centralia was wise—the total value of the town's property was only about $500,000. The cost of saving the town was more than it was worth.

From Beneath, It Devours

The townspeople had started to feel the fire's effects too. A mine fire burning underground can reach 600°F to 1,500°F. And as it burns, it consumes oxygen and leaves behind deadly gases, including both carbon dioxide and carbon monoxide.

The dangerous combination of gases, which miners call "black damp," started seeping into Centralia homes. One resident noticed that his furnace's pilot light kept going out because of the black damp flowing into his basement from the fire. Other residents were short of breath, and government-installed carbon monoxide monitors found elevated levels of the gas inside homes. Then, in 1978, a thermal probe 12 feet from a local gas station registered a temperature of 136 degrees; the ground 20 feet from a natural gas pipeline was measured at 770 degrees. Both were potentially disastrous situations, and fissures opened on nearby Route 61, eventually forcing the state to abandon the road.

The fire gained national attention in 1981 when the ground collapsed beneath a local boy named Todd Domboski, dropping him into a hole four feet wide and about 150 feet deep. His cousin pulled him out, but when a government inspector examined the sinkhole afterward, he concluded that if Todd had not been rescued so quickly, the carbon monoxide would have killed him in minutes.

Division in the Ranks

As residents of the town realized the peril of the advancing fire, they couldn't agree on how to handle the problem. Some people wanted to move but needed government aid to unload their now-worthless property. Others felt that if they could raise the money, it might still be possible to extinguish the fire.

Still others believed the threat of the fire was just an elaborate hoax perpetuated by the government. The reasoning: In 1954, Congress had passed a law that made the owners of old coal mines responsible for half of the expense of the mines' cleanup. Before the fire, the Coates Coal Company, the original owner of Centralia's mines, had decided to dodge the liability by selling the rights for the vein under Centralia to the town for one dollar; Coates would continue to excavate and manage the mine. Centralia residents had seen this as a windfall—proceeds from the sale of the coal under Centralia could potentially bring billions of dollars. But now, with a fire burning beneath them, Centralia's residents were legally responsible for half the cost of the cleanup—a cost they couldn't afford. Some believed the mine fire was a ploy by government officials to reclaim the land and mine the coal themselves.

Exodus

But most residents just wanted to move away, and in 1983, the federal government finally approved $42 million to buy them out. Almost all of the 1,100 residents took the offer, and their homes were demolished after they left. When the state invoked eminent domain a decade later, most of the 80 people who'd stayed behind finally left. The remaining dozen residents, most over 60 years old, have slowly dispersed over the years.

The mine fire still rages today—it advances about 75 feet a year. There are no current plans to put it out, and geologists estimate that it could continue to burn for another 250 years until it consumes all of Centralia's anthracite. The town has become a popular destination for tourists who ignore warning signs at the edge of a field that still emits toxic gas. They even drive down the abandoned Route 61 to snap photos. In the end, the fire caused no human deaths; its only casualty was the town of Centralia. According to Helen Womer, one of the last residents to leave, "Centralia committed suicide."

The U Penn Quiz

How well do you know the history of Pennsylvania's most prestigious university? (Sorry, Penn State grads.)

1. When was the University of Pennsylvania founded?
A. 1740
B. 1749
C. 1751
D. 1755

2. Which Founding Father helped found Penn?
A. Robert Morris
B. Benjamin Rush
C. George Clymer
D. Benjamin Franklin

3. What's Penn's motto?
A. *Vox clamantis in deserto*
B. *Leges sine moribus vanae*
C. *Dei sub numine viget*
D. *In Deo speramus*

4. When did Penn join the Ivy League?
A. 1755
B. 1852
C. 1945
D. 1954

5. Which U.S. president attended Penn?
A. Grover Cleveland

B. Millard Fillmore
C. William Henry Harrison
D. James Buchanan

6. Which famous computer was built at Penn?
A. UNIVAC
B. ENIAC
C. The Colossus
D. The TRS-80 Model I

Answers on page 307.

● ●

Did You Know?

The University of Pennsylvania was the site of the first medical school in the United States—it opened in 1756. Penn was also one of the first universities in America to admit women; they could attend (but couldn't earn degrees) in the 1870s. Finally, in 1882, women began earning graduate degrees and, in 1914, undergraduate degrees in a separate women's school. The school didn't officially become coed until the early 1970s, though, when the women's and men's schools merged.

Revolutionary Documents: The U.S. Constitution

*The colonists had fought the Revolutionary War and cut the
cord with England. Now, all they needed to do was figure
out the new country's operating instructions.*

Within eight days of approving the Declaration of
Independence in 1776, the Continental Congress in
Philadelphia set itself a new task: writing the Articles of
Confederation, a document whose rules would guide the new
nation. Unfortunately, the rules they came up with didn't work
very well. The biggest problem was that, because the delegates
were afraid of duplicating what they considered England's
tyranny, the Articles of Confederation didn't create a strong
central government; it left most of the power up to the individual states. But without any authority, the federal government
couldn't do much—in particular, it couldn't tax its citizens to
raise money for an army. The government was able to ignore
this problem for several years, but in 1786, it suddenly found
that it needed that army. And not to fight off a foreign threat,
but to put down a rebellion right there at home.

The Farmers Revolt

By 1786, most farmers in New England were drowning in debt.
They'd fought against England, and when the Revolutionary
War was over, they headed home with little or no money to
show for their efforts. The new government had issued them
promissory notes, but they couldn't actually use those to buy

anything. And when they arrived home, they found that their families were also in trouble; most of the rural areas' supplies and livestock had been sold aid to the war effort (and paid for with more promissory notes). As the new country plunged into an economic depression, the states began taxing residents to raise money. Faced with the need to feed their families and keep their land, the farmers racked up debts that they had no way of repaying.

Burdened with tax debts of their own, the wealthy businessmen and merchants who'd loaned the farmers money started demanding that the debts be repaid. When the farmers couldn't pay, the businessmen confiscated the farmers' land and assets. In some cases, the farmers were sent to debtors' prison.

In the fall of 1786, a Massachusetts farmer named Daniel Shays had had enough. He and hundreds of other disgruntled farmers banded together to stage an uprising, demanding that the state relieve their debts and protect their assets. When they got no real response, they blockaded the debtors' courts so court cases could not be heard. Shays then led the men to the federal arsenal in Springfield, Massachusetts, determined to storm the building and steal weapons. But a militia raised by the governor beat Shays to the arsenal and fired on the angry farmers, killing several.

The Elite React

As news of the rebellion spread, the wealthy business owners and politicians in Boston had little sympathy for the farmers. The Massachusetts governor called the farmers "knaves and thieves," and founding father Sam Adams demanded that they be put to death for treason. The very fact that the United States had to deal with a rebellion so soon after winning its independence was seen as an embarrassment for the new country. Many in the government were worried that the violence would spread and lead to anarchy.

The men of Shays' Rebellion disbanded and hid until a general amnesty in 1788 convinced most of them to turn themselves in. Two men were executed, but many others were eventually pardoned. Even while the rebellion was going on, though, the members of the Congress of the Confederation in New York (formerly the Continental Congress) knew something needed to be done. Their primary concern was that, because the country had no strong central authority, there had been no federal army to put down the rebellion. The states could send their militias, but many of the men in the militias were the very farmers who were in open revolt. So in the spring of 1787, all the states but one sent delegates to Philadelphia. The exception was Rhode Island, which was worried about losing some of its autonomy, in particular that the new congress would create a central money supply to replace the states' money—and the delegates did do that.

Choosing the Team

The convention began in May, with Benjamin Franklin, governor of Pennsylvania, as the official host. (Franklin was 81 years old and so frail that prisoners from the Walnut Street jail carried him in a sedan chair to and from the State House.) Thomas Jefferson, author of the Declaration of Independence, was absent—he was serving as ambassador to France.

George Washington, retired from the army and living on his Virginia plantation, had to be persuaded to attend. He was deeply troubled by the situation, saying, "I am mortified beyond expression when I view the clouds that have spread

over the brightest morn that ever dawned in any country . . .
What a triumph for the advocates of despotism, to find that we
are incapable of governing ourselves and that systems founded
on the basis of equal liberty are merely ideal and fallacious."
But Washington had gravitas, and the convention would be
taken seriously only if he were present. Plus, Shays' Rebellion
showed him that the country needed a strong central government. So he came.

It's Going to Be a Long Summer

At first, the delegates were charged with the task of revising
the Articles of Confederation. But some of them thought it
would be better to start over. James Madison of Virginia came
prepared with a plan for a written constitution that included a
government very much like the one the United States has today:
a legislative branch that included a house of representative and
a senate, a chief executive who could veto the legislature, and
an appointed judicial branch. The states would send representatives to the legislature based on population—the bigger the
state, the more representatives it would have.

Madison's proposal (called the Virginia Plan) ran into
resistance because it favored the more populated states. So
New Jersey delegate William Paterson countered with a plan
that gave all states equal representation in both houses of
Congress. (New Jersey was a small state.)

The delegates couldn't agree, so Connecticut's representatives stepped in. They suggested an upper house (the Senate)
that had two legislators from each state, and a lower house (the
House of Representatives) that varied in size, depending on
each state's population. Still, questions remained: How would a
state's population be tallied? Would slaves count? After much

debate, the convention decided that each African American man would count as three-fifths of a person. Women and American Indians were excluded.

Debate Is a Good Thing

By mid-July, the delegates had agreed to a rough version of the United States Constitution. Not every question had been settled, but five men were appointed to write up the document based on their notes of the debates. (The rest of the delegates took a 10-day vacation.) The authors who stayed behind in Philadelphia included two men from the South (John Rutledge and Edmund Randolph), two from the North (Oliver Ellsworth and Nathaniel Gorham), and one from the "middle" (James Wilson of Pennsylvania). On August 6, Rutledge announced that a document was ready.

Over the next five weeks, the delegates debated, refined, and tinkered with the phrasing. Some issues, like how to elect the president, were handed over to committees. At the end of the summer, a new group of five was selected and tasked with writing up the final document. Gouverneur Morris of Pennsylvania did most of that work, with the help of James Madison, Alexander Hamilton, Rufus King, and William Johnson, the president of Columbia College in New York. The final document went back to the convention on September 12.

Sealing the Deal

There was little argument this time. Benjamin Franklin delivered the following statement: "Thus I consent, sir, to this Constitution, because I expect no better, and because I am not sure that it is not the best." The other delegates agreed, and the document was complete.

The next step was to have nine of the thirteen states ratify the Constitution. That turned out to be a two-year process that involved promising an entire additional document—the Bill of Rights, which was written later in New York. But finally, on June 21, 1788, New Hampshire became the ninth state to ratify the U.S. Constitution, making the document the law of the land. (Rhode Island, incidentally, finally accepted the Constitution in 1790, the last of the original thirteen to do so.)

To read about other great documents written in Philadelphia, turn to pages 38 and 182.

Did You Know?

Known in her day as the "Diva of Din," Florence Foster Jenkins turned bad singing into a career. Born in Wilkes-Barre in 1868, she started giving concerts in 1912. And even though she spent years taking voice lessons, nothing seemed to improve her terrible singing. Yet her concerts were hits. Why? She wore extravagant costumes (one of her most famous included wings and a crown) and—thanks to her own supreme self-confidence—created a "so bad it's good" experience for audiences. Her shows continued into the 1930s, and she played to increasingly packed rooms. And despite her critics, Jenkins compared herself to the likes of Frieda Hempel, Luisa Tetrazzini, and other opera divas of the era.

Jenkins's fame peaked in 1944 with a concert at Carnegie Hall. The show sold out, and the box office turned away 2,000 people. She died a month later at the age of 76.

The Stall of Fame

We're always amazed by the creative ways people use bathrooms, toilets, toilet paper, etc. So we created Uncle John's "Stall of Fame" to honor them. Here are two Pennsylvanians who made their mark . . . with toilets.

Thomas Suica of Monaca

Notable Achievements: Beating the system and making unique art

True Story: In November 2000, the Sky Bank announced it was building a branch on a vacant lot next to Suica's home in the western Pennsylvania town of Monaca. Suica, a plumber, didn't like the idea of a bank moving in next door—so he fought back by installing 10 "decorative" toilets on the roof of his garage. Every month or so, he rearranged them to create scenes commemorating the changing seasons. (His Christmas display: Santa's sleigh being pulled by 10 toilet reindeer.)

When the city fined Suica $135 and cited him for creating "unsanitary and unsafe conditions" on his roof, he fought back in court—and won. Judge Thomas Mannix threw out the citation, finding that the town "had not proved the toilets, which Suica bought new, were unsanitary." Three years later, the city council tried again, arguing that Suica's toilet display was a health hazard because the bowls would collect water that could breed mosquitoes that might bring the West Nile virus. The council withdrew its complaint when it found that Suica had sealed the bowls shut to prevent them from collecting water.

Update: Sky Bank eventually abandoned its plans to build a bank next to Suica's house.

Joseph Taviani of Bath

Notable Achievement: Decorating his rental properties in a town-appropriate manner

True Story: In July 2001, Taviani put three toilets on the front lawns of three rental properties he owns in Bath: two were plain white, and the third was pink and planted with pink tulips. His neighbors were outraged, but Taviani maintained that his displays were "art." The two white toilets were eventually stolen, and the pink one came under fire when locals complained, but the town council couldn't find any evidence that the toilets violated the town's building codes. Last we heard, the pink toilet was still there.

And why toilets in the first place? Taviani explained, "When you think of Bath, you think of a bathroom. Tubs were too big."

Did You Know?

During the mid-1700s—as the population of Pennsylvania grew and farmland was harder to come by—people started packing up their possessions and heading south along a path that became known as the Great Wagon Road. The road stretched from Pennsylvania through Maryland and Virginia and into North Carolina, which was mostly unpopulated at the time. The colonists' preferred mode of transport? The Conestoga wagon, which had been developed by Pennsylvanians living in the Conestoga Valley (in modern Lancaster county) in the early 18th century.

Keystoners on the Big Screen

Grace Kelly, Will Smith, and Jack Palance all have at least one thing in common: they're Pennsylvania natives who have a movie title in this crossword puzzle. (Answers on page 309.)

Across

1 Margarita need
5 Musical staff insignia
9 Civil rights protest
14 Director Kazan
15 Powerful engine
16 At full gallop
17 James ___ Jones
18 Seed cover
19 Some fountain drinks
20 1954 Grace Kelly movie
23 Ben & Jerry's "___ Gooey Cake" (frozen yogurt)
24 "Bad ___ to them!" (luck)
25 Laps up noisily
28 "Should ___ acquaintance . . ."
30 Vital fluid
33 Shiva worshipper
34 Movie lioness
35 Verdi slave girl
36 1996 Will Smith movie
39 Social equal
40 Not the original color
41 ___ de menthe

42 Armenia, once
43 Letter opener
44 Geneva's nation
45 Perky songbird
47 Hemingway nickname
48 1999 Jack Palance movie
54 "Could you give me ___?"
55 Not counterfeit
56 Ancient Peruvian
57 Beat back
58 Memo starter
59 Oscar winner, e.g.
60 Actress Parker
61 Real estate agent's sign
62 Poop out

Down

1 Parrot morsel
2 Jai ___
3 Italian bread?
4 Formidable task
5 Rubs the wrong way
6 Artist Neiman
7 Islamic leader

8   What soap may leave

9   Like some vows and some cows

10 Modern music holders

11 Is partial

12 Cake decorator

13 Nintendo's Super ___

21 Clean, as a spill

22 Bruin athlete

25 Steamers and icebreakers

26 Come-ons

27 Hidden

28 Tree of the birch family

29 "Pre-owned"

31 *Hitchhiker's Guide* writer Douglas

32 One whose name is on the check

34 One-named Irish singer

35 Daring circus performer

37 Perfect spots

38 Some bra features

43 Lethal

44 Cruised the sea

46 She's Dorothy in *Jerry Maguire*

47 Oyster's prize

48 Telly's character on *Kojak*

49 *Battle Cry* author Leon

50 Get-hitched-quick spot

51 Voting no

52 It's south of Va.

53 Truth alternative

54 Jean of Dada

The Rolling Rock Story

Rolling Rock beer—in its green bottle with a painted-on label—remains the best-known product to come out of the Allegheny mountain town of Latrobe.

On a Roll

In the 1970s, Rolling Rock beer was a Northeast institution. But the brewery's founders were an unlikely bunch—an order of Benedictine monks.

The monks opened the Latrobe Brewing Company in 1893, and various owners brewed beer there until 1920, when Prohibition made the manufacture and sale of alcohol illegal in the United States. That seemed to be the end of the brewery, but in 1933, with Prohibition on the verge of repeal, four brothers—Frank, Anthony, Ralph, and Robert Tito—bought the old plant and started making beer again. They had some missteps, but in 1939, they hit on the brew that would make them millionaires: a pale lager they called Rolling Rock after the smooth pebbles they'd seen in nearby streams.

The Titos were beer makers, though, not marketers, and even though their beer developed a loyal fan base in Pennsylvania, they did little to expand their brand. In fact, their salesmen generally sold only to bars and restaurants that were within a day's drive or less from home. But despite the lack of marketing, word of Rolling Rock spread throughout Penn-sylvania and then the northeastern United States. By the early 1970s, the Latrobe Brewing Company was putting out more than 700,000 barrels of beer per year.

On the Move

But as more beer brewers came on the market, Rolling Rock's lack of a marketing strategy proved to be a problem. In the early 1980s, Latrobe's output dropped by almost half, and the Titos decided to sell. Over the next two decades, various companies (with marketing departments) bought and sold Rolling Rock and helped expand the brand to larger markets. The brewery changed hands several times, but production remained in Latrobe . . . until 2006, when Anheuser-Busch acquired the company and decided to move Rolling Rock production to New Jersey.

It was a blow to locals, who adamantly believed the beer would never be the same. According to the town's former mayor, Jim Gebicki, "It's hard to believe there won't be Rolling Rock in Latrobe. It's a real sadness . . . They can take it to New Jersey, but it will never be Rolling Rock."

A group of concerned citizens used Internet campaigns and boycotts to try to keep Rolling Rock in Pennsylvania, but they failed. The last batch of Rolling Rock rolled out of Latrobe in July 2006. Many in the town feared this would mean the economic downfall of their community, but the Latrobe Brewing Company soon reopened—in 2007, it started brewing the Boston Beer Company's Signature brand, Samuel Adams.

Why 33?

Aside from its green glass bottle and painted-on label (instead of a pasted-on paper label), one of Rolling Rock's most distinctive markings is the number "33" printed on every bottle. Over the years, people have posed theories as to what the number means: some claim it's the number of tanks at the brewery;

others say it stands for 1933, the year Prohibition was repealed.

But both are wrong. Here's the real story: When Rolling Rock was being introduced, several people in the company argued over how long the slogan on the beer's label should be. Eventually, the Tito brothers settled on a long one: "Rolling Rock from glass lined tanks in the Laurel Highlands. We tender this premium beer for your enjoyment as a tribute to your good taste. It comes from the mountain springs to you." The adman who wrote the slogan wrote the number "33" next to the copy to indicate how many words it was.

Next, the slogan was sent to the bottle maker, who thought "33" was part of the slogan and printed it on each glass bottle. Rather than scrap the bottles, the company decided to leave it. And over the years, even though the slogan changed slightly, the number 33 became a recognizable part of Rolling Rock's brand.

Did You Know?

- Most Amish buggies travel between 5 and 8 mph.

- Buggies are usually painted brown, black, gray, or white so as not to draw attention to their owners.

- You can identify how conservative an Amish order is by its buggies; the more plain the buggy, the more conservative the order. Liberal orders have been known to "dress up their buggies" with windshields, wipers, blinking turn signals powered by batteries, and even cup holders.

On the Road (Again)

Three more must-see Pennsylvania roadside attractions.

Ned's Lucky Toe: Pittsburgh

In 1900, the City of Pittsburgh erected a bronze statue of native son Stephen Foster (the 19th-century songwriter who penned classics like "Oh! Susanna" and "My Old Kentucky Home") in the northeastern neighborhood of Highland Park. The statue showed Foster—in a bow tie and long coat, holding his song-book—seated, with a slave named Ned at his feet playing the banjo. But during the 1930s, people vandalized the statue, breaking off pieces of bronze to sell for scrap, and eventually, the city's mayor had Foster and Ned moved to Schenley Plaza. The park was situated along busy Forbes Avenue, which discouraged vandalism.

Over the years, the statue came under fire from civil-rights advocates, who said that the depiction of a slave was racially offensive. But the statue remained, and superstitious visitors started rubbing Ned's bare right big toe for good luck. Why the toe? Bare feet are rare for statues, making Ned unusual. And because one superstition says that good luck sinks (like gold), the toe—being the statue's lowest point—would be where all the luck was.

The Body of Saint John Neumann: Philadelphia

Bishop John Neumann of Philadelphia's Saint Peter's Catholic Church died in 1860 (Pope Paul VI made him a saint in 1977). At Neumann's request, the church enshrined him in a crypt in the basement. Today, his body is still there . . . behind glass beneath the basement's altar. And if he looks especially good for a man who's been dead for more than 140 years, it's because his face is actually a plaster mask, and his body is covered in ceremonial robes.

And If You're Really Hungry . . .

Just off Highway 80 in Clearfield is Denny's Beer Barrel Pub, home to the world's largest hamburger: a 100-plus-pound gastrointestinal glut called the "Main Event Burger." Denny Liegey opened the restaurant in 1977 and started out with smaller burgers: one-half and one-pounders. But in 1990, wondering how big a burger his customers could finish, he got the idea of offering a burger challenge. So he made two-pound burgers, then three-pounders, and so on, all the while offering customers various prizes if they finished their burgers in an hour or less. (Most people couldn't.) It's those challenges and the title of "world's largest" that keep customers coming. Oh, and in case you're wondering; the 100-pounder doesn't come cheap—one burger with all the fixings will set you back about $380.

For more roadside attractions,
turn to page 12.

• •

Did You Know?

Pennsylvania's Susquehanna River provides half of the fresh water found in the Chesapeake Bay—the largest estuary in the United States—even though the bay doesn't touch Pennsylvania at all.

Down in the Valley

*Most people know about George Washington's Revolutionary
War triumph at Valley Forge. But what makes the story
even more remarkable is how many of Washington's
men didn't survive that winter—and why.*

How Bad Was It?

In December 1777, General Washington and the Continental
Army were in full retreat from a British force that was bigger,
better armed, and better fed. With the Americans driven out
of New York and unable to protect the nation's new capital of
Philadelphia, the British took over the city. Washington's troops
were forced to flee to Valley Forge, a village on the Schuylkill
River about 20 miles northwest of Philadelphia. Washington's
force was about 12,000 strong but was facing more than 30,000
British. The Americans were so short of supplies that thousands of them didn't even have shoes.

The exhausted rebels were stuck. Hemmed in by the superior
British forces, they were short on food, there was no shelter
available, and within days of their arrival, six inches of snow
had fallen. According to the French Marquis de Lafayette, "The
unfortunate soldiers were in want of everything; they had neither coats nor hats, nor shirts, nor shoes. Their feet and their
legs froze until they were black, and it was often necessary to
amputate them."

Nature 1, Americans 0

The British expected that the coming winter would bring
defeat to the threadbare American army, but Washington

thought differently. He made shelter his first priority. He divided his men into squads of 12 and ordered each group to build itself a small log hut. As an extra incentive, the general promised $12 to the group that built a shelter in the "quickest, most workmanlike manner." The soldiers lacked the proper tools and had to scrounge for building supplies, but by February, they had created a small town of huts against the freezing landscape.

Survival was still dicey, though. Washington had written to the U.S. government warning that if no supplies came, his hungry army would have to disband to keep from starving. But the new United States was disorganized and lacked experience and money. Plus, with the nation's army outnumbered, the government couldn't get its supply wagons past the British.

They got some help when Chief Shenandoah and the nearby Oneida Indians brought the troops 600 bushels of corn. He also sent an Oneida woman to teach the soldiers how to prepare the vegetable. But Washington's troops subsisted mainly on water and "firecake"—a mixture of flour, water, and salt (if a soldier was lucky enough to have salt) that was baked on hot rocks or in the fire. The soldiers tried to hunt and forage, but winter had left the area nearly barren.

Casualties at Camp

Still, the lack of food, the ever-present British threat, and the cold weren't the worst killers at Valley Forge—sickness was. Spring brought warmer weather and more food, but thanks to the crowded quarters and 18th-century sanitation (there was none), diseases like the flu, typhus, and dysentery spread through the camp.

Washington tried to keep the diseases from turning into an

all-out epidemic. He had two hospitals built and made sure doctors were always available. He also petitioned the government for milk and medicines for his soldiers and ordered that his troops be inoculated against smallpox. But the diseases still took a heavy toll. During the encampment, more than 2,500 soldiers died, all without a shot being fired.

Patience and Obedience Unparalleled

Despite these miserable conditions, the sick, shivering, starving soldiers remained loyal to the patriot cause. Washington wrote:

> To see the men without clothes to cover their nakedness, without blankets to lie upon, without shoes . . . without a house or hut to cover them until those could be built, and submitting without a murmur, is a proof of patience and obedience which, in my opinion, can scarcely be paralleled.

Even more amazing was that the men used their time at Valley Forge to become a superior fighting force. One of the new recruits who arrived in camp at the end of February was Baron Friedrich Wilhelm von Steuben, who had been a member of Frederick the Great's Prussian army. Washington immediately put him in charge of training. Von Steuben drilled and trained the Americans, teaching them new military skills and turning the woodsmen, tradesmen, and farmers of the Continental Army into professional soldiers ready to push their way out of the valley and take on the British again.

Forging Ahead

They got some more help in May 1778 when France came to their aid, giving the patriots new allies and supplies. Then on June 19, six months after their arrival, the Continental Army marched out of Valley Forge. They were still outnumbered and undersupplied, but when they marched into New Jersey nine days later, they took on British troops at the battle of Monmouth and drove them from the battlefield. Washington's men held the area for another three years until the Americans finally beat the British once and for all at Yorktown.

Today, the encampment where Washington's army spent that winter is the 3,600-acre Valley Forge National Historical Park. Washington's original stone headquarters has been restored and furnished, and the log huts that saved the army from freezing have been reconstructed to retell the incredible story of perseverance and survival.

Did You Know?

Many people from northwestern Pennsylvania swear they've seen a 30-foot-long sea serpent named Bessie living in Lake Erie. The legend began as early as 1817 but seems to have picked up steam since the 1960s. Fishermen often report hearing strange slapping noises on the lake, feeling something bumping against their boats, and even seeing a prehistoric-looking monster with scales. Most scientists insist that Bessie is nothing more than lore and claim that it's more likely the fishermen are seeing lake sturgeon, a type of fish that can grow to be four feet long and weigh 100 pounds. Sturgeon also have bony plates on their backs and whiskerlike organs called barbels hanging from their lower jaws. Still, many people of the Lake Erie region remain convinced that Bessie is real—the Ohio city of Huron even offers a reward for her safe capture.

Queen of the Jail

From our archives: a true story of danger,
seduction, betrayal, and a deadly escape.

The Setting

Allegheny County Jail, Pittsburgh, 1901

The Cast

Katherine Soffel (the warden's beautiful wife), Ed Biddle
(famous outlaw), Jack Biddle (Ed's younger brother and
accomplice), Peter Soffel (prison warden)

Prologue

Jack and Ed were known as "the Biddle Boys," leaders of a gang
of small-time outlaws who relied more on brains than brawn to
carry out their nefarious crimes. Sometimes they used chloro-
form to render their victims unconscious; sometimes they used
beautiful women as distractions. They carried guns, too . . . just
in case.

On April 12, 1901, the gang was robbing a house next to a
small grocery store in Mt. Washington, Pennsylvania. A female
accomplice kept the grocer occupied while the boys searched
the adjoining house, looking for a pile of cash. The distraction
didn't work, though—the grocer heard a noise and went to
investigate. A struggle ensued, shots were fired, and the grocer
ended up dead on his living room floor. The Biddle brothers
fled the scene and holed up nearby, but the police soon caught
up with them. After a shootout in which a police officer was
killed, the outlaws were arrested. The trial was quick and the

sentence severe: the Biddle Boys were to be hanged for their crimes on February 25, 1902.

Secret Love Affair

Prison warden Peter Soffel and his wife Katherine were in the midst of a divorce when the Biddles arrived at the Allegheny County Jail. Katherine spent most of her time visiting the prisoners, offering them spiritual advice and bringing them Bibles. For the inmates, Katherine Soffel was a welcome sight—they called her the "Queen of the Jail."

She first went to see the Biddles out of curiosity. Their exploits had made them notorious, and Ed's charm and good looks soon won her over. She became infatuated and visited him more and more often, at least 25 times over the next few months, sneaking him food and books. The warden knew his wife had taken an interest in the outlaw, but he must not have realized how keen an interest it was, because he didn't stop her from visiting.

After a few months, Ed and Jack convinced Katherine that they were innocent and asked her to help them escape so they could live honest lives as coal miners in Canada. She agreed.

Daring Escape

Katherine's room was so close by that Ed could see it from his cell window. The two devised a secret code: Katherine would point to various parts of her body that represented different letters and to spell out messages about the warden's movements. The two brothers then came up with a plan. They asked Katherine to smuggle in two saws and a revolver. Again, she agreed.

On January 29, 1902, the brothers cut through their cell

bars, overpowered three guards, and locked them in a cell. As the Biddles hurried from the prison, Katherine came out to meet them . . . which was not a part of the plan. She was supposed to lie low and meet them in Canada a month later. But to their surprise, she'd taken a page out of their book, chloroformed her husband, and then snuck away in the night.

The warden awoke to a nasty headache and an empty house. When he was told the Biddle Boys had escaped, he knew Katherine was involved and immediately put out an all-points bulletin on the three of them.

On the Run

Meanwhile, Ed had agreed to let Katherine come along, much to the dismay of his brother Jack, who thought she'd slow them down. They stole a horse and sleigh from a nearby farm and made it to Cooperstown, 38 miles north of Pittsburgh. They planned to have a quiet breakfast and slip away unnoticed, but news of the breakout had beat them there and the police were on their trail.

Final Showdown

On January 31, 1902, just outside the town of Mount Chestnut, the Biddle Boys and Katherine Soffel ran into a posse at the crest of a snowy hill. Ed stopped the sleigh, handed the reins to Katherine, and then he and Jack jumped off, each with a gun in hand. The sheriff told them to surrender, but Ed opened fire. The lawmen responded with a hail of bullets.

When the shootout was over, Ed was shot twice, Jack 15 times, and Katherine—who had grabbed a gun and joined in the fray—was shot once by Ed after pleading with him to take her life. (She didn't want to live without him.)

The three were taken to nearby Butler Hospital. Katherine's wound was treatable; Ed and Jack were not so lucky. As he lay on his deathbed, Ed told police he'd never loved Katherine, that he just used her to help him escape. Katherine claimed that Ed was just saying that to protect her, and love letters he'd written her while still in prison seemed to back her up. And Jack? He died, along with his brother, on the night of February 1, 1902.

Postmortem

The Biddle Boys' bodies were put on display at the Allegheny County Jail for two hours. More than 4,000 people came to see the famous bandits. Katherine served 20 months in prison and died on August 30, 1909.

Did You Know?

During the 1700s, it usually took two weeks for a letter to travel from Philadelphia to New York since all mail was carried by ship because the roads over land were poorly maintained and marked. When Benjamin Franklin became Philadelphia's first postmaster in 1737, his first order of business was to improve the postal system. He built roads and set up a 24-hour mail wagon that traveled from Philadelphia to New York during the day and night. Under Franklin's supervision, the travel time for a piece of mail between major colonial cities was cut in half.

Quotable Cosby

Comedian Bill Cosby is one of the most famous people to be raised in Philadelphia. And like fellow Philadelphian Benjamin Franklin, Cosby can be both witty and wise. Here's some of what he's had to say.

"Always end the name of your child with a vowel so that when you yell, the name will carry."

"Decide that you want it more than you are afraid of it."

"I don't know the key to success, but the key to failure is trying to please everybody."

"When you become senile, you won't know it."

"A word to the wise ain't necessary. It's the stupid ones who need the advice."

"I want to die before my wife, and the reason is this: If it is true that when you die, your soul goes up to judgment, I don't want my wife up there ahead of me to tell them things."

"Did you ever see the customers in health-food stores? They are pale, skinny people who look half dead. In a steak house, you see robust, ruddy people. They're dying, of course, but they look terrific."

"Gray hair is God's graffiti."

"Every closed eye is not sleeping, and every open eye is not seeing."

"Immortality is a long shot, I admit. But somebody has to be first."

Pennsylvania's Grand Canyon

. . . and some other natural wonders in the Keystone State.

The Allegheny Petroglyphs

Five miles south of the town of Franklin in northwest Pennsylvania is the Indian God Rock, a large boulder that sits on the bank of the Allegheny River. The 22-foot-high rock is covered with hundreds of ancient petroglyphs: images of people, hands, animals, arrows, and geometric designs. Archaeologists believe they were carved between the tenth and the seventeenth centuries, probably by ancestors of the region's Algonquin Indians. But some historians say the petroglyphs resemble ones made by Europeans and may have been carved by European explorers—possibly Vikings.

Coral Caverns

This deep cave system in south-central Pennsylvania is the only fossilized coral reef cavern known in the world. Discovered by miners quarrying for lime in 1928, the cave's defining feature is a towering wall that was once a living coral reef lying on the seabed of an ancient ocean. It's covered with fossils of tiny sea creatures that lived more than 400 million years ago.

Triple Divide Summit

The Triple Divide Summit, located in Potter County on the New York border, isn't much to look at—it's just a mountaintop about 2,500 feet high. But it has the distinction of being a major "hydrographic triple divide point" of North America, meaning that the water that falls on it can end up in one of the continent's major drainage areas. Depending on where it lands, rain falling on Triple Divide Summit can flow north and end up in the St. Lawrence River and then Hudson Bay; east and into the Atlantic Ocean; or south to the Ohio and Mississippi rivers and then into the Gulf of Mexico.

Archbald Pothole

Archbald Pothole State Park, northeast of Scranton, features one of the world's largest known potholes—depressions cut into solid rock by swirling water . . . in this case, water from glaciers that melted during the last ice age. The massive Archbald Pothole—it's about 40 feet deep and 40 feet across—formed between 10,000 and 30,000 years ago.

Pennsylvania's "Grand Canyon"

Located in Tioga State Forest in the north-central part of the state, Pine Creek Gorge is known as the "Grand Canyon of Pennsylvania." The long, forested gorge runs nearly straight for more than 40 miles, is more than a mile wide, and is more than 1,000 feet deep. Hiking trails line the rim and the gorge floor, and the area is home to a vast array of wildlife, including bald and golden eagles, ospreys, wild turkeys, otters, fishers, porcupines—and lots of black bears.

• •

Did You Know?
Condé Nast Traveler magazine ranks Pittsburgh's International Airport as the eighth-best airport in the world . . . and the best in the United States.

The Sweet Life of Milton Hershey

Today, the name Hershey is synonymous with sweet treats. But did you know that the man behind the brand built an entire community in Pennsylvania—and then kept its citizens employed through the Great Depression?

Hershey, Pennsylvania, is a town built for fun. Not only is it the unofficial "chocolate capital of the world" and the self-proclaimed "sweetest place on Earth," it's also home to a chocolate factory, a theme park, a zoo, and a chocolate spa . . . where guests can take a whipped cocoa bath or get a chocolate fondue wrap. And it was all the vision of one man: Milton S. Hershey.

Milking It

Hershey founded the Hershey Company in 1894 in his hometown of Derry Church, Pennsylvania. The son of Mennonite farmers, he'd become an apprentice to a candy maker in Lancaster when he was a teenager, and in 1875, at the age of 18, he moved to Philadelphia to open his own candy business. That shop failed after just a few years, so he headed to Colorado, where he took on another apprenticeship, this time with a caramel manufacturer.

It was during this trip that Hershey perfected a caramel recipe with extra milk, which resulted in a softer, tastier product. Armed with his new caramels, he headed back to

Lancaster, where there were plenty of dairy cattle to provide milk for his new candy. Then in 1883, after two other shops failed (one in Chicago and another in New York), he had a hit: his Pennsylvania-based Lancaster Caramel Company became a commercial success, and its caramels were popular all over the United States and Europe.

The Chocolate King

Hershey wasn't done coming up with new kinds of candy, though. At the 1893 World's Columbian Exposition in Chicago, he saw an exhibit of German chocolate makers who added milk to the otherwise crumbly candy to create creamy milk chocolate.

Intrigued by the process, Hershey had one of the German machines sent to Pennsylvania and decided to devote his career to manufacturing an affordable domestic version of milk chocolate. He created the Hershey Chocolate Company in 1894 and, six years later, gave up on caramel and turned his attentions entirely to chocolate. He sold his Lancaster Caramel Company and used the profits (about $1 million) to buy 40,000 acres in Derry Church. The area provided everything he needed: access to the nearby Susquehanna River for shipping, abundant dairy farms for milk, and a willing workforce. By 1905, Hershey was operating the largest chocolate manufacturing plant in the world, and a year later, the town of Derry Church was renamed to honor him. Hershey, Pennsylvania, was born.

The Park that Chocolate Built

The chocolate-making business made Milton Hershey one of the wealthiest men in the country. And he decided to invest some of his money in the workers who had contributed to his success. To make the company's town as fulfilling a place to live as possible, Hershey created an entire community around his factory, including homes, an accessible public transportation system, and lavish recreational opportunities. In 1907, he built a small neighborhood park for his employees to enjoy on their days off. Initially, the park was landscaped with trees and ponds, but over the years, Hershey added a swimming pool, a bandstand and pavilion (the site of company-sponsored concerts and theater productions), a bowling alley, and a carousel. By the mid-1930s, the park included a fun house, a water flume ride, a roller coaster, and a penny arcade.

For many years, the park remained just a local attraction. But as more people outside of Hershey started to visit, it seemed logical that the park should incorporate and expand. So in the 1970s, the company park officially became Hershey Park, an amusement complex that today sits on more than 100 acres and boasts 60 rides—including 10 roller coasters. Next door is Hershey's Chocolate World, which offers guests chocolate-themed shopping and restaurants.

Philanthropy Brings Sweet Dreams

The amusement park wasn't all that Milton Hershey gave to his workers. The Great Depression hit Pennsylvania hard, and the craftsmen who'd built the town fell on tough times. Hershey, on the other hand, was producing cheap, tasty chocolate, and his business had barely suffered. So he conjured up the Hotel Hershey and hired 800 local laborers to build it. His primary stipulation was that the dining room not have any corners. Hershey had spent a lot of time in fancy hotels where bad tippers were banished to corner tables, and he didn't want visitors to his hotel to encounter the same fate.

The workers completed the hotel—circular dining room and all—in little more than a year, and since the grand opening in 1933, it has been in continuous operation. Today, the Hotel Hershey is a member of the Historic Hotels of America.

Hershey also invested his money in education. Growing up in rural Pennsylvania, he hadn't had much access to good schools. So he invested millions of dollars in the Hershey Industrial School for orphaned boys. In 1918, he donated much of his fortune—including his controlling interest in the Hershey Chocolate Company—to a trust that would be used to run the school. Today, the 10,000-acre Milton Hershey School educates and houses about 1,700 children (girls and boys) from low-income families or who are in foster care.

Milton Hershey died in 1945, but his chocolate empire now makes about $5 billion a year and employs more than 13,000 people. His town and amusement park are Pennsylvania staples, and his philanthropic endeavors (including his school) have built hospitals, theaters, and gardens throughout the state.

Did You Know?

According to Retail Confectioners International—a Chicago-based company that looks out for the interests of candy makers—Pennsylvania is home to more than 10 percent of its members.

Fly Like an Eagle

A few fascinating facts about the Philadelphia Eagles.

The National Football League's Eagles were founded by Pennsylvanians Bert Bell and Lud Wray in 1933 (the same year as—but a few months before—the Steelers).

Name: Bell and Wray choose Eagles after being inspired by the insignia of a large blue eagle that symbolized President Franklin D. Roosevelt's New Deal program.

Colors: Midnight green, black, white, and silver

Logo: From 1948 to 1996, the Eagles logo changed a few times, but it was always a version of a green eagle with outstretched wings. Since 1996, it's been just the head of an eagle.

Stats

Like most new NFL teams, the Eagles got off to a bad start. They lost their first game to the New York Giants by a humiliating score of 56–0, and over the next 10 years won only 23 games total. (They lost 81, and four games ended in ties.) Things finally got going in the 1940s, and in 1947 the Eagles made it to their first NFL Championship game. They lost, but returned the next year and, in what was known as the "Blizzard Bowl," won their first NFL Championship, beating the Chicago Cardinals 7–0 in a blinding snowstorm. They won a second championship in 1949, beating the Los Angeles Rams 14–0.

The 1960 NFL season, though, is the most celebrated in the franchise's history. On December 26, after a 10–2 season, the Eagles met Vince Lombardi's Green Bay Packers in the NFL Championship game and beat them 17–13. It's the only playoff game that Lombardi's Packers ever lost.

In the years since, the Eagles haven't managed to win another championship. They made it back to the playoffs in 1978 and to the Super Bowl twice, in 1981 and in 2005, but lost both times.

Eagle Extras

- Seven Eagles players have been inducted into the NFL's Hall of Fame: Chuck Bednarik, Bob "Boomer" Brown, Sonny Jurgensen, Tommy McDonald, Pete Pihos, Steve Van Buren, and Reggie White.
- At halftime during a game against the Minnesota Vikings on December 15, 1968—the last game of a season in which the Eagles won just two games—a man in a Santa suit was on the field as part of a Christmas parade. The notoriously bad-tempered Eagles fans booed him . . . and pelted him with snowballs.
- Quarterback Donovan McNabb holds the NFL record for the most consecutive completed passes. Over the course of two games in 2004, McNabb connected with his receivers 24 straight times.
- In 1992, Eagles running back Herschel Walker competed in the Winter Olympics in Albertville, France. He placed seventh in the two-man bobsled competition.
- In 1975, a bartender and former track star named Vince Papale got a chance to try out for the Eagles. He was 30 at the time and had not played football in college (he played only one year in high school). Still, he made the team. He played for two seasons and is the oldest rookie in NFL history. (Papale was the subject of the 2006 film *Invincible*, starring Mark Wahlberg.)

Roll Out the Barrels

On page 268, we told you about Rolling Rock and the Latrobe Brewing Company, but Pennsylvania is actually home to more than 70 breweries, including the nation's oldest.

D.G. Yuengling and Son

German beer brewer David G. Jüngling immigrated to the United States in 1823. He changed the spelling of his name to Yuengling and, six years later, opened his first brewery: the Eagle Brewery in Pottsville. It was the first large commercial brewery in the United States. The brewery's name changed to D.G. Yuengling and Son in 1873, when Frederick Yuengling joined his father. The brewery is still operating, is the sixth-largest in the country, and is still owned by the Yuengling family.

Lancaster Brewing Company

The city of Lancaster, in the heart of Pennsylvanian Dutch country, became a hotbed of beer brewing in the late 1700s, when Scottish and English immigrants brewed beer for their inns and taverns. In the 1840s, German immigrants added their own lagers, and the region became known as the "Munich of the United States." It's been home to several breweries since then, but only the Lancaster Brewing Company is still around today. That company makes several kinds of beer, including Amish Four Grain, Hop Hog IPA, and Milk Stout, a sweet, English-style beer.

Iron City Brewing Company

This Pittsburgh brewhouse has been around since 1861 and has had a tumultuous history. Founded by German immigrant

Edward Frauenheim in 1861 as the Iron City Brewing Company, it merged with 11 other local breweries in 1899 to create the colossal Pittsburgh Brewing Company—the third-largest in the country. The company survived Prohibition by making soft drinks and near-beer (which has little or no alcohol in it). Between 1986 and 2005, the brewery changed owners several times and continually lost money. Finally, in 2005, it filed for bankruptcy. Two years later, the equity firm Unified Growth Partners bought the brewery—and changed its name back to the Iron City Brewing Company. Today, it's the thirteenth-largest brewery in the United States.

Straub Brewery

Straub's story goes back to 1872, when German immigrant Peter P. Straub got a job brewing at Captain Charles C. Volk's Lager Beer and Eating Saloon in St. Mary's (north-central Pennsylvania). Four years later, he bought the business and renamed it the Benzinger Spring Brewery. Peter Straub ran the company until 1912, when his son Anthony took over and renamed it Peter Straub Sons' Brewery. It's been owned by the family ever since and today is just called the Straub Brewery.

Quote Me

"Beer is proof that God loves us and wants us to be happy."

—Benjamin Franklin

Keystone Quiz

*Put on your Keystone thinking caps and see how
well you do. (Answers are on page 309.)*

1. Name the dam in the Allegheny National Forest that created
Pennsylvania's deepest lake. (Extra credit: Name the lake.)

2. Name the five most populated cities in Pennsylvania.
(Feeling extra smart? Name the ten largest.)

3. Name the *Saturday Night Live* comedienne from Upper
Darby who made political-parody history in 2008.

4. What's the shortest route from Pennsylvania to Canada, and
how far is it?

5. Remove a letter from the name of this Pennsylvania river
(and county), and you'll have something to wear comfortably
in Rome.

6. Name three mountain ranges in the Keystone State.

7. Andy Warhol had a stuffed dog named Cecil that's now on
display at the Andy Warhol Museum. Where's the museum?
(Hint: It's in the city where Warhol grew up.)

8. Speaking of dogs . . . the Great Dane is Pennsylvania's official state dog because another famous Pennsylvanian owned
one. Who was it?

It's a Zoo, Too

On page 95 we introduced the mammals found in Pennsylvania.
Here are a few less cuddly animals that call the state home.

Eagles

In 1980, Pennsylvania had only three known nesting pairs
of bald eagles. Even though the birds are still considered
threatened today, conservation efforts over the last three
decades have brought their numbers up to more than 100
pairs. Migrating eagles pass through, too.

Timber Rattlesnakes

Of Pennsylvania's 22 native snakes, timber rattlers are the
largest. They can grow to more than five feet long, and are one
of the most venomous (and dangerous) snakes in North
America.

Burrowing Crayfish

These crustaceans grow to be about three inches long, have
powerful pincers, and live in wet, marshy, or grassy regions,
where they dig burrows about six feet deep. Wondering if you
have burrowing crayfish near your home? Check the edges of
nearby streams or ponds and look for their burrows, which
have a distinct hardened "chimney" made of mud.

Eastern Hellbenders

Twenty-two species of salamanders call Pennsylvania home;
one of those is the eastern hellbender, which live entirely in
water. They're a splotchy olive-brown color, with flaps and

folds of skin hanging from their sides—and can grow to be more than two feet long, making them the third-largest aquatic salamander in the world. Another remarkable feature: their lifespan—one raised in captivity lived for 29 years.

Bog Turtles

These turtles are among the smallest in the world; they grow only to about four inches in length. But they can live for up to 30 years. With their black or deep-brown shells and yellow/orange splotches behind their ears, they're easy to spot.

The turtles get their name from the fact that every fall, usually in September, they bury themselves in mud at the bottom of a bog and hibernate for about six months. Like many turtles, they manage to get oxygen during hibernation not by breathing, but through specialized skin cells on their necks and at the base of their tails that extract oxygen from the water.

Did You Know?

The Hershey Chocolate Company helped Uncle Sam during World War II by supplying chocolate bars to the troops. More than 3 billion "Ration D" bars were manufactured and distributed to U.S. soldiers between 1943 and 1945. By the end of World War II, the Hershey factory was turning out the chocolate bars at the rate of 24 million per week.

Pennsylvania By the Letters

*Uncle John's Bathroom Reader salutes the great
state of Pennsylvania . . . alphabet-style.*

P . . . is for PENSYLVANIA, which is how the state's name was
spelled on the U.S. Constitution's list of signatories. (Earlier in
the document—in Article I, Section II—it's spelled correctly.)
It's also spelled with one "n" on one of the most famous state
symbols . . . the Liberty Bell. (And "P" is for "Pennsylvania,"
the only state that starts with the letter P.)

E . . . is for ERCILDOUN, a Quaker hamlet in the far southeast
corner of the state. The name was taken from a poem by
Scottish writer Sir Walter Scott.

N . . . is for NORTH SIDE, the part of Pittsburgh just north of
the Allegheny and Ohio rivers. North Side is home to Heinz
Field, where the Pittsburgh Steelers play football. It was also
the location of the first modern baseball World Series, in which
the Boston Americans beat the Pittsburgh Pirates five games to
three. The proper pronunciation of "North Side": "Nahth Side."

N . . . is also for Joe NAMATH, a.k.a., Broadway Joe, quarterback of the New York Jets from 1965 to 1976. Namath, a
Pennsylvania sports legend, was born in Beaver Falls in 1943.
His Hungarian grandfather had settled in Pittsburgh to work in
the steel mills, and the spelling of the family name back then
was Nemeth. What does that mean in Hungarian? "German."

S . . . is for STEAGLES. In 1943, the Pittsburgh Steelers and Philadelphia Eagles merged because the military draft during World War II had depleted the number of men available to play. The team was officially known as the "Eagles–Steelers" but became unofficially known as the "Steagles." Most memorable moment: During the third game of the season, against the New York Giants, the Steagles fumbled a record 10 times. More memorable: they still won, 28–14.

Y . . . is for YODEL, which many music historians believe arrived in the United States with German-speaking immigrants, many of whom settled Pennsylvania in the 1600s. (The word "yodel" comes from the German *jödeln* and first appeared in the United States in the 1820s.)

L . . . is for LAST. Pennsylvania was one of the last states to ratify the 18th Amendment to the Constitution, which prohibited the manufacture and sale of alcoholic beverages. (Prohibition passed on February 26, 1919.) Pennsylvania was also the last state to make winemaking legal again after Prohibition was repealed in 1933.

V . . . is for VETCH, as in Penngift Crownvetch, Pennsylvania's official "beautification and conservation plant." The general assembly gave the plant (with its white and lavender flowers) its special distinction in 1982.

A . . . is for ABOLITION. Pennsylvania was the first state to abolish slavery—all the way back in 1780—before the Revolutionary War was even over.

N . . . is for N AGAIN. Pennsylvania is the only state with three Ns in its name.

I . . . is for INDEPENDENCE. It's everywhere: Pennsylvania is officially known as the "State of Independence." Historical items are kept in Philadelphia's Independence National Historical Park, there's a town called Independence, and thousands of businesses in the state have "Independence" in their names, including Independence Blue Cross, Independence Answering Service, Independence Biofuels, and Independence Communications—the state's largest provider of Muzak.

A . . . is for AMERICAN ALPHABET. Of the many things Benjamin Franklin invented, one of the oddest was an alphabet that he thought more accurately reflected American English. It was phonetic, which Franklin believed would make it easier for children and foreigners to learn. Franklin's alphabet consisted of 26 letters, but six of them—C, J, Q, W, X, and Y—were replaced with new ones he invented. Franklin tried to get the new alphabet accepted for decades, but it never caught on.

● ●

Did You Know?

The northern Pennsylvania town of Mansfield proudly claims that it was the site of the first lighted nighttime football game in 1892.

Answers

Welcome to Penn State, page 88

Let Freedom Ring, page 109

1. Legend. The bell traveled on a ship called the *Hibernia*, which was known to have transported dry goods and passengers to the colonies from England and Ireland. Historians do not believe it was a slave ship.

2. A little of both. The bell arrived in Pennsylvania in 1752 and was set up in Independence Square to be tested before it was hung in the State House steeple. On its very first ring, the bell did crack—its metal was so brittle that it broke at the stroke of the clapper. But the ringing and cracking occurred in March 1753, not on the Fourth of July.

3. Fact. Government officials tried to return the broken bell to England, but there wasn't enough room on the ship so the captain left it on the dock. Next, the bell went to John Pass and

John Snow, Philadelphia foundry workers who broke it down and recast it, adding more copper to the bell's metal alloy. Pass and Snow's bell was stronger, but its tone was poor (the result of too much copper), so they recast it again, using silver and other metals to sweeten its sound.

That second casting rang in the key of E flat, but some people (particularly Pennsylvania assembly speaker Isaac Norris) still didn't like the sound. So Norris commissioned a whole new bell from Whitechapel. When that one arrived, though, it sounded no different from the original. So the Pass/Snow bell remained in the State House steeple and was rung to call the assembly to order or to signal important announcements. Today it's known as the Liberty Bell. It's 3 feet high, with a circumference of 12 feet at the lip, and is composed of about 70 percent copper, 25 percent tin, 2 percent lead, 1 percent zinc, 0.25 percent arsenic, and 0.2 percent silver, with trace amounts of gold, magnesium, and nickel. The other bell found a home, too: the Pennsylvania government hung it in a cupola at the State House.

4. Legend. The Declaration of Independence went to the printer on July 4, 1776, and was read publicly on July 8. Other bells did toll in Philadelphia on that day, but the State House belfry was so dilapidated that the Liberty Bell couldn't be rung—people worried that the tower would collapse.

The legend of the Liberty Bell and the Declaration came from an 1847 short story by George Lippard that was published in the *Saturday Currier*. In Lippard's story, the State House bellman rang the Liberty Bell when his grandson came running with news of independence, shouting, "Ring, Grandfather! Ring!" Over time, that fictional story became accepted as historical fact.

The Liberty Bell did ring for other important events leading up to the American Revolution, including the 1757 and 1764 meetings of the Pennsylvania assembly that sent Benjamin Franklin to England to redress colonial grievances. In 1771, the Liberty Bell called the assembly together to petition King George for a repeal of tea taxes, and in April 1775, it pealed to proclaim the Battles of Lexington and Concord.

5. Fact. In September 1777, the British attacked General George Washington's troops at the battle of Brandywine. The Brits won that battle and marched toward Philadelphia. The Americans, afraid the British would capture the bell and melt it down, had the Liberty Bell removed from its steeple, and Colonel Thomas Polk, along with 200 militiamen, escorted the bell to Allentown. Today, visitors to Allentown can see where the bell was hidden under the floor of the Zion Reformed Church.

6. Fact. After the British were defeated, the Liberty Bell was brought back to Philadelphia, but the State House steeple was still too unstable for the bell to be rehung. It wasn't until 1785 that the steeple was rebuilt and the bell rehung. In 1788, it rang to celebrate the ratification of the U.S. Constitution. It also rang to celebrate patriotic occasions such as the inauguration of John Adams and to mourn the deaths of famous Americans like Benjamin Franklin, George Washington, and Alexander Hamilton.

7. Legend. The first known use of the name "Liberty Bell" dates to 1835. An abolitionist publication called the *Anti-Slavery Record* noted that the "liberty bell" was rung to celebrate freedom on the Fourth of July even though "one sixth of all inhabitants of the country" were in "abject slavery." Abolitionists took up the name, and in 1839, an abolitionist poem entitled "Liberty Bell" caught the public's attention. Eventually, Americans came to call Philadelphia's bell by that name.

8. Fact. From 1885 to 1915, the Liberty Bell traveled by train to world's fairs across the United States. In 1902, it was involved in an accident when the locomotive transporting it to an exposition in South Carolina collided with another train. The bell's last tour was in 1915, when it traveled to San Francisco for the Panama-Pacific International Exposition.

9. Legend. Philadelphia reporters noted that the "old bell" tolled on April 7, 1841, when President William Henry Harrison died, and there was no mention of a crack. However, an article published in 1848 in Philadelphia's newspaper the *Public Ledger* mentioned that the bell had cracked in 1845. Whenever it occurred, a hairline crack was repaired so the bell would hold together and ring on George Washington's birthday on February 22, 1846. But as the *Ledger* reported, "It gave out clear notes and loud . . . until noon, when it received a sort of compound facture in a zig-zag direction through one of its sides, which put it completely out of tune." The bell had cracked up to the crown, and it hasn't been rung since.

10. Legend . . . and hoax. On April 1, 1996, Taco Bell ran a full-page ad in the *New York Times* announcing that it had purchased the Liberty Bell to help reduce the national debt and was renaming it the "Taco Liberty Bell." It was just an April Fool's joke, but it backfired—many customers were offended.

Colonial Philly, page 114

B	A	I	T		G	M	A	N		D	A	N	C	E
M	U	T	E		R	A	B	E		A	R	E	A	S
O	R	E	M		U	T	N	E		S	M	I	L	E
C	A	R	P	E	N	T	E	R	S	H	A	L	L	
	L	A	D	E	R		T	E	N					
T	R	E	A	T	Y		S	E	R	I	O	U	S	
S	E	T	T	O		S	I	C	A		G	N	P	
A	T	H	E	N	S	O	F	A	M	E	R	I	C	A
R	I	A		L	A	I	R		S	A	L	L	Y	
S	E	N	A	T	O	R		S	T	I	L	E	S	
	S	A	M		A	T	H	O	L					
N	A	T	I	O	N	S	C	A	P	I	T	A	L	
M	O	G	U	L		I	C	E	R		N	A	N	U
O	N	E	T	O		N	I	L	E		G	R	I	T
P	O	S	E	R		A	I	L	S		S	A	L	E

The Pittsburgh Pirates Quiz, page 169

1. C. The team that eventually became the Pirates started playing in the American Association, an early pro league, in 1882. Other teams in that league that became current major league teams were the Cincinnati Red Stockings (the Reds), the St. Louis Brown Stockings (Cardinals), and the Brooklyn Atlantics (Dodgers). In 1887, the Pittsburgh team became part of the National League. Its first NL game: a win against the Chicago White Stockings (now the Cubs) by a score of 6–2.

2. A. The team originally played in Allegheny City, across the Allegheny River from Pittsburgh. But when it joined the National League, the name changed to the Pittsburgh

Alleghenies, even though technically games were still played in Allegheny City. (The other names listed are from American Association teams in Brooklyn, Cleveland, and Cincinnati, respectively.)

3. D. The team played in Allegheny City until 1908. In December 1907, Pittsburgh annexed the area, so when the 1908 season rolled around, the team finally got to play in the city of Pittsburgh even though it was playing on the same field as the year before.

4. B. The team took the name Pirates in 1891 after "stealing" second baseman Lou Bierbauer from the Philadelphia Athletics. (The Athletics left Bierbauer off their reserve list, but assumed he'd stay with the team. He didn't.) The Athletics complained mightily, calling the signing "piratical." The Pittsburgh team, amused by the outrage, decided to become the Pirates. The name finally made it onto the team jerseys in 1912.

5. B. In 1890, the then-Alleghenies lost many of their players to the competing Pittsburgh Burghers. This weakened the team and led to a 23–113 season. The disastrous showing put the team's owner, Dennis McKnight, in the hole financially, and he had to sell the team. But McKnight had a plan: he bought a stake in the Burghers and then bought the Alleghenies again. That allowed him to merge the two teams (and the lost players) into one strong team.

6. B or D . . . depending on how technical you want to get. The Pirates won the NL pennant in 1901 and 1902, before the World Series existed. Since there's been a World Series, the Pirates have failed to win it only twice after winning the pennant: in 1903 (the very first World Series, which they lost to Boston) and again in 1927 (swept by the Yankees). They notched World Series wins in 1909, 1925, 1960, 1971, and 1979.

A Penn-y for Your Thoughts, page 180

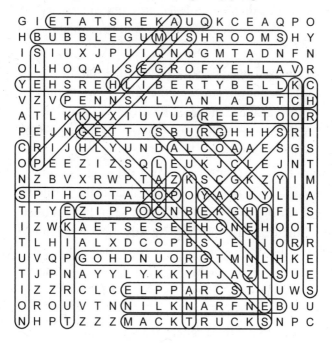

Oh, the Symbolism, page 211

1. **A.** White-tailed deer live all over the United States except in the Southwest, Hawaii, and Alaska.

2. **B.** Pennsylvania's top milk-producing county is Lancaster.

3. **B.** Because it lives in cold-weather areas, the ruffed grouse has adapted to survive. In the winter, the birds grow projections off of their toes that act like snowshoes, and they can even spend the night burrowed under soft snow to keep warm.

4. **C.** Tylerville fisherman Vonada Ranck holds the record for catching the largest brook trout in state history: it was 22 inches long and weighed 7 pounds.

5. **B.** Rumor has it that Governor Pinchot actually preferred the azalea to the mountain laurel and was going to make that the state's flower. But he deferred to his wife, who loved mountain laurels.

6. A. Trilobites went extinct about 250 million years ago.

7. C. There are about 2,000 species of fireflies in the world; they live mostly in warm, humid areas.

8. A. Eddie Khoury and Ronnie Bonner wrote the song's music and lyrics.

9. C. The K4s was the Pennsylvania Railroad's main passenger train between 1914 and 1957. At one time, the "Pennsy" had 425 of these engines in its fleet, but only two are still around today. One is at the Railroad Museum of Pennsylvania in Strasburg. The other used to be on display in Altoona, but suffered so much wear and tear from years outside that's it's being restored.

10. B. Eastern hemlocks can grow to more than 100 feet high and live for 800 years.

The Joy of Sects, page 225

1. A or C. Bravo if you eliminated Quakers and Moravians right away—they don't wear old-fashioned clothes. As for the other two, take another look at the clothes. Color doesn't matter, but patterns do. Are the dresses striped, checked, flowered, plaid, or plain? The Amish wear only solid colors, so anything else suggests the girls are Mennonites.

2. D. Amish communities do not have churches. Instead, they hold Sunday services in different homes each week, so a wagonload of benches is delivered to the designated house. Most Amish homes have dark green window shades. Why the plain, identical window treatments? The Amish community would consider decorative shades or frilly curtains signs of vanity.

3. B. Although a basket of buns and mugs of coffee may be passed around, the Moravian Love Feast is actually a festival that includes the singing of hymns and the playing of devotional music. The practice imitates the "agape" gatherings of the earliest Christians, celebrations held in the morning that included prayer and sharing a meal. Moravian Love Feasts can be held on holidays, anniversaries, or anytime church leaders decide that a little fellowship would bring spiritual blessings to the congregation.

4. B. Although you might see foot washing at a pre-Easter service in a Catholic church, the Amish hold the only ceremony in which everyone gets their feet cleaned. Since the Amish religion was founded in Germany in the 1600s, congregations have held a special adults-only communion service (called Grossgemee) in the spring and fall. The service lasts all day, and the adults wash each other's feet—men wash men's feet, women wash women's—to imitate Jesus, who once washed the feet of his disciples.

5. Most likely, the Quaker. That's the only sect of the four that originated in England, and the British are great tea drinkers. If you said, "None of them would go into a bar!" you may be right. None of these groups approve of drunkenness or partying, but all of them actually do allow moderate drinking. Amish men enjoy beer, and the others have changed their attitudes toward drinking over time. Mennonites in the United States were completely against alcohol during the 19th and early 20th centuries, for instance, but the sect has since relaxed that stance. Today, about 60 percent of Mennonites consider moderate alcohol consumption to be acceptable.

The U Penn Quiz, page 256

1. All of the above . . . which is to say that each date has a claim to being the "real" founding date. Penn itself puts the date at 1740, when the colony granted a charter to a charity school for poor children on the property. However, it wasn't until 1749 that the school's trustees first convened. The first classes weren't held until 1751, and the actual college didn't get a charter until 1755.

2. D. Benjamin Franklin wanted to start a "Publick Academy of Philadelphia" that taught both the arts and practical skills, rather than the religious subjects that the other colonial universities (Harvard, Yale, Princeton, and William & Mary) focused on. So in 1749, he bought an unused property and merged it with the state's charity school, establishing the college as an institution of higher learning. (Franklin wasn't the only Founding Father to found a Pennsylvania college. Benjamin Rush started Dickinson College in 1783.)

3. B. *Leges sine moribus vanae means* "Laws without morals are useless"; the motto was officially adopted in 1932. It's attributed to William Smith, the university's first provost— who nicked it from the Roman poet Horace. (The other mottoes listed here are for Dartmouth, Princeton, and Brown, respectively.)

4. D. The Ivy League is composed of eight elite Eastern universities (Penn, Harvard, Yale, Princeton, Dartmouth, Brown, Cornell, and Columbia), but it specifically refers to a sports league made up of those schools. Sports rivalries among Ivy League schools date back to 1852 (when crew teams from Harvard and Yale squared off), and there was an Ivy Group football agreement in 1945. But it wasn't until 1954 that the

Ivy League—the NCAA Division I athletic conference that exists today—was formally created. And 1956–57 was the first academic year that the schools officially played in league sporting events.

5. C. William Henry Harrison studied medicine at Penn, but didn't like the subject and left the school in 1791. He did all right anyway, becoming a war hero, general, congressman, governor, and ambassador before winning the presidency in 1840. His best-known act as president: dying after just 30 days in office. He caught pneumonia after giving an hours-long inauguration speech in the rain.

6. B. The ENIAC (short for "Electronic Numerical Integrator and Computer") was the first general-purpose electronic computer. Physicist John Mauchly and engineer J. Presper Eckert Jr. began work on it in 1943 at Penn's Moore School of Electrical Engineering. They designed the computer primarily to compute values for artillery tables, which would help make World War II artillery attacks more accurate, but the computer wasn't finished until 1946, so its original purpose was virtually obsolete. Instead, scientists used ENIAC to compute figures for creating a hydrogen bomb.

ENIAC cost $400,000 to build and had 18,000 vacuum tubes, 70,000 resistors, 10,000 capacitors, 6,000 switches, and 1,500 relays . . . all stuffed into a room that measured 30 x 50 feet. An urban legend says that when the engineers at Penn turned ENIAC on, all the lights in Philadelphia dimmed. Eckert denied that in 1989, saying, "That story is total fiction, dreamed up by some journalist."

Keystone Staters on the Big Screen, page 266

S	A	L	T		C	L	E	F		S	I	T	I	N
E	L	I	A		H	E	M	I		A	P	A	C	E
E	A	R	L		A	R	I	L		C	O	K	E	S
D	I	A	L	M	F	O	R	M	U	R	D	E	R	
		O	O	E	Y		C	E	S	S				
S	L	U	R	P	S		A	U	L	D		S	A	P
H	I	N	D	U		E	L	S	A		A	I	D	A
I	N	D	E	P	E	N	D	E	N	C	E	D	A	Y
P	E	E	R		D	Y	E	D		C	R	E	M	E
S	S	R		D	E	A	R		S	U	I	S	S	E
	W	R	E	N			P	A	P	A				
	T	R	E	A	S	U	R	E	I	S	L	A	N	D
A	H	A	N	D		R	E	A	L		I	N	C	A
R	E	P	E	L		I	N	R	E		S	T	A	R
P	O	S	E	Y		S	O	L	D		T	I	R	E

Keystone Quiz, page 292

1. Kinzua Dam and the Allegheny Resevoir.

2. The largest, in order: Philadelphia, Pittsburgh, Allentown, Erie, Reading (Scranton, Bethlehem, Lancaster, Harrisburg, Altoona)

3. Tina Fey

4. From Erie to Long Point, Ontario, a distance of about 30 miles.

5. The Tioga River (and Tioga County). Take the "i" out, and you have a "toga."

6. Allegheny Mountains, Appalachian Mountains (includes the Blue Ridge Mountains), Pocono Mountains

7. Pittsburgh

8. State founder William Penn. A portrait of Penn and his dog hangs in the governor's mansion.

FOR PUZZLE LOVERS: UNCLE JOHN'S BATHROOM PUZZLERS

Find these and
other great *Uncle
John's Bathroom
Reader* titles online at
www.bathroomreader.com.

Or contact us:
Bathroom Readers' Institute
P.O. Box 1117, Ashland, OR 97520
(888) 488-4642

Also available from the Bathroom Readers' Institute...

Test your friends...test yourself! *Uncle John's Did You Know and Uncle John's Bathroom Reader Ultimate Challenge Trivia Quiz* are packed with fun, fascinating facts.

Bathroom Readers' Institute
P.O. Box 1117, Ashland, OR 97520
www.bathroomreader.com

Ahoy, Uncle John!

It's our 21st annual edition—
jam-packed with more than 500
pages of brand-new material!

The Bathroom Readers'
Institute has sailed the
high seas to bring you
**Uncle John's Unsinkable
Bathroom Reader.** You'll
find all your favorites:
obscure trivia, strange
lawsuits, dumb crooks,
forgotten lore, history,
and more. Keep your
head above water as
you read about . . .

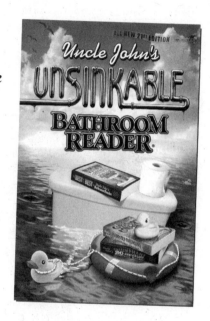

- The CSI Effect
- The Tapeworm Diet
- 7 (Underwater) Places
  to See Before You Die
- Medical Miracles
- 44 Things You Can Do With a Coconut
- The History of the Comstock Lode
- The Godfather of Fitness
- High-Tech Underwear
  . . . and more!

On Sale Now!
www.bathroomreader.com

The Last Page

Sit down and be counted!

Become a member of the Bathroom Readers' Institute! No join-up fees, monthly minimums or maximums, organized dance parties, quilting bees, solicitors, annoying phone calls (we only have one phone line), spam—or any other canned meat product—to worry about . . . just the chance to get our fabulous monthly newsletter (and if you want) some extremely cool Uncle John's stuff.

So send us a letter:
Bathroom Readers' Institute
P.O. Box 1117
Ashland, OR 97520

Or email us at mail@bathroomreader.com.

Hope you enjoyed the book—and if you're skipping to the end, what are you doing reading this page? Go back and finish!